CITIZENSHIP IMPERILLED

ashoka UNIVERSITY

HEDGEHOG AND FOX

HISTORY AND POLITICS SERIES

"The fox knows many things,
but the hedgehog knows one big thing"

General Editor

RUDRANGSHU MUKHERJEE

NIRAJA GOPAL JAYAL

Citizenship Imperilled

INDIA'S FRAGILE DEMOCRACY

permanent black in association with ashoka UNIVERSITY

Published by

PERMANENT BLACK
'Himalayana', Mall Road, Ranikhet Cantt,
Ranikhet 263645
Email: perblack@gmail.com

in association with

ashoka
UNIVERSITY

Distributed by

ORIENT BLACKSWAN PRIVATE LIMITED
Bangalore Bhopal Bhubaneshwar Chandigarh Chennai
Ernakulam Guwahati Hyderabad Jaipur Kolkata
Lucknow Mumbai New Delhi Patna
www.orientblackswan.com

ISBN 978-81-7824-645-1

Typeset in Adobe Garamond Pro
by Manmohan Kumar, Delhi
Printed and bound in India by Manipal Technologies Limited, Manipal

To

The Dons of the WhatsApp University

1. Lore & Gore
2. Baat Cheet
3. The Four Musketeers

Contents

Preface and Acknowledgements

With the exception of the Introduction and Chapter 1, the essays in this volume have been previously published between 2012 and 2019. While the book had been planned for a few years, it has to be acknowledged that, were it not for the pandemic, it may have remained in the realm of mere possibility for a bit longer.

I am most grateful to Rukun Advani for encouraging me to put together this collection, and for the honour of bringing to bear his sharp editorial skills on the manuscript. As always, I am indebted to my family for anchorage; and, in the pandemic, for some delightful and intensely competitive scrabble evenings.

Thanks are due to the Oxford University Press and Taylor and Francis for permission to republish the journal articles and book chapters in which they hold the copyright.

Chapter 1 is an expanded version of a Public Lecture titled "Citizenship Imperilled: Struggle and Solidarity in India Today", delivered on 6 February 2020 at the London School of Economics. It also draws upon my article, "Faith-Based Citizenship", published in *The India Forum,* 1 November 2019, https://www.theindiaforum.in/article/faith-criterion-citizenship. My special thanks to Professor Sumi Madhok for the lecture and the discussion of fraternity in the work of Hannah Arendt. Thanks also to Aman Wadud for helping me with fact-checking numbers.

Chapter 2 was published under the title "Citizenship", in Sujit Chowdhry, Madhav Khosla, and Pratap Bhanu Mehta, eds, *The Oxford Handbook of the Indian Constitution* (Delhi: Oxford University Press, 2016). The version herein is lightly edited but not updated.

Chapter 3 was published with the same title in Engin F. Isin and Peter Nyers, eds, *Routledge Handbook of Global Citizenship Studies*, Abingdon: Routledge, 2014.

Chapter 4 was in its first version the Keynote Address at the South Asian Studies Association of Australia, at the 22nd Biennial Conference of the Asian Studies Association of Australia (ASAA), in July 2018, at the University of Sydney. It was subsequently published under the same title in *South Asia: Journal of South Asian Studies*, vol. 42, issue 1, 2019.

Chapter 5 was originally published under the same title in *Oxford Development Studies*, vol. 39, no. 2, June 2011.

Chapter 6 was originally published with the same title in the *Journal of Human Development and Capabilities: A Multi-Disciplinary Journal for People-Centered Development*, vol. 10, no. 3, November 2009.

Chapter 7 was originally published with the same title in Ira Katznelson and Partha Chatterjee, eds, *Anxieties of Democracy*, New Delhi: Oxford University Press, 2012.

Introduction

Citizenship Imperilled

In 2013, I published a book titled *Citizenship and Its Discontents: An Indian History*. In this citizenship-framed rumination on the long twentieth century in India, I discussed the fragile and contingent quality of the constitutional consensus on the civic-national conception of citizenship, and how the "many-faceted and multiply contested idea of citizenship was forged and continues to be fashioned through contestation."[1] Even so, it was impossible to anticipate at the time that the consensus could be so easily overturned and the contestations sharpen so rapidly, revealing irreparably deep fractures. It was unimaginable then that even what had seemed to be lamentably slow progress in realising meaningful citizenship could so quickly slip away from our grasp; that we would be called on to mourn the absence of what was, till only the year before, a discontent about its imperfections; and that, far from accelerating progress on the road to citizenship, we would find ourselves facing not just an unexpected roadblock but an uncontrolled backward movement. The Indian idea of citizenship – in the law and the Constitution, as well as in social and political life – appeared, in the years that followed, to have been irretrievably undermined. Until, that is, the winter of 2019, when matters worsened.

The introduction of the Citizenship Amendment Bill 2016, which had lapsed with the Sixteenth Lok Sabha, had already sent alarm bells ringing. A slightly altered version of this Bill

[1] Jayal, *Citizenship*, 23.

was reintroduced on 4 December 2019 and by 11 December it had been passed – one might even say steamrolled – by both Houses of Parliament to become the Citizenship Amendment Act (CAA). This became a flashpoint, with the question of citizenship commandeering the headlines as never before. Though the concept of universal equal citizenship adopted by the Republic of India in 1950 had undoubtedly been incrementally eroded over the preceding three decades, the CAA signalled its definitive end. But the public interrogation of this calculated undermining of the civic-national idea of citizenship brought it into the public sphere in an unexpectedly dramatic way. The moment when the original ideal of citizenship was legally extinguished thus curiously became also the moment in which it appeared to have been recovered rather than irretrievably lost. It was a moment in which citizenship was sought to be reclaimed through its re-enactment. In the history of independent India there had never been such a demonstration of *acts* of citizenship provoked by a heightening of popular consciousness around a hitherto unapprehended and even obscure legal provision. The issue of citizenship now became the subject of energetic debate and resistance.

The legal provision in question and the movement against it are discussed in greater detail in Chapter 1 below. Here, to put it briefly, the CAA provided members of specified religious communities with a fast track to citizenship by naturalisation, and simultaneously, by its silence, excluded members of one religious community, Islam, from receiving the same benefit. Muslims are the largest religious minority in India, and their exclusion from this provision reinforced the pronounced majoritarian shift – visible most clearly with the electoral victory of the Bharatiya Janata Party (BJP) in 2014 – in India's polity and society. With the simultaneous announcement of the National Population Register (NPR) and the National Register of Citizens (NRC), the CAA promised a route to non-Muslims to naturalise if they happened to have been excluded from the NPR/NRC, thus implying the introduction of gradations of citizenship.

For Muslims, their legal status as citizens threatened to become a function of their religious identity. This drastic move was a major step forward in a direction that had already been fed into the nation's GPS. Beginning with state-backed campaigns centred in Uttar Pradesh (UP) of "Love Jihad" and "Ghar Wapsi", the lynching of Mohammad Akhlaq by a mob in 2015 on suspicion of possessing beef, and the connivance of the police in protecting the perpetrators, a template was forged for vigilante hate crimes in several states. Meanwhile, the amplification of majoritarianism and hate speech through the artful and insidious use of the social media accentuated the existing exclusion and marginalisation of India's Muslims documented in the Sachar Committee Report of 2006. The report had signalled welcome, if long overdue, official recognition of the poor social indicators of Indian Muslims, as well as of the discrimination experienced by them in every domain from education to employment. The Sachar Report represented a moment of exhilaration – that the promise of equal citizenship in the Constitution was finally on its way to being realised. It was unthinkable then that within a matter of years minorities would be rendered so insecure and policies to improve their condition stigmatised. Everyday forms of social discrimination soon came to be legitimised, to the point that people grew hardened to a regular abuse of the law and unmoved by law-enforcement agencies punishing innocent citizens for no crime other than their identity. It looked like India was moving from treating Muslims as second-class citizens to formalising their status as such.

In the violence that erupted after the protests against the CAA, the playbook perfected since 2014 – of protecting the perpetrator and punishing the victim – was deployed more and more, with full confidence in the indulgence of an executive court to ensure that injustice must not only be done but must also be seen to be done. The fact that a much larger number of Muslim lives and properties were destroyed in the organised and systematic violence is hard to square with the fact that it was the rioters the police were seen sheltering whereas it was the victims that ended up being punished, with a disproportionate number of those incarcerated being Muslims.

Along with and in the wake of the Delhi violence, the pandemic laid bare the deception of universal equal citizenship more starkly than perhaps any other event in recent memory. The virus, far from being the great leveller that it was blithely proclaimed to be, was particularly harsh on two sections of marginalised citizens, against both of whom the law was deployed antagonistically: disciplining and punishing one, and disowning, even forsaking, the other.

The law was used punitively against Muslim minority citizens, who could be forgiven for not knowing what hit them worse, the virus or the law, because the lockdown offered an opportunity for the state to clamp down on dissent and arrest activists, mostly Muslim, who had participated in the protests against the CAA over the preceding months. An international gathering of an Islamic sect was attacked as a conspiracy termed "corona jihad", leading to Muslim patients elsewhere and more generally being turned away from hospitals, and to Muslim vegetable vendors being accused of spitting on their wares with the intent of infecting buyers. The congregation became, in short, a pretext for blaming Indian Muslims at large for the spread of the virus, completely ignoring the many other large gatherings, religious and secular, that the government had also permitted at the same time. Such politically motivated stigmatisation was achieved by abstracting only the religious identity of Muslim citizens from their citizenship identity, with complete silence on their rights as citizens.

Almost hand in hand with this punishing of Muslims, approximately thirty million poor migrant workers in the cities – an estimated 60 per cent of them Dalits and Adivasis – were effectively abandoned by the law. A sudden announcement of lockdown – apparently because the coronavirus had to be contained at four hours' notice – left workers jobless and without money to survive in the city, and no trains or buses to take them home.

Millions – including children, pregnant women, and the elderly – started walking homewards on the highways, covering hundreds of miles, often barefoot, in blistering heat without food or water. Several hundred people died: of exhaustion, road accidents, or run over by a train.[2]

Thirty-two days into the lockdown, four out of five workers who reached out to the Stranded Workers Action Network did not have access to government rations.[3] More than 97 per cent had received no cash relief from the government. Only 6 per cent had received their full wages, 16 per cent had been partially paid, and the rest not at all. Initially, the government asked private employers to pay their workers the wages due to them. The employers got the Supreme Court to agree that they could not afford to pay because their enterprises had been locked down. However, the Indian government did not – as many others across the world did – step into the breach and provide compensation to laid-off workers. One study reported over 60 per cent of those surveyed having gone hungry the entire day for between one and seven days.[4] Livelihoods were devastated, and millions of households rendered food insecure and vulnerable. Dalits and women were disproportionately affected.[5]

When such workers leave their villages in search of work, they leave behind their identities as citizens and acquire the identity of mere workers in the city, invisible and faceless. Leaving home to find work means giving up a modest array of citizenship rights – to vote, to food security, and to work – all of which are tied to their place of residence. The documents they typically possess – the Aadhaar (ID) card, a ration card, and a voter ID – are validated by this residential address. Even when home, and despite showing these

[2] For a computation of non-virus deaths, see https://thejeshgn.com/projects/covid19-india/non-virus-deaths/

[3] Stranded Workers Action Network, "32 Days and Counting".

[4] Centre for Equity Studies and Delhi Research Group, "Labouring Lives".

[5] Deshpande, "The Covid-19 Pandemic".

documents, they are often deprived of basic welfare entitlements like medical aid and food.[6] When they migrate, they are denied these meagre welfare entitlements altogether, because such benefits can be accessed only in the place where their existence has been certified. During the lockdown, food insecurity prevailed despite a Delhi High Court directive to provide food to the poor and needy regardless of registration under the Public Distribution System (PDS).

To migrate, then, is to acquire the identity of a mere worker, giving up one's rights as a citizen. As for workers' rights, there is mostly no formal contract, little protection from labour laws, no guarantee of a minimum wage, and no social security of any kind. Appallingly, even as the reverse migration was ongoing, key labour laws were being suspended in UP, extending working hours and reducing the modest protections that workers notionally enjoy under existing labour laws.

Over and above the deprivation of wages as well as their most basic needs, migrant workers were subjected to police brutality while trying to obtain food or to use a toilet. When they started walking home, lawsuits were filed against them for violating the lockdown rules, and it was only on Day 77 of the lockdown that the Supreme Court directed a reconsideration of these rules. Even as the labouring poor were denied access to public transport, airplanes were sent overseas to fetch a section of citizens called "stranded Indians". Poor Indians stranded within India were ignored; when they finally got home, some were reported to have been hosed down with chemical bleach.[7] Much of all this was made possible by the application, at the onset of the pandemic, of the National Disaster Management Act 2005. While constitutional rights are not technically suspended, the attribution of extraordinary powers to

[6] In past years, starvation deaths have occurred because the Aadhaar card had not been "seeded" with the ration card.

[7] https://thewire.in/government/coronavirus-bareilly-migrants-sodium-hypochlorite

the executive at this time enabled the denial of protective provisions of the law and the Constitution to poor and vulnerable citizens.

Informality in the workplace signals precarity. It amounts to a depletion of the legality of not just the worker but also the person, an attenuation of their moral and juridical personhood. Such individuals have effectively been abandoned and disowned by the law instead of being protected by it. Substantive citizenship has long eluded the marginalised sections of Indian society – Dalits, Adivasis, Muslims, and the poor in whose ranks these groups find substantial representation. Despite constitutional guarantees of equal citizenship and special provisions for disadvantaged communities, the impact of the pandemic and lockdown, of the punitive use of the law as well as its evasion, has fallen far too considerably on those disadvantaged by their identities of caste, tribe, religion, and gender. These categories of marked citizens – long unequal and disenfranchised in multiple ways – had already, as Chapter 4 documents, been rendered more vulnerable to violence and discrimination. Even as those responsible for the lynching of Dalits and for the rape and killing of Dalit citizens are afforded impunity, those working for the rights of Dalits and Adivasis are thrown into prison on fabricated charges.

This descent into violence motivated by prejudice and the collapse of the rule of law only illustrates further the enduringly unequal citizenship of variously marked citizens, and indeed the widening distance between them and the prospect of any meaningful enjoyment of citizenship. While those disadvantaged by inequality have remained dispossessed of opportunities for greater equality, those who hitherto enjoyed the privileges of the unmarked citizen are also experiencing some truncation of their citizenship – if not always in economic terms, certainly in terms of an evisceration of their civil rights and political freedoms.

At first, the free expression of critical opinion earned the unmarked citizen of privilege a regime-manufactured sobriquet – "anti-national"; this was later "improved" into a regime-coined neologism – “urban Naxal”. The deprivation of basic civil liberties and political rights – previously withdrawn only during the eighteen-month national Emergency of 1975–7 – gave the unmarked Indian a taste of second-class citizenship. The exercise of the democratic rights of dissent and protest invited punitive action, including arrest under laws of sedition and other extraordinary laws that permit incarceration without trial, enacted to protect the sovereignty and integrity of the nation against terrorism. A large number of the arrests made under the Unlawful Activities (Prevention) Act 1967 (UAPA) since 2018 have been of human rights activists, many of them working in the areas of Dalit rights and Adivasi rights, and some simply for participating in the protests against the CAA. Little wonder then that India, along with the United States, Brazil, Turkey, Russia, and Poland, was pronounced a backslider on the scale of democracy by the V-Dem Annual Democracy Report of 2018.[8] This was echoed again in the Democracy Report 2020, which characterised India as affected by autocratisation, as slipping from Liberal Democracy to Electoral Democracy in terms of regime type, and as having “continued on a path of steep decline, to the extent that it has almost lost its status as a democracy”.[9] An assault on democracy, or even the hollowing out of democratic institutions, cannot but have a deleterious impact on the quality of citizenship. Uncoupled from democracy, the prospects for citizenship for citizens of all descriptions – privileged and unprivileged, marked and unmarked – are bleak indeed.

With the exception of Chapter 1, which is published herein for the first time, the chapters in this volume were earlier published as individual essays between 2012 and 2019. While they have been lightly edited, they have not been updated. This is largely because they register temporal shifts in the law on citizenship: those published in or before 2015 obviously contain no mention

[8] Varieties of Democracy Institute, “Democracy for All?”

[9] Varieties of Democracy Institute, “Autocratization Surges”.

of the Citizenship Amendment Bill 2016, while the introduction of this initially failed legislation (the precursor to the Citizenship Amendment Act 2019) finds mention in the essays published after that date. Only the first chapter of this book – the most recently written – has a detailed discussion of the Citizenship Amendment Act 2019. It is mainly in the detailing of the trajectory of *legal* citizenship that there are some unavoidable overlaps across the first four chapters. This repetition is infrequent, has seemed unavoidable, and been countenanced to preserve the integrity of the argument within each chapter. I have also not presumed that every reader will read every chapter, or read them in sequence. It is with the same object of keeping each chapter self-contained that tenses have been preserved.

The Citizenship Amendment Act 2019 and its aftermath is the subject of the opening chapter, followed by one on the legal architecture and jurisprudence of citizenship from the enactment of the Constitution in 1950, through the enactment of the law of citizenship in 1955, and onwards through the multiple amendments that have transformed the original conception altogether. Together, the first two chapters, comprising the first section, "Laws", provide a comprehensive account of the legal journey from the civic-national conception of citizenship of the founding moment to its antithesis, faith-based citizenship, in the present.

The chapters of the second section, "Contestations", provide a wide-angle view of citizenship in its three central dimensions of legal status, rights, and identity. Chapter 3 provides the historical background for an appreciation, in Chapter 4, of the changes wrought since 2014. Both chapters are organised around the three dimensions of citizenship, and both delineate the contestations in these three spheres: who is or can be a legal citizen and by implication who cannot; how claims to welfare contributed to the expansion of the rights of social citizenship, and their attrition in subsequent years; and the mediation of citizenship by identities given at birth in ways that undermine relentlessly the inclusionary provisions of the Constitution for minorities and historically disadvantaged communities.

The final section, "Antinomies", comprises three chapters that reflect on the relationship between citizenship and the cognate concepts of inclusion and democracy, doing so both theoretically and by marshalling empirical materials. Chapter 5 deals with the false dichotomy of universal versus group-differentiated citizenship; Chapter 6 with the question of why democratic citizenship rather than inclusion offers a superior normative and conceptual tool for addressing the formidable challenge of human development; and Chapter 7 reads the Indian experiment with democratic citizenship through a Tocquevillian lens, with a particular focus on the women's question.

The discontents of citizenship are infinitely and disconcertingly greater today than they were in 2013, when my (eponymous) book on citizenship was first published.

PART I

LAWS

1

From Birthright to Faith-Based Citizenship

For 101 days, beginning in December 2019, thousands of women began a 24x7 sit-in on Road 13A, which passes through a south Delhi neighbourhood called Shaheen Bagh. At this site of protest, women gathered in large numbers late each evening and stayed through the night, flying the national flag, singing national songs, listening to talks, and watching performances. They belonged to all age groups – young college goers were the most visible, but so were young mothers with babies, middle-aged housewives, and what came to be called the *dadis* (grandmothers) of Shaheen Bagh, elderly women who braved the coldest December that Delhi has seen in 118 years, sitting on the road in temperatures of 2° Celsius.

Inevitably, comparisons were made – some called this India's Tahrir Square or Taksim Square, others recalled Buenos Aires in 1977 – the "Mothers of the Plaza de Mayo" demanding to know where their children had disappeared. The protest was spontaneous and, in cities and towns across India, inspired as many as 426 women-led protests – marches, rallies, and sit-ins – that were similarly peaceful and non-violent.[1]

However, while the women of Shaheen Bagh and of similar protest sites across India were leading the protests, the protests themselves were about an issue that concerns all Indians and not

[1] https://www.behanbox.com/women-led-protest-map-against-citizenship-laws-in-india

women alone. Politicians tried to dismiss it as an all-Muslim protest, but there was enough evidence to suggest the opposite – that it brought people of all faiths together, such as through the performativity, on more than one occasion, of a simultaneous observance, side by side, of Muslim, Hindu, Sikh, and Christian prayers and rituals. Most significantly, there was a revitalisation of the symbols and slogans of the freedom movement a century ago. The anthem of the movement was an Urdu poem, *Hum Dekhenge* (We Shall See), written in 1979 by the Pakistani communist poet Faiz Ahmed Faiz against the military regime of Zia ul Haq. It found translation in multiple Indian languages, and was sung at protest sites across the country and overseas. The slogan that emerged from the movement – *Hum Kagaz Nahin Dikhayenge* (We Will Not Show Our Documents) – spoke to the related issue of the National Register of Citizens (NRC). Above all, the resistance was most poignantly expressed through collective readings of the Preamble to the Indian Constitution, and on posters calling for Saving the Constitution, which frequently found representation as a holy book. What brought the protests to a close at the end of March 2020, however, was not the fulfilment of the demands of the protesters but the pandemic.

The proximate trigger for these protests was a recent amendment to the law on citizenship, but the connection between this and the larger question of constitutionalism was not lost on the protesters. It is in fact the clash between this amendment to an ordinary statute and the constitutional values that are endangered by it that was so powerfully expressed through the collective readings of the Preamble. The central theme of the resistance, in Shaheen Bagh and the many Shaheen Baghs across the country, was nothing less than a defence of India's Constitution and its founding ideals of equality, secularism, and democracy. The peg on which this multifaceted defence hung was the constitutional vision of who is or should be an Indian citizen.

The Public and the Clandestine Pre-History of the Citizenship Amendment Act (CAA)

India's Constituent Assembly wrestled with the question of citizenship chiefly to deal with the massive movement of people in the aftermath of the Partition. Provision had to be made for citizenship for Hindus and Sikhs fleeing to India from the newly created state of Pakistan, but also for those Muslims who had fled India, gone to Pakistan, and later applied to return to India when the violence had abated.

At the end of a debate so fractious and interminable that Dr B.R. Ambedkar described it as a headache, the Constituent Assembly expressed unambiguously its preference for birth on the soil of the country (*jus soli*) as a modern, civilised, enlightened, and democratic principle over the racial principle of *jus sanguinis* (blood, descent, or race) as the primary means for the acquisition of citizenship. In terms of what citizenship offered, the Constitution provided for a universalist conception of equal citizenship to all, regardless of religion, race, caste, and gender. Both these dimensions – who is eligible for citizenship and what are the entitlements it guarantees – are integral to the promise of citizenship, and on both counts the Indian Constitution adopted egalitarian and inclusive principles.

In a polity encompassing such staggering civilisational diversity, this was both a normative and a practical imperative. What tied it together was the idea of civic nationalism, a sense of belonging that transcended – celebrating rather than obliterating – the multitudinous identities of cultural community. The Constitution recognised this diversity through its core commitment to equal citizenship and an inclusive architecture of governance with both normative and institutional commitments to democracy, secularism, and federalism built into its design.

Having provided for the exigencies of citizenship in the extraordinary time of the Partition, and having provided the normative framework for citizenship in the new republic, the Constituent Assembly left it to Parliament to legislate on citizenship for ordinary times. This it did by the enactment of the Citizenship Act in 1955, and the recent controversy is about the latest amendment to this statute, called the Citizenship Amendment Act 2019 – the CAA.

An amendment of less than a hundred words to an ordinary law, the CAA has managed to unsettle the basis of nationhood and citizenship without a constitutional amendment. It signals a foundational shift in the conception of the Indian citizen embodied in the Constitution and the Citizenship Act 1955, in two ways: it entrenches the move from soil to blood as the basis of citizenship and openly introduces a religious category into a religion-neutral law. Both these were presaged in earlier legislation, and it is important to record both the public and the clandestine pre-history of exclusion before the enactment of the CAA. There are three intertwined aspects of this pre-history, feeding into and off each other, that deserve attention: the politics of immigration in Assam which provoked earlier amendments to the law on citizenship, arrived at through political negotiation with the then ruling Congress party; the politicisation of religious identity by the BJP, normalising hate speech and legitimising violence; and both of these finding expression in a range of changes to laws and rules since 2015 that are not specifically about citizenship but bear an uncanny resemblance to the CAA.

Over time, triggered chiefly by political unrest in Assam, India moved decisively from the *jus soli* conception of citizenship adopted in the Constitution, and enshrined in the Citizenship Act 1955, towards a *jus sanguinis* or descent-based conception of citizenship. Assam has a long and complex history of in-migration, mostly from Bengal, starting in the nineteenth century. More recently, the region witnessed substantial in-migration from 1947 on, peaking in 1971 when East Pakistan (now Bangladesh) split from West Pakistan, and continuing steadily thereafter. It was no secret that many of these immigrants had acquired forms of what has been called "documentary citizenship" through "networks of complicity" and "networks of profit".[2]

In 1985, in the wake of the gruesome Nellie massacre of 1983, the Assamese students' organisations that had led the agitation against the enfranchisement of migrants from Bangladesh entered into the Assam Accord with the Rajiv Gandhi government, leading to an amendment in the provisions relating to naturalisation in the Citizenship Act. This amendment created categories of eligibility for citizenship based on the year in which a person had migrated to India. All those who came before 1966 were declared citizens; those who came between 1966 and 1971 were struck off the electoral rolls and asked to wait ten years before applying for citizenship; and those who came after 1971 were deemed illegal immigrants. Though these provisions were a response to the genuine grievances of the Assamese, they contained the seeds of the politicisation and incipient communalisation of the issue of migrants. The amendment also inserted a new requirement into the provisions relating to citizenship by birth. Only those born before 1987 were now to be citizens regardless of their parentage. And, in order for a person born in India between 1987 and 2003 to be a citizen by birth, she now had to have one parent who was an Indian citizen.

An even more stringent requirement was introduced in 2004,[3] making ineligible for citizenship by birth any person born in India with one parent who was at the time of his or her birth an "illegal migrant". This was also when the term "illegal migrant" entered the law, signifying a person who had entered India without legal authorisation or stayed on without it. This introduced, albeit covertly, a religion-based exception to the principle, since the term "illegal migrant" signalled the religious identity (Muslim) of many of the migrants from Bangladesh, against whom there was so much

[2] Sadiq, *Paper Citizens.*

[3] Citizenship (Amendment) Act 2003 (6 of 2004).

political ferment in Assam – though in fact the anti-immigrant sentiment in Assam had more to do with language than religion. Simultaneously, an amendment to the Citizenship Rules excluded "minority Hindus with Pakistani citizenship" from the definition of "illegal migrants", thus legally destigmatising Hindu migrants who had come into the border states of western India from Pakistan. This introduced an explicitly religious category into the margins (the Rules) of what was until then a religion-neutral law.

Political developments in India since the 1990s, when Hindu nationalism came to be mobilised as political ideology, but especially after 2014 – when the BJP became India's first majority government since 1984, and the first non-Congress government to win such a majority since independence – are key to understanding the CAA. This is because the general election of 2014 inaugurated a period in which hate speech and hate crimes against Muslims were accelerated, as was violence against minorities, especially by vigilante lynch mobs which thrived on the promise of legal impunity. The BJP also set in motion a series of government policies towards minorities, including the forced "amelioration" of Muslim women by the criminalisation of the triple talaq, and a clampdown in early August 2019 in the erstwhile state of Jammu and Kashmir. In a matter of six years, a new and patently hostile ecosystem had been ruthlessly put in place for India's Muslim minority, effectively undoing the constitutional commitment to secularism as a doctrine governing the conduct of public life, as well as provisions relating to minority rights and the special status of Kashmir.

This is the broad context within which the Assam question, for reasons both electoral and ideological, was effectively instrumentalised in the widespread legitimisation of an anti-Muslim discourse, fortified with anti-immigrant sentiment. In the run up to the Assembly elections in Assam in early 2016, the BJP had made an electoral promise to "free" the state from illegal Bangladeshi migrants by evicting and deporting them. This was a dog-whistle reference to Muslims, as it simultaneously promised to give Indian citizenship to all Bangladeshi Hindu immigrants if it won the election, which it did. The passage of the Citizenship Amendment Bill (CAB) – as it was at the time – was key to the fulfilment of this election promise. The ideological motivation was fuelled by the decision of the Supreme Court, under Chief Justice Ranjan Gogoi, himself an Assamese, to conduct a National Register of Citizens in the state of Assam.

The first National Register of Citizens for Assam was compiled in 1951 but remained largely dormant until political considerations gave it a new lease of life. In 2005, a meeting between the Centre, the Assam government, and the All Assam Students' Union (AASU), chaired by Prime Minister Manmohan Singh, resolved to take steps towards updating the NRC to fulfil the requirements of the Assam Accord. In 2009, a petition was filed in the Supreme Court by an NGO called Assam Public Works asking for the NRC to be updated. The court gave a direction to this effect, and the exercise began in 2015, with the objective of recording all those who had documentary proof of being Indian, and of them or their ancestors having been in India before midnight on 24 March 1971. In a society as historically undocumented as India, and in a region regularly visited by natural calamities such as floods, there are far too many who cannot produce documents to establish their ancestry. In fact, there are native inhabitants who for generations remain undocumented even as there are immigrants who have acquired "paper citizenship".[4]

The result of the NRC demonstrated the very real possibility that undocumented nationals may be unfairly deprived of their citizenship status. At the end of its first round, 4 million people of the 32.9 million who had applied were excluded. Fresh claims for inclusion were filed by 3.6 million, but, even at the end of this process in August 2019, 1.9 million remained unauthenticated. Champions of the NRC were surprised and disappointed by this

[4] Ibid.

outcome as large numbers of Hindus were unexpectedly among the excluded, and the percentage of exclusion was larger in areas inhabited by indigenous people and lower in border areas where illegal migrants had settled. Among those left out were people who had served in the Indian Army or the Border Security Force for decades; the nephew of former Indian president Fakhruddin Ali Ahmed; and even Syeda Anwara Taimur, the only woman chief minister Assam ever had.[5] Ironically, a former anti-immigration activist and even a local BJP leader found their names missing. In some cases, children's documents were found to be acceptable but not those of their fathers. As the factual outcomes of the process contradicted the political expectations of its enthusiasts, the political messaging sought to assuage fears by affirming that no Hindus would be deported. They were reassured of their being reinstated as citizens on the basis of their religious identity when the Citizenship Amendment Bill (as it then was) became law. It was tacitly acknowledged that only undocumented Indian nationals belonging to the Muslim faith, and therefore having no recourse to the CAA, would be excluded, while documented (and possibly illegal) migrants who belonged to other faiths would be included. This was the promise of the CAA, which also serves to explain why, notwithstanding the unexpected outcome of the NRC, public pronouncements from the ruling party and government continued to affirm its determination for the nationwide implementation of a National Register of Citizens.

It is notable that both the entrenchment of the move from soil to blood as the basis of citizenship and the open introduction of a religious category into a religion-neutral law were presaged in earlier legislation. This clandestine pre-history of the CAA is relevant to appreciate the convergence in the legislative design of exclusion.

[5] Syeda Anwara Taimur passed away in Australia on 28 September 2020.

An apparently unrelated aspect of this secret genealogy is to be found in the history of protective coverage being incrementally extended to the same groups from the same set of countries as those specified in the CAA. These are mostly administrative, rather than legislative, amendments, over the last five years, in laws other than the law on citizenship.[6] In September 2015, the Passport (Entry into India) Rules, 1950, and the Orders under the Foreigners Act, 1946, were amended to exempt the very same religious groups as the ones mentioned in the CAA from the requirement of holding valid passports and visas, and consequently exempt them from being prosecuted or deported. Both these amendments refer to "persons belonging to minority communities in Bangladesh and Pakistan" – Afghanistan was not included here – "who were compelled to seek shelter in India due to religious persecution or fear of religious persecution."[7]

In March 2018, the Reserve Bank of India amended the FEMA (Foreign Exchange Management (Acquisition and Transfer of Immovable Property in India) Regulations, such that

> A person being a citizen of Afghanistan, Bangladesh or Pakistan belonging to minority communities in those countries, namely, Hindus, Sikhs, Buddhists, Jains, Parsis and Christians who is residing in India and has been granted a Long Term Visa (LTV) by the Central Government may purchase only one residential immovable property in India as dwelling unit for self- occupation and only one immovable property for carrying out self-employment subject to the following conditions . . .[8]

[6] Nationals of Pakistan and Bangladesh are ineligible for the status of Overseas Citizens of India.

[7] Notification of the Ministry of Home Affairs, 7 September 2015, G.S.R. 685(E), https://indianfrro.gov.in/frro/Notifications_dated_7.9.2015.pdf

[8] Reserve Bank of India, Foreign Exchange Management (Acquisition and Transfer of Immovable Property in India) Regulations, 2018, Notification No.

With the CAA, discrimination based on religious identity, having already found its way into the rules and orders relating to passports and foreigners, as well as putative investors, has now found its way into the law on citizenship.

The Citizenship Amendment Act 2019

The CAA pertains to citizenship by naturalisation for immigrants without proper papers, officially labelled "illegal migrants" rather than the less humiliating and internationally accepted term "undocumented migrants". The antecedent law provided for such migrants to be eligible for citizenship by naturalisation after a waiting period of eleven years. The amendment reduces that period to five years, but such fast-track citizenship is offered only to select groups among such migrants: specifically, Hindus, Sikhs, Christians, Buddhists, Jains, and Parsis, from three countries, Afghanistan, Bangladesh, and Pakistan. The obvious exclusion of Muslims from this list of faiths, as well as the exclusion of Sri Lanka and Myanmar as neighbouring countries from which migrants may and do come, has been officially justified by saying that the new law will only cover persecuted religious minorities in the three specified countries.

Despite the claim that there are hundreds of thousands of such persecuted minorities clamouring for citizenship, the report of the Joint Parliamentary Committee (JPC) on this Bill provided a figure of 31,313 persons on the basis of inputs from the Intelligence Bureau (IB). It stated that in response to its query as to the numbers of people who would benefit from the Bill, it received the following response from the IB: "As per our records, there are 31,313 persons belonging to minority communities (Hindus - 25447, Sikhs - 5807, Christians - 55, Buddhists - 2 and Parsis - 2)

FEMA 21(R)/2018-RB, 26 March 2018, https://www.rbi.org.in/Scripts/BS_FemaNotifications.aspx?Id=11248, accessed 29 June 2020.

who have been given Long Term Visa on the basis of their claim of religious persecution in their respective countries . . ."[9] An earlier draft of the Bill, as well as the Statement of Objects and Reasons of the version that was enacted, had specifically mentioned religious persecution, but, as the rationale for the amendment, this is conspicuously missing from the Act. As the Intelligence Bureau testified before the JPC:

> The individuals claiming religious persecution and seeking Indian citizenship had entered India decades ago, mostly in the aftermath of [*sic*] partition of the country when a large scale migration between India and Pakistan took place. *It is not possible to verify their claim now.* However, for recent cases, if any, due verification would be made before their claim for Indian Citizenship is entertained.[10]

It is moreover implied that all persecution ended on 31 December 2014 – for that is the cut-off date in the law. The official reason for this is to prevent "misuse by infiltrators from neighbouring countries such as Pakistan."[11] The actual explanation, going by the submission of the Ministry of External Affairs to the JPC, is that the date was chosen as "a natural corollary" of the Ministry of Home Affairs notifications of 7 September 2015 – amending the Passport (Entry Into India) Amendment Rules and the Foreigners (Amendment) Order, both of which "regularised the stay of such people who entered into India on or before 31st December, 2014."[12] These, the ministry says, were "essentially in the nature of a one-time waiver or amnesty granted to these

[9] Sixteenth Lok Sabha, "Report of the Joint Committee on the Citizenship (Amendment) Bill 2016", sec. 2.17, p. 39.

[10] Ibid., sec. 2.14, p. 38. Emphasis added.

[11] "CAA cutoff date will prevent misuse: Official", *The Economic Times*, 6 January 2020, https://economictimes.indiatimes.com/news/politics-and-nation/caa-cutoff-date-will-prevent-misuse-official/articleshow/73114719.cms, accessed 27 June 2020.

[12] Sixteenth Lok Sabha, "Report of the Joint Committee on the Citizenship (Amendment) Bill 2016", sec. 2.7, p. 36.

migrants from minority communities."[13] The same notifications from the Ministry of Home Affairs were repeatedly referenced in questions relating to why the term "persecuted minorities" (as opposed to religious minorities) was used, or why the term "religious persecution" was not mentioned in the Bill. On both these questions the Ministry of Home Affairs drew reference to its notifications of September 2015 which mention the term "Religious Persecution".[14] It is unusual that the silences in the language of a *statute* should rely on more explicit but unrelated *notifications* to give them meaning. This circumspection is suggestive of political wiliness as it minimises the risk of accountability while retaining a legally plausible excuse in the event of judicial scrutiny.

Two implications are notable. First, that only Muslim states are persecutors, and their targets are people belonging only to these six faiths; and second, that non-Muslim (Buddhist) states like Sri Lanka and Mynamar do not persecute anyone at all. This flies in the face of the well-documented persecution of Ahmadiyyas in Pakistan, Hazaras in Afghanistan, Rohingyas in Myanmar, and Tamil Hindus in Sri Lanka.[15] States like Myanmar that share a border with India are excluded, while those that do not share a border, such as Afghanistan, are included in the ambit of the Act. It also fails to account for why people who have suffered other forms of persecution – ethnic, racial, political, or any other – should not be entitled to our compassion. Indeed, Indians are required to restrain their compassion from being intemperately extended; this virtue must scrupulously follow the territorial and religious boundaries laid down by the law,

[13] Ibid.

[14] Ibid., sec. 2.11–2.12, p. 36.

[15] Not just the CAA, but also its critics have been accused of homogenising identities through their "exclusion of ethnic, tribal and other religious minorities, such as Shias, Ahmadiyas, Baluchis, and Sufis in Pakistan; Hazaras in Afghanistan; Uyghurs in China, and Bihari Muslims in Bangladesh": Parthasarathy, "Citizenship (Amendment) Act".

and respect the exclusions that are so entailed, however morally repugnant they may be.

The latest amendment facilitates a pathway to citizenship by naturalisation for people who have been "illegal migrants" from these three countries and promises citizenship by birth to their descendants – so long as they are not Muslims. The Statement of Objects and Reasons of the Bill makes it clear that this provision was meant to help religious minorities who were victims of persecution. However, the text of the amended law nowhere mentions religious persecution, and only the rules, as and when they are formulated, will clarify if there is any requirement to establish persecution, or any procedure to validate it, or indeed even to validate the religious identity of an individual. What the text of the law does say is that such persons will no longer be called "illegal migrants"; by implication, only Muslims qualify for the insult.

The Supreme Court is yet to decide on whether this apparently discriminatory provision violates the constitutional right to equality, as also the principle of secularism – which has long been pronounced a part of the basic structure of the Constitution. The shift from soil to blood as the basis of citizenship, which started just over fifteen years ago, is now consolidated in a definitively exclusionary way by openly introducing a religious category into a hitherto religion-neutral law. As noted earlier, ostensibly innocuous developments of this kind have occurred but gone unnoticed since 2015, when the Rules under the Passport Act and the Orders under the Foreigners Act were amended. The CAA echoes this covert history of protective coverage incrementally extended to the same groups from the same set of countries, as well as its accompanying exclusions. The difference lies in the wide field of application of the CAA and its authoritative finality in determining who may or may not be naturalised as a citizen of India. Indeed, the organic link between the 2015 notifications and the 2019 Act has not been sufficiently remarked upon, though it is made amply clear in the JPC Report which treats the 2015 notifications as a sort of *fait accompli* for their extension into the 2019 Amendment Act:

> The Committee observe that the Government by amending the Passport (Entry into India) Rules, 1950 and the Foreigners Order, 1948 through Notification dated 7th September, 2015 *have already regularised* the entry and stay of persons belonging to six identified minority groups from Afghanistan, Bangladesh and Pakistan so that they can stay in India without attracting the penal provisions of the Foreigners Act, 1946 and the Passport (Entry into India) Act, 1920 and the Rules made thereunder.[16]

This also became the argument that trumped the concerns about provoking Bangladesh, a friendly neighbour.[17]

Article 14 of the chapter on Fundamental Rights in the Constitution guarantees that "The State shall not deny to *any person* equality before the law or the equal protection of the laws within the territory of India." This is not a right that is dependent upon such a person being an Indian citizen; it is available even to foreigners who happen to be within the territory of India. Differential treatment to individuals on the basis of their religious faith would appear to be in contravention of the right to equality. The settled jurisprudence on the matter has two requirements: first, to be reasonable the classification created must be based on intelligible differentia; and second, the differentia must have a rational relationship to the object sought to be achieved by the statute. The Department of Legislative Affairs reassured the JPC on both counts, arguing that the classification met the tests of intelligible differentia, based on the fact that it pertained to minority communities in the specified countries that had suffered religious persecution. Further, while the relationship to the object of the

[16] Sixteenth Lok Sabha, "Report of the Joint Committee on the Citizenship (Amendment) Bill 2016", sec. 2.40, p. 49. Emphasis added.

[17] Ibid.

Act was admittedly not clearly specified in the proposed law, it was "*specifically mentioned in the Cabinet Note seeking approval of the Cabinet for introduction of the Bill.*"[18] It was further stated that Article 11 of the Constitution endows Parliament with the power to determine citizenship, and that "the Legislature is competent to exercise its discretion and make reasonable classification."[19] Under normal circumstances, an independent judiciary might quite likely find such claims unconvincing.

The very admissibility of the idea that it is acceptable to discriminate on the basis of religion seems to strike at the root of everything the Indian nation-building and constitutional projects have stood for. It provokes the concern that once the principle of discrimination on the basis of religion – barred by Article 15 of the Constitution – is admitted on the question of who can be a citizen of India, it may not be possible to limit or contain its further application to other realms; it could plausibly be extended to a graded citizenship in which different sets of rights and entitlements accrue to different tiers of citizens.

As the CAA opens up pathways to citizenship for favoured groups of migrants, deemed acceptable only on grounds of their faith and countries of origin, it is complemented by another initiative, the National Register of Indian Citizens (commonly referred to as the NRC), which opens up paths to statelessness for groups that are disfavoured only on the basis of their faith. The CAA and the NRC are manifestly conjoined in their objectives, as faith is set to become the exclusive criterion for determining who is an Indian citizen and who is not, for inclusion as well as for exclusion. Together, they have the potential of transforming India into a majoritarian polity with gradations of citizenship rights that undermine the constitutional principle of universal equal citizenship, with privileges of inclusion being

[18] Ibid., sec. 2.33, p. 46. Emphasis added.

[19] Ibid.

attached to some categories of citizens while others suffer the disabilities of exclusion.

The political dissimulation around this twinning has been bewildering. On 20 November 2019, the Home Minister told Parliament that the NRC would be conducted nationwide. In Parliament, and in several political meetings, he stated that all concerns were baseless if the "chronology" was appreciated: first the CAA, then the NPR (the National Population Register on which the NRC is based) and finally the NRC.[20] On 20 December, the Prime Minister informed Parliament that "*till now* the government has not taken any decision to prepare the NRIC at the national level." Even as this limited the reassurance to a "not yet", the Cabinet announced budgetary approval for the NPR, readied for roll out alongside the Census. The Census was initiated in a few places, where its lack of transparency and the fear among citizens of not owning the right documents led to attacks on Census enumerators. The arrival of Covid-19 in March 2020 led to the (presumably temporary) suspension of both the Census and the NPR.

The NRC is technically based on the innocuous sounding National Population Register, both of which have been on the statute books since 2003. The repeated attempts at assuaging anxieties by citing sequence (or "chronology") hold the key to understanding it. The NPR is just that: a register of *usual residents*, not of citizens, but of people who have lived in that particular area for a period of six months and who anticipate living in the same place for the next six months. When the NPR is compiled, it will be the prerogative of the local sub-registrar, an official of rather modest status, to identify "doubtful persons", or to put down as "doubtful persons" all those individuals whom non-doubtful persons in the locality identify as "doubtful persons". A robust

[20] https://scroll.in/article/947436/who-is-linking-citizenship-act-to-nrc-here-are-five-times-amit-shah-did-so; also, https://www.newsclick.in/Modi-Shah-NRC-Chronology-Yes-Yes-No-Yes-No, both accessed 7 October 2020.

rent-seeking economy in the manufacture and certification of papers can be reasonably expected to flourish. Those on this list who get authenticated will appear on the NRC; those categorised as "doubtful" will have to prove through appeals that they legally exist, first in the Foreigners' Tribunals and then through the courts.

It is not clear what precisely their doubtful status will involve as the adjudication of claims meanders slowly up from one level to another, but disenfranchisement and disqualification for government benefits would obviously be entailed. In the final analysis, there is the horrific prospect of incarceration in detention centres, for which generous financial provision has already been made. In Assam alone, the construction has begun of a large detention camp with a capacity of 3000 detainees, with ten others planned to fit a thousand people each.[21] Given the potential numbers, deportation is unlikely, but large-scale statelessness as the outcome is plausible.

It might be argued that the worry over exclusions being faith-based is unwarranted, for the process envisaged could arguably affect anyone who is undocumented. But that pushes us to consider who the undocumented are: the poor, the marginalised, and the vulnerable. It is no secret that the social groups among the poor and marginalised are Dalits, Adivasis, and Muslims. This is why the repeated insistence on minding the "chronology" points to the path to citizenship that has thoughtfully been made available in advance, enabling some to declare their undocumented selves as members of a persecuted religious minority. The only group without such recourse to the CAA is the Muslims.

The rationale for a nationwide NRC, its feasibility, and above all its moral legitimacy, are questionable. Under the Foreigners'

[21] Post-Holocaust, it is difficult to escape the symbolism of detention centres in any part of the world: even if those being set up in India are only for large-scale incarceration and in no way resemble the Nazi death camps, their association with the Russian Gulag and the "retraining" camps for China's Muslim Uighur population seems unavoidable.

Act 1946, the burden of proof rests on the individual charged with being a foreigner. Since the Citizenship Act provides no independent mechanism for identifying aliens, the NRC effectively places an entire population under suspicion of alienage. With what justification a state that does not have the ability to "detect" aliens, or even secure its borders against illegal immigrants, can set about finding aliens by elimination is not clear. As one commentator puts it in the context of the Assam NRC, the universalisation of "the suspicion of foreign-ness" meant that "everyone in the state was an alien until proven not."[22] The nationwide NRC seeks to universalise this suspicion across India. Experts have also questioned the legality of the NRC on the grounds that a provision under the Rules cannot contravene the provisions of the parent Act. Authorised by the Registration of Citizens and Issue of National Identity Card Rules, 2003, the NRC uses the cut-off date of 1971, which is based on the Assam Accord, rather than the date of 1987, which is the defining criterion of citizenship by birth according to the Citizenship Act.

To find aliens by elimination is arguably a task requiring greater state capacity than that involved in detecting aliens and securing borders against illegal migration. Even were such a task morally unexceptionable, it is questionable if India has the state capacity required to accurately sift and sort citizens from non-citizens. The costs entailed by the NRC – financial, logistical, and administrative – are enormous. In Assam alone, the huge expenditure on the NRC and the number of officials deployed to enrol just 3.3 million people resulted in an exercise that yielded unanticipated outcomes, especially unwelcome to those who were most enthusiastic about it, as it ended up excluding 1.9 million people. Extrapolating from Assam for a back-of-the-envelope calculation of what a nationwide NRC might cost yields a mind-boggling figure – two and a half times the combined budgetary outlay for health and

[22] Bhat, "Stateless and Hyperlegalized".

education in the Union Budget of 2020. And this does not include the costs involved in deploying approximately 40 per cent of the total number of existing government employees in India. In other words, practically every other service provided by the state, and every other administrative function performed by it, would need to come to a standstill for this to be implemented.

While the limitations of Indian administrative capacity are a public secret, the prospect of millions of poor and unlettered citizens being unable to produce acceptable documentation makes the scenario doubly nightmarish. The practices of "paper citizenship" acquired through "networks of kinship" and "networks of profit" are well documented.[23] As in Assam, such an enrolment drive could actually put undocumented nationals at risk of losing their citizenship as a consequence of the questionable search for non-national – essentially Muslim – migrants who are frequently better documented. Its impact will fall most grievously on the undocumented poor whose forebears have lived in India for generations but who could, for lack of documentation, be rendered stateless and incarcerated in detention centres.

The minutiae of implementation are however only cautionary arguments. The compelling argument against it lies in its adverse repercussions for the delicate but fraying plural social fabric of the Indian nation; for the civilisational qualities of humaneness and hospitality that have marked its history; and above all for the equality of citizenship, based on birth and without regard to creed, that its Constitution guarantees.

From a Civic to an Ethno-National Community

India was constituted as a civic rather than a cultural community. The CAA in combination with the NRC signals a transformative shift from a civic-national conception to an ethno-national

[23] Sadiq, *Paper Citizens*.

conception of India, as a political community in which identity will determine gradations of citizenship. This is a slippery slope to a new conception of Indian nationhood defined in religious majoritarian terms. Access to citizenship determined differentially by religious identity redefines Indian nationhood and threatens to convert citizens into aliens. Alienage may not lead to expulsion, but it can entail disenfranchisement and the comprehensive deprivation of civil and political rights, including the right to own property. The tragedy is that this production of alienage arises out of nothing except prejudice and a hatred based on faith, to which political morality, to say nothing of constitutional morality, is hopelessly hostage.

Though the CAA ostensibly relates only to migrants seeking the legal status of citizenship, it is arguably not just about migrants. The threat, rhetorical or otherwise, of a nationwide NRC shows that the fig leaf of illegal immigration is being used to bring the citizenship of *all* Muslim citizens into question. Migrants – beginning with those in Assam – are fast becoming a pretext to fabricate and advance a much more ambitious and nationwide project of "othering". The multiple identities that have historically been at play in Assam make it disingenuous to present the animosity towards migrants exclusively in terms of Hindu sentiments against Muslims. On its visit to Assam in May 2018, the Joint Parliamentary Committee on the CAB was petitioned by hundreds of organisations agitating against the Bill. The petitioners expressed not only the secular constitutionalist objection to introducing religion-based citizenship provisions, but also the fear of both Assamese speakers as well as indigenous tribal communities – such as the Tai tribes, the Garos, and the residents of the Barak Valley – of becoming minorities in their own land. The attempt to extrapolate lessons for a national-level Hindu political consolidation from the Assam situation is based on a possibly deliberate misrecognition of identities in that state, and on a flawed singularising of its plural identity-related anxieties.

Following the NRC, 3331 people have already been placed in six detention centres in Assam, living in sub-human conditions;[24] 335 of these have spent 3 years in camps; 30 persons declared foreigners have died in the detention camps;[25] and an estimated 33 persons have been driven to suicide by the fear of not possessing papers.[26] Although the Supreme Court has passed orders for the improvement of the conditions in these centres, there is a genuine moral concern about the very idea of such detention centres, for they are so obviously at odds with India's constitutional values, and more generally with the idea of human rights.

In democratic states, stripping a person of citizenship and rendering them stateless is not taken lightly. Criteria for such a stripping being "conducive to the public good" have to be formally established. In the United Kingdom, for instance, it gathered momentum from 2017 onwards, and has mostly been used for IS recruits and "jihadists". Even so, the courts and the House of Lords have weighed in on the issue, and the Home Secretary has enjoyed the power to cancel the citizenship of dual- or multiple-nationality holders, so that no statelessness ensues. The propensity to formalise exclusion through the law of citizenship always exists and requires vigilance. In 1950, Hannah Arendt pointed out that universal human rights were of no avail to people without membership, i.e. citizenship, in a polity. The condition of statelessness is a necessary prelude to rightlessness. That was why, she argued, the Nazis stripped the Jews of their citizenship before marching them off to concentration camps to be exterminated.

[24] "Govt Lodged 3,331 People in Assam Detention Centres, 10 Died Last Year", *Business Standard*, New Delhi, 17 March 2020, https://www.business-standard.com/article/pti-stories/10-inmates-of-detention-centres-in-assam-died-in-last-one-year-govt-120031700816_1.html, accessed 29 June 2020. It is estimated that the number of individuals currently in detention does not exceed 500.

[25] Karmakar, "30 'Foreigners' Dead".

[26] https://www.news18.com/news/immersive/assam-nrc-suicides.html

The Universal Declaration of Human Rights (UDHR) gives every human being, regardless of identity, the right to moral and legal personhood. It was unusual but not altogether surprising that the United Nations High Commissioner for Human Rights filed an intervention application in the Supreme Court of India against the CAA, seeking to remind India of the duty, placed on states by the UDHR, to avoid taking actions that result in statelessness and the deprivation of citizenship. Likewise, over 600 Members of the European Parliament moved six resolutions opposing the CAA, but the vote on this was deferred as a result of diplomatic intervention. Sardar Vallabhbhai Patel seemed to have been prescient when, in his defence of the principle of birthright citizenship in the Constituent Assembly, he said: "It is important to remember that the provision about citizenship will be scrutinised all over the world. They are watching what we are doing."[27]

India's neighbours – especially friendly neighbours like Bangladesh and Afghanistan – were indeed watching, and hearing the implied accusations of their treatment of minorities.[28] Alert to this possibility, the JPC had already expressed concern over "whether it would be prudent to raise the issue of religious persecution in Bangladesh with whom India was maintaining friendly and cordial relations."[29] The Ministry of Home Affairs assured the committee that the government of Bangladesh was committed to protecting and preserving the rights of minority groups in their country and ensuring their security. The committee, however, allowed itself to wonder aloud on the "violent incidents impacting the minority community in Bangladesh in the past."[30] In the end, Bangladesh

[27] Constituent Assembly of India Debates (Proceedings) – Volume III, 29 April 1947, http://164.100.47.194/Loksabha/Debates/cadebatefiles/C29041947.html

[28] Bhadrakumar, "India has Wounded Afghan and Bangladeshi Self-respect", cites a television interview by the Afghan envoy to India, taking vocal exception to the idea that there is state persecution of the minority Sikh community in his country.

[29] Sixteenth Lok Sabha, "Report of the Joint Committee on the Citizenship (Amendment) Bill 2016", sec. 2.38, p. 48.

[30] Ibid.

was persuaded at the highest inter-governmental level that the Indian political rhetoric of sending "termites" and "infiltrators" back to Bangladesh was an internal matter and that there would be no deportation. In fact, the impressive economic indicators of Bangladesh today give rise to the speculation that there may be less migration from Bangladesh to India now than in the reverse direction. Already host to 1.1 million illegal Indian immigrants, Bangladesh is the fifth largest sender of remittances to India.

India's intelligence agencies were also worried that the provisions of the CAA could be taken advantage of by neighbouring countries. In its deposition, the Research & Analysis Wing said: "the agencies who are inimical to us should not have a legal framework within which they can exploit our situation and infiltrate their own people into our own country. That is a matter of great concern for us . . ."[31]

While it is chiefly legal citizenship that is at stake in this discussion, the implications for social citizenship are not insignificant. Even as the CAA excludes Muslim migrants from the provisions for fast-track citizenship, Indian Muslims who are full citizens by birth have long been experiencing the abrogation of their constitutionally guaranteed rights of equal citizenship. Their endemic under-representation in India's public institutions is well known. The Sachar Committee Report established their abysmal education and employment indicators, as well as their poor indicators of social and economic development as being even worse than those of Dalits and Adivasis. Their political representation has always been disproportionately low, but it was, until recently, at least tokenistically accepted as desirable. The unprecedented increase in incidents of vigilante violence against them over the last few years, and the impunity enjoyed by the perpetrators of such violence, signifies a systematic political and ideological attempt to render them second-class citizens. Along with everyday practices

[31] Ibid., sec. 2.22, p. 40.

of social discrimination, and living in an ecosystem of violence, fear, and insecurity, the citizenship of the vast majority of Indian Muslims has been substantively second class. With this amendment to the law, even their formal citizenship is endangered. Should the nationwide NRC disenfranchise the insufficiently documented and thence deprive them of citizenship, it will only complete the political marginalisation of Muslims. Since 2014 it has been repeatedly made clear that they are not deserving of representation; this could make them legally unrepresentable.

Secondly, the gap between formal and substantive citizenship will widen not just for Muslims but for all poor and document-poor Indians, including and especially Dalits and Adivasis. Given the marginalisation and vulnerability of these groups, the convergence of poverty with the absence of documents, and the histories of prejudice in Indian society, these groups more than others will – through the instruments of the CAA and NRC/NPR – be pulled backwards, perhaps even deprived of the formal legal status of citizenship. This would be a move from the substantively second-class citizenship they currently hold to formal legal second-class citizenship – or worse.

As the NRC threatens to convert legitimate citizens into illegal immigrants and illegal immigrants into stateless people, both destined for the camp; as the CAA selectively legalises illegal migrants; and as minorities are rendered second-class citizens by an insidious use of the law, India stands on the edge of a dangerous precipice where its constitutional values and moral compass are at grave risk.

The Rearticulation of Constitutional Values in the Protests

In conclusion, let me return to the protests against the CAA in the winter of 2019 and offer an interpretation of how these sought to retrieve and reinvigorate the core but presently endangered constitutional values of Equality, Secularism, and Democracy.

As they held aloft the Constitution and portraits of Dr Ambedkar, the protesters reaffirmed the principles of equality and inclusion enshrined in this founding document of the Indian republic. Their invocation of the symbols of the constitutional order – the Constitution, the national flag, and the national anthem (with the additional verses that resonate so much today) – were also invocations of the self-definition of India's nationhood, a civilisational understanding of who we are and how our lives interpenetrate, of our similarities of language and culture rather than our differences of worship. What was unique about this moment was the treatment of the Constitution as a hallowed sacrament – a kind of non-denominational sacralisation of the document that enshrines equality.

The second constitutional value that was rescued and reinstated as legitimate in the public imagination was that of secularism, a defining principle of India's constitutional democracy that had been snidely discredited since the 1990s with coinages like pseudo-secular, or sickular, and the charge that secularism meant only minority "appeasement". Proponents of secularism have, over the last two decades, been put on the defensive by the advance of the idea of religious majoritarianism as legitimate state policy. Through the protests, this came to be strenuously repudiated across communities, and there seemed to be a new resolve to reject discrimination on the basis of religion, finding expression in a confident assertion of the idea of secularism, resurrected from the dustbin of political incorrectness and restored to its rightful place in popular discourse.

The protests indicated, thirdly, a reinvention of the vocabulary of democracy beyond electoral participation, with an assertion of the right to protest on the streets even in the face of police brutality. In a typically electoralist interpretation of democracy, those in government argued that the CAA was a manifesto commitment, and its legislative majority of seats was adequate to confer legitimacy on the amendment. In the run-up to the Delhi Assembly elections in February 2019, the ruling party advice to voters – to press the button on the electronic voting machine to send an electrifying current through it – was an attempt to weaponise electoral democracy against participatory democracy, the voting machine against the raw power of the protesting people. Its further denigration of the challenge in the Supreme Court as an interference with the democratic mandate rested on not just a spare understanding of democracy but also an implicit repudiation of the concept of judicial review, and thus the very idea of a constitutional democracy.

Federalism is a core element of the institutional design of India's democracy and the government's brute majority in Parliament has meant that the only institutional pushback could come from the states. However, citizenship is part of the Union list, on which the Centre has the exclusive power to legislate. Though it would probably be unconstitutional for state governments to refuse to comply, the resolutions passed in a few state assemblies and the promise of some states to withhold implementation of the NPR and the NRC are signs of resistance, and of a revival of the federal spirit.

Finally, the protests witnessed the repeated invocation and even the enactment of fraternity from the last few lines of the Preamble. The idea that we should, through the Constitution, resolve to promote fraternity "assuring the dignity of the individual" is attributed to Dr Ambedkar, who held that liberty, equality, and fraternity formed a trinity in which the divorce of any one from the other would defeat the very purpose of democracy. "Without equality, liberty would produce the supremacy of the few over the many. Without fraternity, liberty would produce the supremacy of the few over the many. Without fraternity, liberty and equality could not become a natural course of things. It would require a constable to enforce them."[32]

It has been argued that the addition of fraternity – the only preambular value not to have been mentioned in Nehru's

[32] Dr B.R. Ambedkar's Speech in the Constituent Assembly on the adoption of the Constitution, 25 November 1949, Volume 11, Document No. 165, Paragraph No. 325, https://www.constitutionofindia.net/constitution_assembly_debates/volume/11/1949-11-25

Objectives Resolution – was the distinctive contribution of Ambedkar, whose attachment to this idea was inspired initially by the ideals of the French Revolution and later related by him to the Buddhist conception of *maitri*.[33] Earlier iterations sought to assure the dignity of the individual without distinction of, variously, caste, class, or creed. The final version spoke only and sparely of the dignity of the individual. In his *The Annihilation of Caste* (1936), Ambedkar had already reflected on the concept of fraternity, describing it as "only another name for democracy. Democracy is not merely a form of Government. It is primarily a mode of associated living, of conjoint communicated experience. It is essentially an attitude of respect and reverence towards fellow men."[34]

In the winter of 2019, this notion of fraternity resonated especially with Arendt's argument that the natural place of fraternity is among the pariahs – the persecuted, the exploited, and the humiliated.[35] Indeed, the presence, at Shaheen Bagh, of so many people who had hitherto been what Arendt called "inner emigrants", was an affirmation of fraternity.

While their sit-in aimed to protect the Constitution, there was gratifying irony in the fact that Muslim women – doubly disadvantaged by religious identity and gender – were in the frontlines challenging majoritarianism and redefining gender norms. It took a greatly oppressed minority within a minority to question Hindu majoritarian politics. Only a few months earlier, passing a law to criminalise the triple talaq mode of divorce, the discourse of this majoritarian politics had adopted the language of protection – of saving "Muslim sisters" from their husbands. Now, these same Muslim sisters were being diminished with insinuations about the motives of their protests, as they (or *because* they?) squarely confronted and challenged religious majoritarianism.

[33] Rathore, *Ambedkar's Preamble*, Chapter 4.

[34] Ambedkar, *Annihilation of Caste*, 57.

[35] Arendt, *Men in Dark Times*, p. 13.

Two iconic images of this struggle convey this challenge better than any anodyne academic description can. In one, a group of hijab-wearing students are protecting their male colleague and challenging the policemen attacking him; in the other, it is a young woman holding and escorting the young man whose bleeding hand bears the marks of the gunshot wound he has just sustained. These images subvert familiar stereotypes of masculinity, and the hitherto gendered idea of protection – whether of the Constitution or of fellow citizens – acquires a new meaning.

The arrogant and hasty passage of a discriminatory and deeply flawed law was followed by the eruption of popular resistance, sustained over three months, invoking constitutional values. This was in turn followed by the politicisation and communalisation of the protests by BJP leaders. The BJP's defeat in the Delhi election and the continuation of the protests resulted in the Delhi riots of 23–26 February 2020 in which 53 people were killed and 250 injured. The Report of the Delhi Minorities Commission identifies the incendiary speech of a local BJP leader, with a senior police official by his side, as the trigger for the violence.[36] It documents the systematic and organised nature of the violence; the targeted destruction of Muslim properties and vandalisation of Muslim places and symbols of worship; and, above all, the "refusal/delay/obfuscation" by the police to register First Information Reports. Activists and students who participated in these protests remain imprisoned on grave charges of inciting the very violence of which they were the victims. On 7 October 2020, the Supreme Court pronounced that such protests, even if peaceful, are not acceptable and may not occupy public places indefinitely. In *Amit Sahni vs Commissioner of Police and Ors,* a three-judge bench of the Supreme Court made a distinction between the mode and manner of dissent against colonial rule and dissent in a democracy. "Democracy and dissent," it said, "go hand in hand, but then the demonstrations

[36] Government of NCT of Delhi, "Report of the DMC Fact-Finding Committee".

expressing dissent have to be in designated places alone."[37] It is notable that this judgment was pronounced a full six months after the protests had been suspended due to the pandemic. It is especially notable that the court has, as of the end of 2020, not found the time to hear, let alone adjudicate, the petitions challenging the constitutionality of the CAA.

Although the articulation of the politics of fraternity and solidarity was vitiated by violence, interrupted by the pandemic, and discredited by the court, it is undeniable that the imperilment of legal citizenship produced exemplary citizens of practice. Whatever the future of citizenship, the fact that the politics of hyper-masculine cultural nationalism gave an impetus to the reclaiming and rearticulation of a feminised civic nationalism can only be normatively reassuring.

[37] Amit Sahni versus Commissioner of Police & Ors. SCC Civil Appeal No. 3282 of 2020, 17, https://www.livelaw.in/pdf_upload/pdf_upload-382531.pdf. A review petition has since been filed in the Supreme Court, though it is yet to be heard. Instead, and inconsistently with its position on the Shaheen Bagh protests, the court appears to be unusually receptive, in December 2020, to claims about the right to protest of farmers agitating against the three farm laws.

2

Law, Politics, and the Architecture of Citizenship

Introduction

The chapter on citizenship in the Indian Constitution has two distinctive qualities. First, more than any other set of provisions in the Constitution, the articles on citizenship have a pronounced quality of immediacy, of belonging only to the moment of their enactment. This is unusual because constitutions generally reflect a sense of timelessness in their phrasing, of having been enacted for perpetuity rather than for some fleeting moment. This avowedly momentary character is accentuated, secondly, by the self-limiting provision that a more permanent and enduring law on citizenship will be enacted by Parliament in due course. When he recommended the adoption of these articles to the Assembly, Dr Ambedkar clearly stated that they were not intended to lay down a permanent or unalterable law of Indian citizenship, but "all that we are doing is to decide *ad hoc* for the time being" who will be citizens on the date of the commencement of the Constitution.[1] Every other matter relating to citizenship would be determined by Parliament. The phrasing of Article 11 – "Nothing in the foregoing provisions of this Part shall derogate from the power of Parliament to make any provision with respect to the acquisition and termination of citizenship and all other matters relating to citizenship" – reaffirms the transience and self-limiting character of these provisions.

[1] *Constituent Assembly Debates*, vol. 9, 347, 10 August 1949.

Their immediacy and impermanence were dictated by the particular circumstances of the Partition of India in 1947 which substantively shaped their deliberate temporariness. Ironically, however, it is the legacy of this historical context that has proved the most enduring feature of citizenship law and jurisprudence in India. The present chapter provides an account of the constitutional provisions on citizenship in the Constituent Assembly of India and the debates that preceded their adoption. It also examines the subsequent legislation of the Citizenship Act of 1955, the case law on citizenship, as well as the amendments effected in the Act and its rules from the mid-1980s to the present. All of these, it is argued, strongly reflect the context of the Partition in which the constitutional provisions were drafted and adopted. The legal and judicial trajectory of citizenship in independent India is thus illustrative of the ways in which the Partition legacy continues to inflect this body of law and jurisprudence. Indeed, the imprint of this event is more, rather than less, deeply entrenched with the passage of time. The Citizenship Act of 1955 encapsulates that innocent moment after the physical and emotional upheaval of the Partition has settled and a fresh attempt is made to legislate citizenship in a way that does not reflect this legacy. However, the legacy creeps in again after the break-up of Pakistan and the influx of immigrants on the eastern border of India. It also becomes more evident on the western border with the influx of Hindu refugees from Sindh and Punjab in Pakistan in the 1990s and beyond.

As reflected in the amendments to the citizenship laws and rules, this legacy is visible in the way in which *jus soli* citizenship came to be first inflected and then eclipsed by elements of *jus sanguinis*. The Constituent Assembly witnessed a contest between these two principles, and the first section below, "Citizenship for Extraordinary Times", offers an interpretation of the debate and documents the constitutional settlement of citizenship. It also identifies the core issues that are most contested and remain central to citizenship jurisprudence, much of which speaks to the legacy of the Partition.

This is done through a focus on four terms whose interpretation has been central to the case law on citizenship: domicile, intention, migrant, and passport. The subsequent section, "Citizenship Laws for Ordinary Times", explicates the main provisions of the Citizenship Act 1955 and contextualises the amendments to the Citizenship Act from the mid-1980s to the present. The third section, "Three Parts to *Jus Sanguinis*", documents the gradual shift from a *jus soli* conception of citizenship to a *jus sanguinis* conception, reflecting the peculiar quality of the imbrication of the constitutional and statutory law of citizenship in the Partition of India. The apparent exception of recent amendments, which are intended to accommodate the claims of the diaspora, is actually less of an exception than it appears, as it echoes the shift from *jus soli* to *jus sanguinis*, albeit in a context discontinuous from that of the Partition. The concluding section reflects on the patterns of change and continuity in the constitutional and post-constitutional law of citizenship.

Citizenship for Extraordinary Times

Constitutions do not ordinarily define citizenship. Despite its invocation of the Declaration of the Rights of Man (1789), its vesting of national sovereignty in the French people, and its canonically inclusive conception of citizenship, the Constitution of the Fifth Republic in France does not actually define this concept. In the American Constitution, citizenship remained undefined till after the adoption of the Fourteenth Amendment in the aftermath of the Civil War and as a reaction to the Supreme Court's decision in *Dred Scott v Sanford* (1857).[2] Even the famously progressive

[2] *Dred Scott vs Sanford*, 60 US 393 (1857). Section 1 of the Fourteenth Amendment to the United States Constitution reads: "All persons born or naturalized in the United States, and subject to the jurisdiction thereof, are citizens of the United States and of the state wherein they reside." Rogers M. Smith's magisterial history of American citizenship, however, provides a compelling account of the ambiguities

Brazilian Constitution of 1988, which privileges the value of citizenship as a founding principle of the republic and defines expansively the social and economic rights of the people, does not actually indicate what the source and basis of citizenship will be.

When India's Constituent Assembly began its deliberations in December 1946, there was no thought of a separate chapter on the topic of citizenship. By the time the Constitution was adopted, the Partition had intervened and citizenship had become the subject of Part II of the Constitution, following the first part, "The Union and Its Territory". The seven articles that comprise this section took two years to be finalised, leading Dr Ambedkar, Chairman of the Drafting Committee, to say of what eventually became Article 5, the opening article of the section: "Except one other article in the Draft Constitution, I do not think that any other article has given the Drafting Committee such a headache as this particular article. I do not know how many drafts were prepared and how many were destroyed as being inadequate to cover all the cases which it was thought necessary and desirable to cover."[3] Article 5 was originally a part of the Fundamental Rights chapter. The discussion on citizenship was in fact initiated in the Sub-Committee on Fundamental Rights in March 1947, where there was consensus on a single citizenship for the Indian Union. There was also some preliminary discussion of the alternative bases of citizenship (*jus soli* and *jus sanguinis*) as members of the Constituent Assembly were anxious to avoid giving the impression that they were adopting the same "racial" principle against which the Indian nationalists had offered solidarity to the struggles of Indians in South Africa. As Vallabhbhai Patel said, "It is important to remember that the provision about citizenship will be scrutinised all over the world."[4]

---

in the Fourteenth Amendment in relation to foreign-born Blacks as well as tribes. Smith, *Civic Ideals*, Chapter 10.

[3] *Constituent Assembly Debates*, vol. 9, 347, 10 August 1949.

[4] Sardar Vallabhbhai Patel, 3.18.178, https://www.constitutionofindia.net/constitution_assembly_debates/volume/3/1947-04-29.

The announcement of the Partition in June 1947 gave a new impetus to the debate on citizenship in the Constituent Assembly. The division of British India along broadly religious lines triggered the massive movement of population from one country to another and, in some cases, back again to the first. It was accompanied by large-scale violence, displacement, and homelessness, which made it impossible to discuss even fundamental rights without some clarity about who the bearers of rights, or citizens, would be in the new republic.[5] An ad hoc committee was set up to re-examine the question of citizenship in the wake of the changed circumstances of the Partition. In the early discussions, a variety of possible challenges were articulated, ranging from provisions for marriages between citizens of India and Pakistan to provisions for residents of seceding areas who wished to retain their Indian citizenship. There was also some debate on the entitlements of Indian residents of Burma, Ceylon, Malaya, and other countries that had sizeable Indian populations. Determining an appropriate cut-off date to determine citizenship entitlements for persons migrating to India from Pakistan was obviously important. But the most contentious issues were around the concepts of domicile, migration, and the intention to settle, to which we will return after a brief delineation of the constitutional provisions on citizenship in Articles 5–11 of the Constitution.

Article 5 confers citizenship, at the commencement of the Constitution, on "every person who has his domicile in the territory of India and

[5] See *Constituent Assembly Debates*, vol. 2, 338, 30 August 1947. In the discussion on fundamental rights, B. Das said: "Many things have happened since we discussed Fundamental Rights in April last. India has been divided up and Indian citizens who are born in both parts of India now can claim citizenship in either Pakistan or Hindustan. There may be families that may have a brother in Pakistan acquiring the citizenship of Pakistan while others may be citizens of India. So it is natural that Government should legislate that everybody must declare whether he is a citizen of Pakistan or Hindustan. One would not like the best brains of India to go to Pakistan and when they come back to India will they be taken as Indians or only recognized as citizens of Pakistan because they have served after the separation in that country?"

(a) who was born in the territory of India; or
(b) either of whose parents was born in the territory of India; or
(c) who has been ordinarily resident in the territory of India for not less than five years immediately preceding such commencement

Article 5 was a preliminary foundational statement of *jus soli* citizenship, albeit one that applied only to those already living rather than to those born after the commencement of the Constitution. It was chosen as a form of "enlightened, modern civilised" and democratic citizenship, over the rival principle of *jus sanguinis* – described by the constitution-makers as "an idea of racial citizenship".[6] If Article 5 was an enunciation of citizenship for ordinary times, Articles 6 and 7 were articulations of citizenship for extraordinary times. Article 6 provides for citizenship for those who migrated to India from the territory now included in Pakistan if either of their parents or grandparents was born in India. If such a person migrated to India before 19 July 1948, he should have been resident in India since the date of his migration;[7] and if he migrated after that date, he should have been registered as a citizen of India by a designated government official. If Article 6 was intended to accord rights of citizenship to those who migrated from Pakistan to India around the time of the Partition, Article 7 was correspondingly designed to exclude from citizenship those who migrated from India to Pakistan after 1 March 1947. However, it provided for rights of citizenship for those who had so migrated from India to Pakistan but had returned to India with a permit of resettlement or permanent return issued by an authorised government official after the same date and by a process similar to that provided for in Article 6. As

[6] Ibid., vol. 9, 347, 29 April 1947.

[7] I retain here the constitutional usage of the masculine gender with some unease, and only in the context of the constitutional provisions.

we shall see, Article 7 was a hugely embattled provision in the Constituent Assembly.

Article 9 states that individuals who voluntarily acquire the citizenship of a foreign state cannot be citizens of India. Article 10 provides for the continuance of the rights of citizenship for anyone deemed to be a citizen under the earlier provisions "subject to the provisions of any law that may be made by Parliament"; and Article 11 gives Parliament complete power to "make any provision with respect to the acquisition and termination of citizenship and all other matters relating to citizenship".[8] The last two articles underscore unambiguously the stopgap and ad hoc nature of the constitutional provisions on citizenship, which are intended to provide for the specific situation of the extraordinary event of the Partition while a conception of citizenship for normal times awaits the attention of an elected Parliament.

Echoes of the communally charged atmosphere of the Partition resounded in the Assembly as it debated what eventually got enacted as Article 7. Though the markers of religious difference were not openly displayed, they are easily recognisable in the debates on Articles 6 and 7 of the Constitution. Article 6 was obviously unexceptionable as it guaranteed rights of citizenship for those that were largely Hindu migrants from Pakistan, commonly described in the discourse of the time as refugees. Article 7, however, implicitly referred to Muslims who had fled India for Pakistan in the wake of Partition-related violence but had later returned to reclaim their lives, livelihoods, and property. This article was necessitated by the fact that the numbers of such people were considerable, the High Commission claiming that it daily received a thousand applications from Muslim refugees.[9] Such people were euphemistically described as "migrants", and this was the most intensely

[8] Constitution of India 1950, Article 11, https://www.india.gov.in/sites/upload_files/npi/files/coi_part_full.pdf

[9] Zamindar, *The Long Partition*, 86.

contested article on citizenship in the Constituent Assembly. It is important to note that though the Constitution does not use the terms refugee and migrant, the words occurred frequently in Constituent Assembly speeches and subtly encoded religious identity in a shared universe of meaning.

There was heated contention in the Assembly about the necessity for a provision such as this. Jaspat Roy Kapoor labelled Article 7 the "obnoxious clause", arguing that "Once a person has migrated to Pakistan and transferred his loyalty from India to Pakistan, his migration is complete. He has definitely made up his mind at that time to kick this country and let it go to its own fate, and he went away to the newly created Pakistan, where he would put in his best efforts to make it a free progressive and prosperous state."[10] Other detractors of the article declared that Indian citizenship was being "sold too cheaply" and that the migration of these people from India to Pakistan had been intentional. Returning, they could now be saboteurs, spies, and fifth columnists. At best, they might have changed their minds about where to settle on finding Pakistan a less comfortable place than they had anticipated; or they might be returning to restore control over properties they had abandoned when they fled. Loyalty and intentionality were recurring themes in this view, and intention was to become, as we shall see, a central motif in the adjudication of cases in subsequent years.

In contrast, those who advocated Article 7 favoured a more inclusive conception of legal citizenship. They argued that Muslim migrants who had left India because of the communal riots and violence should be welcomed back. Their loyalties and intentions could not be treated as suspect because they had, to quote Mahajan CJ in *Central Bank v Ram Narain* just a few years later:

> [I]n October or November 1947, men's minds were in a state of flux. The partition of India and the events that followed in its wake in both Pakistan and India were unprecedented and

[10] *Constituent Assembly Debates*, vol. 9, 366, 11 August 1949.

> it is difficult to cite any historical precedent for the situation that arose. Minds of people affected by this partition and who were living in those parts were completely unhinged and unbalanced and there was hardly an occasion to form intentions requisite for acquiring domicile in one place or another. People vacillated and altered their programmes from day to day as events happened. They went backward and forward; families were sent from one place to another for the sake of safety . . . No one, as a matter of fact, at the moment thought that when he was leaving Pakistan for India or vice versa that he was forever abandoning the place of his ancestors.[11]

The intention to acquire domicile in Pakistan was not only difficult to establish but also seen as an unreasonable assumption since rational and deliberate intent was difficult to establish in a situation dominated by the raw emotions of fear and insecurity. All these – domicile, intention to permanently settle, and the meaning of migration – became points of contention in the case law.

Even as the Citizenship Act was passed by Parliament in 1955, the legacy of the Partition continued to be unsettled and ubiquitous in citizenship jurisprudence. In the body of case law following 1950, there are only a few cases – such as *State Trading Corporation* on whether or not a corporate entity enjoys the fundamental rights of a citizen – that are altogether unrelated to the event of Partition.[12]

Since the term "domicile" in Article 5 was not defined in the Constitution, it came to be contested in several cases which invariably referred to the basic principles of English law making a distinction between domicile of origin and domicile of choicc. While there is a wealth of legal commentary on the term in the

[11] *All India Reporter* (hereafter AIR), 1955 SC 36 [11].

[12] *State Trading Corporation of India v The Commercial Tax Officer*, AIR 1963 SC 1811.

context of the Conflict of Laws,[13] what is relevant for our purposes is the relationship between domicile and citizenship adjudicated in a number of cases, including as recently as 1991. In *Louis de Raedt v Union of India*, a Belgian missionary who had been living in India since 1937 petitioned the court in 1987 claiming that he had, on 26 November 1949, become a citizen under Article 5(e) of the Constitution.[14] The Supreme Court ruled that mere residence in the country did not constitute domicile; it must be accompanied by the intention to make a permanent home in the country, which de Raedt had not demonstrated. The court's verdict was that de Raedt had applied for a one-year extension of his permission as recently as 1980, which did not indicate a decision to reside permanently in India. At best it indicated the petitioner's uncertainty about his permanent home:

> For the acquisition of a domicile of choice, it must be shown that the person concerned had a certain state of mind, the *animus manendi*. If he claims that he acquired a new domicile at a particular time, he must prove that he had formed the intention of making his permanent home in the country of residence and of continuing to reside there permanently. Residence alone, unaccompanied by this state of mind, is insufficient.[15]

While intent or *animus manendi* was an important consideration in several cases, the Supreme Court had, as early as 1955, held that both factum and animus were essential, and neither by itself was sufficient. In *Central Bank of India v Ram Narain*, Ram Narain was being tried in India for an offence committed in Pakistan in November 1947.[16] On behalf of his firm, Ram Narain had taken an advance from the Central Bank of India in Multan District,

[13] Seervai, *Constitutional Law of India*, vol. 1, 319–25.

[14] (1991) 3 SCC 554.

[15] *Louis de Raedt* (n 14) [10].

[16] AIR 1955 SC 36.

against stocks (bales of cotton). In the disturbances that occurred during the Partition, the guard of the bank's warehouse fled and the stocks disappeared. In January 1948, an enquiry found that Ram Narain had himself stolen the goods and booked them to Karachi. Ram Narain had already moved his family to Gurgaon, India, and himself moved to India in November 1947. The bank demanded that he refund the money, but to no avail. It then got a sanction from the Government of East Punjab to prosecute Ram Narain, whose plea was that he was not an Indian citizen, but a Pakistan national, at the time of the offence and therefore Indian courts did not have jurisdiction. The High Court upheld this plea, arguing that the courts had no jurisdiction over an accused who was not a citizen of India at the time of the commission of the offence. The Supreme Court dismissed the bank's appeal, saying that both factum and animus were essential, and that in this case even if animus could be inferred from Ram Narain relocating his family to India in advance of his own move, the factum was found wanting and hence it could not be established that he was indeed domiciled in India at the time the offence was committed.[17]

It is worth noting that the domicile of women and minor children was inferred from the domicile of their husbands and fathers, respectively. A woman migrating from India to Pakistan with her husband in December 1947 would lose her Indian domicile and terminate her citizenship by virtue of such a move. However, Article 7 overrides Article 5, and domicile is not a criterion in Articles 6 and 7. This means that if a woman, born and domiciled in India, migrated to Pakistan after 1 March 1947, she would lose her Indian citizenship and domicile even if her husband remained in India. Minors were also considered to have migrated if they accompanied their fathers, though there was uncertainty about situations in which a minor migrated to Pakistan independently of a father who remained in India. Could such a minor be deemed

[17] *Central Bank of India* (n 16) [11].

to have migrated, or to have formed an intention to make Pakistan his permanent home? In *Rashid Hassan Roomi v Union of India*, the petitioner was the son of Indian parents who had lived in India for five years before the commencement of the Constitution.[18] His father migrated to Pakistan, while the son continued to live in India and eventually went on to become the Chairman of the Town Area Committee. He retained his domicile and citizenship on the grounds that his father had deserted him.[19]

The relationship between domicile and migration was no more obvious than that between domicile and citizenship. In *Shanno Devi v Mangal Sain*, the court adopted a narrow interpretation, in accordance with Article 6, defining migration as coming to India with the intent of permanent residence.[20] In *Kulathil Mammu v State of Kerala*, by contrast, a broader view prevailed as the court interpreted migration as coming and going from one territory to another, a meaning that could attach to both Articles 6 and 7 without bringing in the concept of domicile.[21] This was justified by the argument that both these articles began with a *non obstante* clause, as they were designed to deal with the abnormal situation of the movement of populations between India and Pakistan. This particular case pertained to a twelve-year-old boy who had

[18] AIR 1967 All 154.

[19] The presumption of equivalence between domicile and citizenship also provoked the question of whether a single all-India citizenship implied that an individual could not be domiciled in a particular State. This came up as a Conflict of Laws question in *DP Joshi v Madhya Bharat*, AIR 1955 SC 334, in which a constitution bench of the Supreme Court upheld State domicile in relation to college admissions, ruling that domicile and citizenship were two distinct concepts and that discrimination based on residence was not violative of Article 15(1). In *Pradeep Jain v Union of India* (1984) 3 SCC 654 [8], Bhagwati J stated that it was "highly detrimental to the unity and integrity of India to think in terms of state domicile." Jurists have argued that the reality of legal pluralism – especially with respect to personal laws – makes State domicile compatible with all-India citizenship. See Seervai, *Constitutional Law of India*, vol. 1, 317–28, n.13.

[20] AIR 1961 SC 58.

[21] AIR 1966 SC 1614.

migrated to Pakistan with his father in 1948, had returned to India on a Pakistan passport with an Indian visa, gone back and forth a few times, and finally returned to live in India. In October 1964, Aboobacker – whose late father had held Indian nationality – was arrested and detained by the State government. His plea before the court – that he was an Indian citizen and "had simply gone to Karachi in search of livelihood as he was poor" – was contested by the State, which treated his migration as intentional and therefore not attracting the provisions of Article 7.[22] The Kerala High Court had upheld the State's view, but the Supreme Court settled on a wider interpretation that focused only on movement from one place to another – "whether or not there is any intention of settlement in the place to which one moves" – and held that such an interpretation was indeed the intent of the Constitution makers.[23] The wide interpretation adopted in this verdict then implied that the idea of *animus manendi* did not apply in the abnormal situation of the Partition.[24]

A piece of evidence frequently cited in judicial decisions at this time as a decisive criterion for determining intention was the passport. In *Louis de Raedt*, it was argued on behalf of the petitioning Belgian missionary that his case could not be rejected only because he held a foreign passport. Around the time of the Partition, people often had to acquire a Pakistan passport in order to return to India. In some cases, such as *State of Andhra Pradesh v Abdul*, the court took the view that passports were not conclusive evidence of the person having voluntarily obtained Pakistani citizenship or of having renounced Indian nationality.[25] In others, such as *Izhar Ahmad Khan v Union of India*, the possession of a Pakistan passport was interpreted as evidence of such volition and

[22] *Kulathil Mammu* (n 21) [4].

[23] *Kulathil Mammu* (n 21) [5].

[24] Seervai, *Constitutional Law of India*, vol. 1, 331, n.13. Seervai was sharply critical of this judgment which he argued wrongly overruled the verdict in *Shanno Devi*.

[25] AIR 1961 SC 1467.

intent.[26] In *State of Gujarat v Saiyad Aga Mohmed Saiyed Mohmed*, the Supreme Court prevented the government from deporting the plaintiff despite his possessing a Pakistani passport because

> If a plea is raised by the citizen that he had not voluntarily obtained the passport, the citizen must be afforded an opportunity to prove that fact. Cases may be visualised in which on account of force a person may be compelled or on account of fraud or misrepresentation he may be induced, without any intention of renunciation of his Indian citizenship to obtain a passport from a foreign country.[27]

In the next section, we shall see how the exercise of judicial reasoning in the early decades is, on some of these terms, inverted when the determination of citizenship for people presumed to be illegal immigrants from Bangladesh comes to be litigated.

Citizenship Laws for Ordinary Times

The Citizenship Act 1955 was enacted in pursuance of Article 11 of the Constitution. It provides for the acquisition of citizenship in five ways: by birth, descent, registration, naturalisation, and the incorporation of territory. The most significant amendments to the Citizenship Act have been to Sections 3 (citizenship by birth) and 6 (citizenship by naturalisation) to address concerns about illegal immigration from Bangladesh. Section 7 (citizenship by incorporation of territory) has also been substantively amended to provide for overseas citizenship of India.

There were originally two exceptions to citizenship by birth: (a) if the father possessed diplomatic immunity and was not an Indian citizen, and (b) if the father was an enemy alien and the birth occurred at a place under enemy occupation. While these (obviously infrequent) exceptions remain, another set of exceptions

[26] AIR 1962 SC 1052.
[27] (1979) 1 GLR 71 [15].

was later introduced that have immediate relevance to migrants from Bangladesh. This is expressed in two sub-clauses of the amended Section 3, which now accords citizenship to those born in India (a) on or after 26 January 1950 and before 1 July 1987; (b) those born on or after 1 July 1987 but before the commencement of the Citizenship (Amendment) Act 2003 and "either of whose parents is a citizen of India at the time of his birth"; and, in 3(c):

> [O]n or after the commencement of the Citizenship (Amendment) Act, 2003, where –
>
> (i) both of his parents are citizens of India;
>
> (ii) one of whose parents is a citizen of India and the other is not an illegal migrant at the time of his birth.

Thus, only those born in India after 26 January 1950 and before 1 July 1987 enjoy the right to unconditional citizenship based on *jus soli*. To be citizens by birth, those born between 1 July 1987 and before the amendment of 2003 must have one parent who is a citizen of India at the time of their birth. Section 3(c) excludes all those born – after the commencement of the amendment of 2003 – with one parent who is an illegal migrant at the time of their birth. The explanation of this lies in the amendment to the provision relating to citizenship by naturalisation in Section 6 of the Citizenship Act.

Meanwhile, Section 4 relating to citizenship by descent for those born outside India to Indian parents has been rendered gender-neutral. Until 1992, this applied to anyone whose *father* was a citizen of India at the time of his birth. Since 1992, citizenship by descent is available to those born outside India *either of whose parents* is a citizen of India at the time of his birth. In 2004 and 2005, the provisions of citizenship by registration (Section 5) were amended to, on the one hand, exclude from such citizenship all illegal migrants, and, on the other, to lower the residence requirement for those registered as Overseas Citizens of India (for five years) from two years to one.

The most significant amendments to the Act have however been to the provisions of Section 6, which deals with citizenship by naturalisation. Section 6A was introduced in 1985 to make special provisions for the citizenship of those covered by the Assam Accord. Migration from Bangladesh peaked in 1971, at the time of the break-up of Pakistan, and continued steadily thereafter. The subsequent enfranchisement of large numbers of refugees/migrants took on a communal colour and generated massive protests by the All Assam Students' Union, between 1979 and 1985, against the swamping of Assam by "foreigners". In February 1983, in the midst of elections based on electoral rolls that allegedly included a large number of "illegal" voters, a terrible massacre took place in Nellie, killing over two thousand people.

The Assam Accord, the political settlement arrived at between the Assam movement and the central and state governments, provided that (a) all those who had migrated before 1966 would be treated as citizens; (b) those who had migrated between 1966 and 1971 could stay by putting themselves through the designated process of registration as foreigners; and (c) all those who migrated after 1971 would be deemed illegal immigrants. The numbers of such illegal immigrants are commonly estimated to be upward of ten million. Many of them had acquired forms of what has been called "documentary citizenship", including ration cards and election cards which enabled them to vote in elections.[28] The amendment to the Citizenship Act in 1985 was intended to ensure that the names of those who came in after 1966 would be deleted from the electoral roll. They would then have to wait ten years from their "detection" as foreigners before becoming legal citizens and voters once again.

In 2003 (effective 2004), the section on Citizenship by the Incorporation of Territory into India was substantially amended to include a section (7A) on the registration of Overseas Citizens

[28] Sadiq, *Paper Citizens*.

of India. This provides for anyone who is an adult citizen of another country, but either was or was eligible to be a citizen at the time of the commencement of the Constitution, or is a child or grandchild of such a citizen. A year later, the Central Government specified the rights of such citizens, which include the grant of a lifelong multiple-entry visa to India, but exclude such citizens from voting or contesting election to public office or recruitment to government jobs. Citizens of Pakistan and Bangladesh, or even those who have ever held citizenship of these two countries, are ineligible for registration as overseas citizens of India.

The restrictions on citizenship for migrants deemed illegal, on the one hand, and the expansion of citizenship to include the diaspora, on the other, are suggestive of the increasing encroachment of elements of *jus sanguinis*. Three issues that reflect the move from *jus soli* to *jus sanguinis* in the citizenship law of India need careful consideration.

Three Paths to *Jus Sanguinis*

Two of three paths to *jus sanguinis* have been briefly mentioned: first, the constraint applied to the *jus soli* principle by the provision excluding from citizenship those Indian-born people who had at least one illegal-migrant parent at the time of their birth; and, secondly, the provisions relating to overseas citizenship of India which give recognition to members of the diaspora not born in India but who are the children or grandchildren of those who were citizens by birth. The third aspect of the citizenship law that indicates such a move is contained in the 2003 (effective 2004) amendment to the Citizenship Rules 1956 in respect of their application to the States of Gujarat and Rajasthan. Here I will first return to the amendments excluding the Indian-born children of illegal migrants, and the events leading up to these; then turn to the amendments to the Citizenship Rules for migrants from Pakistan to Rajasthan and Gujarat; and finally to the amendments relating to Overseas Citizenship.

The amended Citizenship Act is not shy of acknowledging that these amendments or "special provisions" are a product of the Assam Accord. As such, the reference to illegal migrants is a thinly veiled reference to Muslim migrants. In the previous section, we noted that a large number of these migrants had acquired the franchise by means that have been labelled "networks of profit" and "networks of complicity".[29] In other words, kinship networks and money were reasonable guarantees of registration on the electoral rolls. Assiduously courted by the Congress party, the vulnerability of these people on account of their religious identity had made them Congress sympathisers and eager voters. In 1983, the Congress government at the Centre responded to the political unrest in Assam by enacting the Illegal Migrants (Determination by Tribunals) Act (IMDT Act) which provided for complaints about illegal migrants to be filed and adjudicated by tribunals especially instituted to detect and expel foreigners. While this conveyed the impression of assuaging nativist Assamese sentiment, networks of ethnic solidarity could be and were relied upon to render such complaints meaningless. The law also entailed making an Assam-specific exception to India's law on foreigners, which ordinarily places the burden of proving citizenship status on the individual in question. The IMDT Act removed the burden of proving their citizenship from those suspected of being illegal immigrants. The presence of illegal immigrants in the area could now be reported by their neighbours, and if the tribunal decided upon its examination of the complaint that those so accused were indeed illegal migrants, it had the power to order their deportation.

The IMDT Act was challenged in the Supreme Court by a writ petition filed by Sarbananda Sonowal, one of the leaders of the

[29] Ibid., 56–69, n.28.

students' agitation against immigration. The plea was that the Act was *ultra vires* of the Constitution because it made it "impossible for citizens who are resident in Assam to secure the detection and deportation of foreigners from Indian soil."[30] Its legality was brought into question because, though the professed aim of the IMDT Act was to facilitate the detection and deportation of illegal foreign migrants in Assam, the procedure prescribed did not conform to the Foreigners Act 1946, which is applicable to all foreigners throughout India. An exception had effectively been made for non-Indians who had entered Assam clandestinely after 1971 and were alleged to have brought about a change in the "whole character, cultural and ethnic composition of the area".[31] Such migration, it was claimed, had the potential to create internal disturbance and needed to be treated as aggression under Article 355 of the Constitution, which binds the Union to protect States against such aggression.

The petition was supported by the National Democratic Alliance coalition headed by the BJP when it came to office at the Centre. The new government communicated to the Supreme Court its intention to repeal the Act both because of the internal security implications of the population influx, and also because the application of the Act to only one State was clearly discriminatory.[32] In 2000, the State government in Assam headed by the Asom Gana Parishad (AGP) – the All Assam Students' Union had grown into the political party of this name – claimed that the provisions of the IMDT Act actually *protected* illegal migrants. To support its case that the small numbers of foreigners detected and deported could be directly attributed to the provisions of the Act, it showed that while it had initiated 310,759 enquiries, the total number declared illegal immigrants was 10,015, of whom only 1481 had actually

[30] *Sarbananda Sonowal v Union of India* (2005) 5 SCC 655 [2].

[31] Ibid. [2].

[32] Ibid. [3].

been expelled. The court was therefore asked to order a repeal of the IMDT Act for being "an ineffective piece of legislation" which was obstructing rather than facilitating the detection, deportation, and deletion of the names of illegal migrants from the electoral rolls.[33]

Religious bias was writ large in the claim, common enough in contemporary political discourse, that while the Hindu population of the State had risen by 41.89 per cent during 1971–91, the Muslim population of Assam had risen 77.42 per cent during the same period.[34] In 2004, the Congress party returned to power at the Centre and informed the Supreme Court that the Union government would retain the IMDT Act in its current form. Thus, the AGP and the BJP interpreted the small numbers actually deported as a sign that the Act was performing its intended purpose of protecting illegal immigrants for electoral gain by the Congress party. For its part, the Congress interpreted the same small numbers of those deported as showing that the Act was effective in ensuring that true Indians were not wrongfully deported on the suspicion of being foreigners.

The case was decided in 2005, with the Supreme Court striking down the Act as *ultra vires* of the Constitution and transferring all cases pending before the tribunals to the tribunals constituted under the Foreigners (Tribunals) Order 1964, to be decided in the manner provided in the Foreigners Act. The court concerned itself chiefly with determining the constitutional validity of the Act and especially the question of its applicability only to Assam, thus creating a State-specific exception to a national law. It ruled that the Act violated Article 14 of the Constitution to the extent that the exception was based solely on geography rather than any substantive connection with the object and policy of the Act.[35] It refused to entertain any consideration of the election manifesto of

[33] Ibid. [8].

[34] Ibid. [7].

[35] Ibid., Para 45.

a political party as a relevant factor in judging the constitutional validity of a law.[36] The judgment affirmed the procedure laid down in the Foreigners Act, which places the burden of proving citizenship upon the person in question, and noted that not only did the IMDT Act not contain any provision similar to Section 9 of the Foreigners Act regarding burden of proof, it was "conspicuously silent about it".[37] This, it argued, placed a very heavy burden on both the applicant and the authorities of the State to prove that a person was an illegal migrant liable for deportation. Indeed, said the court:

> Not every person feels that he owes a duty towards the nation and he should initiate proceedings for deportation of an illegal migrant. The applicant also incurs risk to his own security and safety besides spending time and energy in prosecuting the matter . . . This shows how one-sided the provisions of the IMDT Act are. They have been so made that they only result in giving advantage and benefits to an illegal migrant and not for achieving the real objective of the enactment, namely, of detection and deportation of a Bangladeshi national who has illegally crossed the border on or after 25th March, 1971.[38]

Accordingly, the court upheld the contention of the petitioners that the Act itself was the biggest obstacle to the identification and deportation of illegal migrants, that citizens were hardly likely to initiate such proceedings for deportation, and that, as it had resulted in expulsions in less than half of one per cent of all cases initiated, the Act seemed to have been deliberately designed to protect and shelter illegal migrants rather than to identify and deport them.[39]

[36] Ibid. [19].
[37] Ibid. [40].
[38] Ibid. [47].
[39] Ibid. [47].

The verdict quoted extensively from a 1998 report of the Governor of Assam stating that illegal migrants coming into Assam from Bangladesh were "almost exclusively Muslims".[40] The xenophobic sentiments expressed in the report raised fears of swamping and even terror: "The influx of these illegal migrants is turning these districts into a Muslim majority region. It will then only be a matter of time when a demand for their merger with Bangladesh may be made. The rapid growth of international Islamic fundamentalism may provide for [*sic*] driving force for this demand."[41]

The view that illegal migrants had reduced the people of Assam to a minority in their own State was endorsed by the Supreme Court, which echoed the petitioner's concern that their presence represented a threat of "external aggression and internal disturbance".[42] It thus came to the conclusion that the IMDT Act contravened Article 355 of the Constitution, which mandates the Union government to protect states against external aggression and internal disturbance.[43] However, the fact that the IMDT Act was struck down by the court has had no impact whatsoever on the law on citizenship, in particular the amendment to the Citizenship Act that modified the provision of citizenship by birth to exclude from it those born in India who have an illegal migrant as a parent at the time of their birth (Section 3(c) (ii)).

It is instructive to contrast this with the amendments to the Citizenship Rules. These were enacted to address the claims to citizenship of Hindu migrants from Pakistan migrating across the western border into the States of Rajasthan and Gujarat.[44] This region has experienced several waves of such immigration: from

[40] Ibid. [17].

[41] Ibid.

[42] Ibid. [63].

[43] Ibid., Para 42.

[44] For a detailed account of this case, see Jayal, *Citizenship and Its Discontents*, Chapter 3.

the wars between India and Pakistan in 1965 and 1971, and after the demolition of the Babri Masjid in Ayodhya in December 1992. Following the demolition, the insecurity of the Muslim minority in India found parallels in the insecurity of the Hindu minority in Pakistan, approximately 17,000 of whom migrated to India. Most of these, being Pakistan passport holders, travelled on Indian visas and overstayed. They then became applicants for citizenship. The Union government had already, in response to widespread allegations about the manipulation of citizenship certification in Assam, withdrawn to itself the powers of District Collectors all across India to confer citizenship in accordance with the law. To enable the grant of citizenship by District Collectors in Rajasthan and Gujarat, the Union government had to make an exception to this withdrawal of powers; this was accomplished in 2003 (effective 2004), through an amendment to the Citizenship Rules 1956, for a specified and limited period and within a limited jurisdiction. This made it possible for District Collectors in these specific States to hold "Citizenship Camps" to process the applications for citizenship of migrants from Pakistan. There still remain a few thousand people who are awaiting the legalisation of their citizen status. The most significant feature of this amendment is its open declaration of the religious identity of the migrants. Until this point, the religious identity of migrants (illegal or otherwise) was covertly indicated, but never explicitly mentioned. This amendment to the rules dispenses with such signalling. It even avoids the description of these people as migrants, much less illegal migrants, the coded dog-whistle label indicating immigrants from Bangladesh. Rule 8A of the Citizenship Rules 1956 reads:

> In respect of *minority Hindus with Pakistan citizenship* who have migrated to India more than five years back with *the intention of permanently settling down in India* and have applied for Indian citizenship, the authority to register a person as a citizen of India . . . shall be the

> concerned Collector of the district where the applicant is normally resident.[45]

Let us return to Article 7 of the Constitution and compare the amended rules to what was once described as "the obnoxious clause":

> Notwithstanding anything in articles 5 and 6, a person who has after the first day of March, 1947, migrated from the territory of India to the territory now included in Pakistan shall not be deemed to be a citizen of India:
>
> Provided that nothing in this article shall apply to a person who, after having so migrated to the territory now included in Pakistan, has returned to the territory of India under a permit for resettlement or permanent return issued by or under the authority of any law and every such person shall for the purposes of clause *(b)* of article 6 be deemed to have migrated to the territory of India after the nineteenth day of July, 1948.[46]

A quick reading shows that though the history of the Partition and the debates in the Constituent Assembly make it clear that Article 7 of the Constitution was intended to cover returning Muslims who had migrated to Pakistan, it forbore from making any mention of the religious identity of these people. The amendment to the Citizenship Rules, by contrast, does not hesitate to assume and name the religious identity of the recent migrants from Pakistan, who are explicitly referred to as "minority Hindus with Pakistan citizenship". Further, recall the repeated questioning of the *intention* of returning Muslims, both in the Constituent Assembly as well as in a vast range of case law. By contrast, Hindu migrants are not required to prove their ***intention to permanently settle in India*** so long as they have been resident for at least five

[45] Citizenship Rules 1956, Rule 8A (emphasis added).

[46] Constitution of India 1950, Article 7 (emphasis added).

years. The requirement for a permit of resettlement has naturally been done away with.

In both these amendments to the Citizenship Act and the Citizenship Rules, it is clear that elements of *jus sanguinis* have infiltrated the constitutional regime of *jus soli.* On the one hand, those born in India, but with one parent an illegal migrant at the time of their birth, have become ineligible for citizenship. On the other hand, a special dispensation has been made for "minority Hindus with Pakistan citizenship". Both these, one covert and the other explicit, suggest that religious identity has acquired a greater role in the construction of legal citizenship than might be supposed by simply looking at apparently identity-neutral constitutional provisions.

A third path to *jus sanguinis* has become manifest in the amendment of Section 7 of the Act, allowing for Overseas Citizenship of India (OCI). This is by no means dual citizenship. The website of the Ministry of Overseas Indian Affairs is at pains to labour the point that "OCI is not to be misconstrued as 'dual citizenship'."[47] Despite political promises made and reiterated over the years, India still has a regime of single citizenship and does not recognise dual citizenship. This means that unlike, for instance, the possibility of an American citizen being also simultaneously a German or Irish citizen, or the possibility of a Pakistani citizen being simultaneously a British citizen, Indian law requires that an Indian citizen who is acquiring British or American citizenship must renounce her Indian citizenship. Moreover, those who have at any time held citizenship in Bangladesh or Pakistan are specifically excluded from the purview of this provision.

Around the time India became independent, it had been the consistent position of its political leadership that Indians living in other countries must give their complete allegiance to their adoptive homes. This position was adopted despite the anxiety of

[47] Ministry of Overseas Indian Affairs, "Overseas Citizenship of India Scheme".

Indians in other countries of South and South East Asia as well as Africa of being rendered second-class citizens in the countries where they lived. There was a shift in this approach when India was facing international sanctions for its nuclear tests. In 1998, the Prime Minister announced the constitution of a high-level committee to examine the question of dual citizenship for Non-Resident Indians (NRIs) – Indians who live abroad even as they retain their Indian citizenship. The government floated the Resurgent India Bonds scheme to attract investment but these were offered only to select Indians (NRIs as well as former citizens) in the US, Canada, and Europe. The explicit exclusion of citizens of the less prosperous members of the diaspora in places like the Caribbean, Mauritius, and Fiji elicited accusations of "dollar and pound apartheid". The high interest rates and tax exemptions offered by the bonds scheme made it hugely popular and the success of the scheme led to a second, the India Millennium Deposit scheme, in 2000. Together, these two bonds schemes raised close to USD 10 billion. The demand for dual citizenship from such Indians has been a longstanding one.

Meanwhile, the High-Level Committee on the Indian Diaspora submitted its report (also known as the Singhvi Report) in 2001.[48] Lyrically eulogising the diaspora as the "National Reserve of India" and "the National Resource of India", it recommended dual citizenship by an amendment to the Citizenship Act.[49] The substantive argument made in support of dual citizenship invoked the emotional ties of emigrants to their land of origin and referred to their desire for dual nationality as "a higher form of the acknowledgement of their linkage with Mother India".[50] The Singhvi Report rejected outright arguments against dual citizenship that pertained to national security concerns. In fact, it remarked that

[48] Government of India, "Report of the High Level Committee on the Indian Diaspora".

[49] Ibid., 526, n.46.

[50] Ibid.

the IMDT Act (which was still undecided in court at the time) had failed to check illegal migrants into the country. By contrast, people entering the country with dual citizenship would, it argued, be easier to monitor and regulate. It also betrayed a class bias in promising that the process of dual citizenship would be extremely selective. For instance, those whose ancestry could be traced back to first-wave émigrés (indentured labourers) would be kept out. As regards the common anxieties about divided allegiance and disloyalty, the Singhvi Report offered the assurance that overseas citizens would not be allowed to join the bureaucracy, the police force, or the defence services. It specifically ruled out the grant of political rights, such as the right to vote or hold public office, for these groups.[51]

In 2002, a scheme was inaugurated allowing for individuals of Indian origin within a select group of sixteen countries, all advanced industrial societies of the global North, to be registered as Persons of Indian Origin (PIO). The justification for the choice of countries invoked the principle of reciprocity in that it was limited to those that recognised dual citizenship. In 2005, the Citizenship Act was amended to introduce the category of "Overseas Citizen of India", and the privileges accompanying the status were expanded. Today, it is only those who are or have been at any previous time citizens of Pakistan or Bangladesh that continue to be excluded from this category.

In *Talat Jamal Siddiqui v Union of India* (2011) the Delhi High Court upheld a rejection order of the government that denied a PIO card to a woman holding a British passport because she had once held a Pakistani passport.[52] This was despite the fact that both her parents were born in pre-independence India, that she was the spouse of a PIO, and the parent of two PIOs. Among the grounds on which the petitioner contested the rejection in the High

[51] Ibid., 567, n.46.

[52] *Talat Jamal Siddiqui v Union of India* (Delhi High Court, 21 January 2011).

Court was the gendered language used in the official notification, claiming that the use of words such as "he" and "himself" clearly did not apply to her. The court was unfortunately not persuaded even to the modest extent of ordering a gender-neutral rewriting of the rules.

Over the last decade, overseas Indians have clamoured for dual citizenship, and rhetorical promises to this effect have in fact been made almost on an annual basis. Some OCIs, professionals such as doctors and dentists, advocates and chartered accountants, have been given permission to practice their professions in India.[53] The rights that OCIs do not enjoy include the right to vote and to contest elections for political office. They are also "normally" ineligible for public employment, though exceptions can and have been made from time to time. OCIs also do not have to pay taxes. Nevertheless, the manifestly greater engagement of the diaspora in a range of political activities in recent times – from mobilising funding to providing technical expertise for election campaigns – suggests that its members have, even without dual citizenship, become more politically engaged in India. This may well betoken the impending realisation of dual citizenship.

Conclusion

The core features of contestation and the central anxieties around the legal status of citizenship in India exhibit certain significant continuities and inversions. Some of the core principles on which judicial verdicts were based in the early decades after the adoption of the Constitution retain their centrality even as they are inverted after the 1990s. Two examples suffice to demonstrate this. In the earlier phase, courts viewed an individual's possession of a Pakistan passport in either of two ways: as something that indicated that

[53] Ministry of Overseas Indian Affairs, Notification Number SO 36E, *Gazette of India*, 6 January 2009.

individual's intention to permanently settle in Pakistan, or, more uncommonly, as a document acquired more or less involuntarily. In 1991, the court saw de Raedt's possession of a Belgian passport as conclusive evidence of his lack of intent towards residing permanently in India. And now even the possession of an *Indian* passport has lost its evidentiary value: towards those showing Indian passports as proof of Indian citizenship when alleged to be illegal immigrants from Bangladesh, the courts have expressed cynicism. In *Motimiya Rahim Miya v State of Maharashtra*,[54] as also in *Razia Begum v State*,[55] the courts have ruled that Indian passports may have been acquired by misrepresentation and fraud. "Documentary" citizenship thus comes to be mistrusted, with passports being potentially as suspect as ration cards and election cards.[56]

Similarly, the question of intention to settle has retained its importance, albeit in an inverted manner. In the post-Partition period, as we have seen, the determination of citizenship rested heavily on the intent to permanently settle. Intention was positively valued as a condition of entry into the privileged circle of citizenship. In the present, such intention continues to carry positive connotations with reference to Hindu migrants from Pakistan who, as the amended Citizenship Rules say, have come with "the intention of permanently settling down in India". However, in the context of Bangladeshi immigration the intention to permanently settle by acquiring a ration card, election card, or passport is thought dubious. Intention is here ascribed and deployed to deny, rather than affirm, claims to citizenship.

This chapter has sought to demonstrate the contention over citizenship from the Constituent Assembly to the present. It has also shown that the divisive legacy of the Partition and the

[54] AIR 2004 Bom 260.

[55] (2008) 152 DLT 630.

[56] Sadiq, *Paper Citizens.*

religious identities implicated in it continue to lie at the core of this contention. This is the reason why, despite the victory of the *jus soli* conception of citizenship at the constitution-making stage, a gradual and subtle shift occurred towards a *jus sanguinis* conception. Whether it is the issue of "illegal immigrants" from Bangladesh on the eastern border of India, or that of "minority Hindus with Pakistan citizenship" on the western, the law and rules have tended to view these very differently, seeing the latter, but not the former, as people with a rightful claim to Indian citizenship. This reconfiguration of Indian citizenship based on *jus sanguinis* is reflected also in the expansive approach latterly adopted towards the Indian diaspora.

PART II

CONTESTATIONS

3

Indian Citizenship

A Century of Disagreement

The idea of the Indian citizen is at once the defining aspiration of modern India and its most contested political idea. With independence in 1947 and its Constitution in force from 1950, India's citizenship story is a saga of sorts that straddles the twentieth century: the dominant idea of citizenship is formed in the colonial first half of the century, finds embodiment in the constitutional settlement at its mid point, and is simultaneously unravelled and strengthened in the century's second half. At no point in this considerable span of time, and in no aspect of this complex idea, is there an absence of contestation – frequently deep contestation. If the resilience of these ideational contests is surprising, the continuity in the debates and even the arsenal of arguments deployed across the period is startling, considering that the constitutional settlement of 1950 was expected to resolve contention with a consensual and authoritative conception of citizenship. This chapter provides an account of a century of disagreement over the issue in three of its core dimensions: citizenship as legal status; citizenship as rights and entitlements; and citizenship as identity.

Citizenship as Legal Status

Across the world, there is evidence of an increase in the hybridisation of legal citizenship. Even countries that historically adopted the ethnic descent-based model are now moving towards a more inclusive territorial birth-based model, or at least incorporating elements of it. In India, however, we observe the reverse, from the more inclusive principle of legal citizenship articulated in the constitution to a less inclusive conception; from a birth-based to a descent-based principle. The laws, rules, and jurisprudence on citizenship have come to be increasingly inflected by religion. This is apparent in the contrasting ways in which the Indian state deals with, on the one hand, illegal migrants, and, on the other, an Indian diaspora clamouring for dual citizenship.

In the late-nineteenth century, the historical fault lines of legal subject-citizenship were race and class rather than religious identity; by the late-colonial period, religious difference began to inform the discourse of citizenship in ways that would prove consequential. In the movement for freedom from colonial rule, the idea that India would adopt the principle of *jus soli* as the basis of citizenship was frequently repeated. Freedom from British rule in 1947 was accompanied by the Partition, a movement of fourteen million people across newly demarcated borders. The disruption, violence, and trauma of this event informed, in no small measure, the debate on the articles pertaining to citizenship in the drafting of the Indian Constitution. The adoption of *jus soli* as the defining doctrine of Indian citizenship was a hard-won battle, and the contention over citizenship in this period prefigures the gradual shift towards a *jus sanguinis* regime in statutory law, administrative rules, and jurisprudence.

In its most raw form, this shift is first seen in the legislative amendments of the 1980s that sought to manage the flow of illegal – usually Muslim – migrants from Bangladesh on India's eastern border. One of these amendments modified the provision of citizenship by birth to exclude those born in India who had at the time of their birth an illegal migrant as one of their parents. On the western border, another set of refugees – low caste but Hindu – from Pakistan triggered the formulation of rules that made explicit mention of their religious identity, and also made it possible for them to more easily obtain citizenship precisely because they were seen as members of a vulnerable minority in the country of their origin.

The irony is that while many of the migrants from Bangladesh acquired forms of "documentary citizenship" through "networks of complicity" and "networks of profit",[1] those on the western border found it much harder to acquire such documents, even as the visibly gentler official approach towards their predicament explicitly recognised their religious affiliation. The modifications introduced into the laws (and appurtenant rules) of citizenship by the presence of migrants, both east and west, more or less covertly introduced religion as a criterion into the law. It is notable, however, that the migrants on the western border – towards whom the state adopted a benign attitude on account of their religious identity – themselves repudiated arguments of blood and belonging in favour of a largely instrumental understanding of what citizenship meant to them: access to basic public services, from electricity connections to admission into government schools, from caste certificates to subsidised food.

As is well known, undocumented aliens in several states in the US enjoy rights to public schooling, drivers' licences, and property. These policies tend to make rights and status somewhat independent of each other.[2] Meanwhile a public debate continues over whether giving undocumented aliens access to social provisioning diminishes the citizenship of the native born.[3] The practice of according some rights even to those lacking documentation of their legal status is inverted in India: there are approximately ten million technically illegal migrants who are "citizens" only through their possession of illicitly

[1] Sadiq, *Paper Citizens*.

[2] Bosniak, *The Citizen and the Alien*, 89.

[3] Macedo, "The Moral Dilemma of U.S. Immigration Policy".

acquired documentation.[4] In an implicit acknowledgement of the impossibility of telling the citizen apart from the denizen, the Unique Identity Card (Aadhaar) project of the Indian government decided to confer identity documents on all residents rather than only citizens.

In terms of legal status, even as citizenship has become more inclusive in one Indian region and more restrictive in another, the predominant *jus soli* conception has thus been modified by *jus sanguinis*, reflected also in the receptiveness of successive Indian governments to the wealthy Indian diaspora's claim to some form of dual citizenship. Following the liberalisation of the Indian economy in the 1990s and the sanctions imposed by Western countries following India's nuclear tests, the Indian political establishment was inspired by the hope that the Indian diaspora would, like its Chinese counterpart, start pouring investment into India and so contribute to rapid economic growth. An annual festival celebrating the achievements of members of the diaspora was inaugurated, invariably addressed by the Prime Minister, making grand promises of dual citizenship as well as professional and economic opportunities. It is hardly accidental that the more powerful and articulate sections of the diaspora, arguing for dual citizenship on the basis of blood and belonging, happen to be prosperous Hindus based in the countries of the global North. Though the claims of the (mostly Hindu) migrants into western India and of the Indian diaspora are both based on the principle of *jus sanguinis*, there is a stark difference between the state response to those who are stateless and to those who aspire to be citizens of two states simultaneously. For stateless migrants, legal citizenship is entirely devoid of affect, and merely an instrument of access to basic public services.

[4] This was the figure quoted by the Union Home Minister in a statement to Parliament in 1997. Cf. Supreme Court of India, *Sarbananda Sonowal vs. Union of India and Anr.*

Citizenship as Rights

That India's movement for freedom was led by lawyers and intellectuals inspired by ideas of civic freedoms and political rights is scarcely surprising. It is, however, quite extraordinary that, from as early as the 1920s, the understanding of citizenship amongst these nationalist elites encompassed social and economic rights. The Congress party, which led the nationalist movement, pledged its commitment to an impressive range of economic rights as early as 1931. However, the project of social and economic rights remained embattled, and only very recently has a slew of such enactments begun to hold out some promise of their realisation.

Despite propitious beginnings in nationalist thinking and a sympathetic international environment increasingly engaged in every aspect of human rights, the history of social and economic rights (SERs) in India is one of deep ideological ambivalence and profound political compromises. The Constituent Assembly was the principal theatre for the enactment of this script. Though a powerful case was made to include various social rights in the Fundamental Rights chapter of the Constitution, these were eventually sequestered in a non-justiciable section of the Constitution – the Directive Principles of State Policy. Two arguments were used to achieve this. The first questioned the propriety of a constitutional document spelling out what were essentially social policies. Being programmatic rights, and substantively ideological in nature, the argument was that they ought to be decided upon by elected legislatures as they entailed public decisions about the distribution of social resources. A distinction was thus introduced between rights and policies: a Constitution could guarantee rights but was deemed inappropriate as an instrument of policy.

Secondly, resting on what is now widely acknowledged to be a fallacious distinction between, on the one hand, civil and political rights that require state abstinence, and, on the other, social and economic rights that demand positive state action, it was argued that the latter were simply unaffordable for a poor country.[5] So in India negative rights were privileged, while positive rights were held hostage to the inadequacy of resources – an inadequacy which made it difficult for the state to provide, say, a decent standard of life to all workers. This is an argument that is, of course, frequently heard even today in the adjudication of social rights from India to South Africa.[6]

Ultimately, the Constitution's Directive Principles transformed the obligations of the state to its citizens into principles that were expected to guide state action, not rights that were enforceable. In the early decades after independence, this ideological ambivalence between Fundamental Rights and Directive Principles came to be expressed as a contradiction that took two shapes: on one side the state and its socialistically inclined policies and on the other individual rights such as property; on one side a judiciary that stood for the protection of individual rights and on the other an executive that championed the progressive cause of social equality. A role reversal occurred in the 1990s, when the government adopted policies of economic liberalisation and reform favouring capital and individual enterprise, while the judiciary came to be viewed as the champion of the underprivileged and their rights.

In 1991, under the shadow of a huge fiscal deficit and a balance of payments crisis, the government initiated economic policies of reform and liberalisation. The economic reforms resulted in higher growth rates but failed to make a correspondingly big dent in poverty or to achieve significantly higher levels of human development. The voting out of a government that had tried in 2004 to sell the electorate the dream of "India Shining" led the opposition to foreground the ordinary citizen in its political strat

[5] The fallaciousness of this distinction has been most powerfully argued in Holmes and Sunstein, *The Cost of Rights*.

[6] Pieterse, "Eating Socioeconomic Rights".

egy. Not long after, a right to work, in the form of the National Rural Employment Guarantee Act, was legislated in 2005. The right to information was also enacted in the same year. In 2009, the right to education was given constitutional status, and in 2013 a national law on food security was enacted. It suddenly began to appear as if an altogether new regime of social citizenship had begun in an ideological environment not usually associated with such concerns.

The troubled career of SERs is, however, by no means over, as, even in the moment of its apparent triumph, the new welfare regime shows a double-edged quality. The impetus for these enactments of social and economic rights came from a combination of judicial activism and civil society mobilisation, with a responsive political leadership eager to show its oneness with the *aam aadmi* (common man). But these rights have also been interrogated, in ways reminiscent of the Constituent Assembly debates, by arguments about the cost of social rights. The neo-liberal argument against redistribution, underwritten by a manifest lack of social solidarity amongst vocal sections of middle-class citizens, has however been more prominent. There also remain serious policy challenges to the implementation of SERs on account of weak state capacity, as well as because the actual delivery of many of the public goods provided for as rights is being contracted out to non-state entities, or being delivered in partnership with them.

Quite apart from the many challenges of realising social rights, there is a deeper conundrum here. The Indian state has typically approached citizens through the construction of categories of exception, classifying different sections of the population for the delivery of welfare goods. In the 1950s, the objects of social welfare policy were women, children, and the young; the physically and mentally challenged; criminals and those placed under correctional administration. Over the next two decades, social welfare came to encompass special plans for the Scheduled Castes and Scheduled Tribes, as well as rural artisans, small and marginal farmers, and the elderly, which meant giving subsidies for the construction of houses and wells, and self-employment or wage-employment schemes. As the special categories of entitlement proliferated, providing such welfare became not just politically controversial but also administratively complex.

In the name of substantive citizenship, and with the ostensible object of bridging the gap between the formal and the real, the official strategy of special rights for special groups detached the benefits of social provisioning from the status of citizenship. Since such provisioning was not universal, it was not integral to citizenship in the way in which civil and political rights were. This severance of welfare entitlements from the status of equal citizenship entrenched the prior separation between civil and political rights on the one hand, and social and economic rights on the other. All citizens are entitled to civil and political rights – those with additional entitlements to social and economic provisioning are also formal citizens in this sense. However, their enjoyment of such provisioning is derivative of, and conditional upon, their placement in particular categories. The ostensible rationale of these categories is that greater substance will be given to their equal civic status through socio-economic provisioning. In reality, because such provisioning is invariably of a much inferior quality – poor services for poor people – the creation of such categories of exception, with its apparent objective of facilitating the conditions of substantive citizenship, seems to work as a strategy of what T.H. Marshall famously labelled "class abatement".[7]

In the global North, citizenship had historically played a role in assuaging the tension between capitalism and democracy, and even pre-empting the class struggle.[8] As it eliminates social conflict and seeks to incorporate the working class, citizenship tends to legitimise, rather than mitigate, the inequalities of social class. The

[7] Marshall, *Citizenship and Social Class*.

[8] Dahrendorf, "Citizenship and Social Class".

socialist rhetoric of the pre-1991 *dirigiste* regime, however hollow in terms of material outcomes for the poor, had been a successful form of ideological class incorporation, obviating the need for assertive class politics. This was in fact the period in which the working class movement was weakened, and the vacuum created by it filled by, on the one hand, social movements mobilised around livelihoods, displacement, environment, etc., and, on the other, by political mobilisations around caste identity. It was in this context of weakened class politics that the language of rights emerged, often obscuring the many difficulties encountered in their effective realisation. Indeed, the language of welfare has ironically become more strident as the state and capital have grown more audaciously rapacious, separately and in partnership. The central questions about the content of these new social rights remain: are they universal and realisable? Are constitutional sanctions adequate guarantees of their realisation? Does the move from the rhetoric of welfare to the rhetoric – and some legislation – of rights indicate that the goal of social policy is now to mitigate social inequality, or merely to alleviate poverty?

Even as citizenship discourse has become more rights oriented, governance has become less citizen-friendly, with an increasing abrogation of the language of citizenship in favour of the new vocabulary of customers, clients, and users. In this new regime of social citizenship, older categories of "beneficiaries" endure, even as the categories are sometimes finessed or expanded. It is significant that the moment of state acknowledgement that the nation can afford to help the poor coincides with the moment when the responsibility for social assistance has already been diffused among a multiplicity of agencies, often non-state entities. The pre-eminence of the principles of the New Public Management, including the commodification of public services, Public–Private Partnerships, network governance, and the outsourcing of public services to NGOs is manifest. Simultaneously, the citizen has been released from her earlier duty to participate in production; her duty now is to consume, for it is this that makes India become a globally competitive economy.

Citizenship as Identity

The third, and arguably most contested, aspect of the citizenship question in India is its project of balancing the multiplicity and diversity of cultural identities – caste, language, tribe, and religion – with the civic identity. Universalist and group-differentiated conceptions of citizenship have struggled for supremacy for more than a century. This is a difficult contest, because both these conceptions of citizenship have a deep moral appeal. The former affirms the equality of all citizens in terms of moral worth and recognises no gradations of citizenship, as all citizens are guaranteed the enjoyment of equal rights and equality before the law. Formally, the rights of citizenship attach equally to all members of the political community. However, equal rights for all citizens can imply that the special needs of groups of citizens – victims of exclusion or discrimination because they belong to a minority – may be neglected. The distinctive culture of indigenous peoples or of religious, linguistic, or racial minorities may thus be threatened or even extinguished. There is a legitimate concern that difference-blind policies which represent themselves as policies of liberal neutrality may in fact be purveyors of dominant cultures. Cultural difference is typically the source of claims to differentiated citizenship rights, with their institutionalisation taking many familiar forms, such as language rights, affirmative action, or rights of self-government.

Strategies of group-differentiated citizenship (GDC) are widely acknowledged as a normatively satisfactory solution of the concern that universalism is a masquerade promoting the socially dominant culture/race/religion. In Iris Marion Young's formulation of this principle, group-differentiated rights are a way of addressing oppression – which she defines as encompassing exploitation, marginalisation, powerlessness, cultural imperialism, and vulnerability to violence motivated by hatred and fear.[9] In India, as elsewhere, claims to GDC have tended to be faithful to Young's script, treating identity claims arguing cultural difference as the only relevant candidates for such forms of citizenship. Again, in India, as elsewhere, the question that arises from the practice of GDC is this: if "all is particularity", as Ronald Beiner puts it, where might citizenship be practised?[10]

India may well be the first country in the world to have experimented with policies described as affirmative action or positive discrimination. The politics of recognition can be traced back to the 1880s, when the British introduced separate electorates in local government and quotas in the civil service for Muslims in the province of Punjab. Through the late-colonial period, a variety of claims were articulated for GDC through the same mechanisms. Women and Muslims were – so long as they qualified on other criteria such as education and property, of course – given the franchise in separate electorates, i.e. constituencies in which all voters and candidates had to belong to the same community. The claim of the Scheduled Castes/Dalits to separate electorates was effectively, if controversially, stymied in 1932 by Gandhi, who insisted on seeing Dalits as belonging to the Hindu fold.

The dominant perspective – shared by the colonial state and sections of its subjects – was of Indian society as a community of communities, and of the appropriateness of devising institutions for the representation of "classes, races and interests".[11] Citizenship came to be viewed as properly mediated by community, rather than as an unmediated relationship between the individual and the state. The Congress party's espousal of a universal conception of citizenship was a determined attempt to construct a modern state in which

[9] Young, "Polity and Group Difference", 199.

[10] Beiner, *Theorizing Citizenship*, 10.

[11] Aitchison Commission Report on the Public Services, cited in Wolpert, *Morley and India*, 147.

this could be an unmediated relationship, within the framework of a nation that, defined as a civic community, could accommodate diversity. The challenges to this inclusionary universalist conception were many and diverse. They ranged from the exclusionary universalism of the Hindu nationalists to the multiple claims to GDC justified as antidotes to, variously, religious majoritarianism, caste discrimination, and caste-based "backwardness". The latter have endured into the post-colonial period, in one form or another, often justified in almost identical terms.

The Indian Constitution of 1950 abolished separate electorates altogether. It provided instead for "reservations", or quotas, in the legislatures, public employment, and public education for members of the Scheduled Castes and Scheduled Tribes. Intended initially for ten years, these have been regularly extended every ten years since. The creation of Pakistan was treated as the fulfilment of the Muslim claim to differentiated citizenship, and the sizeable Muslim minority that remained in India was therefore given rights of cultural community rather than quotas. The possibility of special provisions for "socially and educationally backward" groups was also admitted in the Constitution, under which such quotas came to be extended, at the national level, to a range of "backward caste" groups in the 1990s. This rather broadly and imprecisely defined category describes a population group whose numbers have been variously estimated as 35 per cent or 50 per cent of Indian society.[12] It has proved to be a quagmire, to the

[12] The First Backward Classes Commission estimated the "socially and educationally backward" section of the Indian population as 32 per cent. Its Chairman, Kaka Kalelkar, disavowed his own report, saying he was uncomfortable with the idea that backwardness should be determined primarily on the basis of caste rather than educational or economic criteria. Government of India, *Report of the Backward Classes Commission*, vol. 1, xiv. The Second Backward Classes Commission, popularly known as the Mandal Commission, adopted a methodology that also placed overwhelming emphasis on caste and ritual aspects rather than on other social and economic indicators like poverty, yielding a figure of 50 per cent. Government of India, *Report of the Backward Classes Commission* (1980). The

extent that the label precludes recognition of its deeply stratified implications; the Most Backward Castes (a political appellation for a sub-group) are generally disgruntled because quota benefits are creamed off by groups better placed to take advantage of them. This resentment persists despite the fact that the economically better off – "the creamy layer" – among these groups are ineligible for such benefits.

It is well known that the institutional incentives for the invention and articulation of identities tend to reinforce and entrench such identities. These are frequently also administratively difficult to arbitrate, given the diversity of ritual and social practices across a vast geographical and social canvas. To enable a more objective identification of "backwardness", India has very recently embarked upon a Caste Census, after having abolished such a census in 1931.

As demands have multiplied for quotas – and even for dedicated sub-quotas for particularly disadvantaged groups within already entitled beneficiary groups – the idea of the nation as a civic community has been rendered fragile. Universal citizenship was the default notion of citizenship under the Constitution, with GDC projected as a temporary exception necessitated by the legitimate demands of social justice. Over time, however, in a curious throwback to the late-colonial era, and often inverting the constitutional principle, GDC now appears to have become the dominant mode of citizenship. The new frontiers in this debate are the defining of newer sub-identities, claims to sub-quotas, and attempts to establish greater backwardness as a way of claiming more redress. As the making of claims on the state tends to be expressed, more often than not, in identitarian terms, it occludes recognition of the fact that many of these historically disadvantaged groups suffer not merely discrimination but also material deprivation. However, because the state is noticeably

governmental category OBC (or Other Backward Classes) is today shorthand for caste groups that have been so identified.

more responsive to such claims, especially at election time, than it is to claims based on material deprivation, identity tends to be the dominant idiom in which such claims are expressed.

Paradoxically, assertions of GDC rights from a multicultural perspective have served to revive and reinforce the colonial argument that Indian society is little more than a community of communities. This was the premier argument offered by the colonial state against the possibility of an Indian citizenship unmediated by community, an argument that most nationalists railed against. Today, it takes the form of an acceptance that it is appropriate for citizenship to be mediated by community, with the civic identity appearing to be a suspicious legacy of modernity and nationalism. The problem remains a variant of the one that Rousseau identified when he said: "We have physicists, geometricians, chemists, astronomers, poets, musicians, and painters in plenty; but we have no longer a citizen among us . . ."[13]

Conclusion

The idea of citizenship typically characterises the relationship between citizen and state, but also that amongst citizens. In contemporary India, both these are unstable relationships. The relationship between the citizen as a rights-holder and the state as the guarantor of rights is far from straightforward. In recent times, for instance, the expansion of rights – to information, to work, to education, and possibly to food – has been simultaneously celebrated and resisted. On the one hand, the middle classes empowered by economic reforms do not display the civic solidarity that must underwrite such redistributive initiatives. On the other hand, amid the celebration of rights, the troubling question remains: what does it mean for a citizen to hold a right that sanctifies a claim on the state when the responsibility for the

[13] Rousseau, *The Social Contract*, 22.

actual provision of what it takes for that right to be realised lies elsewhere? The provider of the good that that right guarantees is frequently no longer the state, but a variety of non-state agencies.

Another irony of independent India's attempts at providing inclusive citizenship is the career of the positive-discrimination regime which constructed and marked citizens in particular ways, as beneficiaries, as labelled objects of special provision, e.g. Scheduled Castes and Scheduled Tribes. In the 1990s, additional markers of citizenship were devised, ostensibly intended to achieve a more effective targeting policies of poverty reduction for groups marked BPL (Below Poverty Line). Both types of markers were intended to render citizens "legible" for the better implementation by the state of its policies of inclusion. Both have ironically tended to entrench exclusion.

The access of members of these groups to the substantive attributes of the real citizen is through these markers. However, their citizenship is rendered qualitatively different from and arguably inferior to the real citizenship of the unmarked citizen. When services for the poor – such as public health and public education – become, as they inevitably do, poor services, they too are stigmatised as inferior. Another form of inferiority that has been constitutionally sanctified, and almost sanitised of its negative connotations, is the doctrine of backwardness. Post-independence politics has been about increasing incentives to backwardness, invariably defined in identitarian terms, because the greater the backwardness, the greater the entitlements that flow from it.

In an atmosphere where competing identity claims cover a large part of the surface area of everyday politics, there is some anxiety about the fragility of the civic project, and the fear that the aspiration of a shared common purpose for the political community as a whole may be unattainable. As the political class hesitates to take ownership of this idea for fear of losing elections, it is not clear whether a civic community that transcends boxes and labels is any longer even an aspiration. In intellectual circles, the post-national imagination in any case precludes such an appeal. The fragmentation generated by identity claims is moreover at odds with the creeping majoritarian impulse reflected in the laws on citizenship.

These varied disputations underline the fragility of the constitutional settlement and signal the erosion of its vision of citizenship. India has historically lacked the kind of social solidarity that could underwrite an egalitarian project, in the way in which Nordic social democracies did. The combination of social intolerance and weak civic solidarity does not make for a promising outlook for the future of citizenship. Recent citizens' mobilisations on issues of corruption, sexual violence, and legal reform have generated some optimism about the performative aspect of Indian citizenship. Indeed, these campaigns do signal a new citizen engagement amongst social groups hitherto alienated from politics. However, it is difficult to detect in them the seeds of a substantive social transformation – for that would require sensitivity to the diversity and plurality of Indian society, as well as to poverty and inequality as challenges to a political community of equal citizens.

4

Reconfiguring Citizenship in Contemporary India

Among the many dualities that India continues to negotiate is the one between marked and unmarked citizens, and the form taken recently by this and related dualities is the subject of the present chapter. In *Citizenship and Its Discontents: An Indian History* (2013), I had argued, among other things, that citizenship is the privilege of the unmarked, because for those in the variously disadvantaged groups the road to citizenship lies only and paradoxically *through* being marked as different, and implicitly even inferior. We could identify broadly two types of markers, apparently distinct, though there are overlaps. The first type, such as "Below Poverty Line" (BPL), is necessary to secure even minimal access to the entitlements of social citizenship, but the affectation of inclusion hides the deceit of exclusion. Statist markers such as this may be contrasted to a second type, comprising those that are descriptive of identities – Hindu, Muslim, Dalit – but transmit signals, implicitly or explicitly, of the privilege of inclusion for some and the detriment of exclusion for others. The difference is deceptive. Both sets of markers implicitly stigmatise groups, diminish citizenship, and, in the case of groups like poor Dalits, are jointly complicit in negating the possibility of citizenship itself. While assessing the major reconfigurations of citizenship in the years since 2014, when the Bharatiya Janata Party (BJP) assumed power in New Delhi, I will argue that we observe, with respect to both types of markers, not the realisation of substantive citizenship but in fact a substantive erosion of even formal citizenship.

I propose while making this argument to revisit some of the themes I explored in *Citizenship and Its Discontents*, with a view to identifying and analysing some reconfigurations of citizenship in India that have occurred since that book's publication. What are the pre-eminent challenges to citizenship today? How does the landscape of citizenship in India look now, when viewed through the prism of the three components of citizenship – status, rights, and identity – which structured that volume?

In the book, the story of Indian citizenship is one that straddles the twentieth century, a century of disagreement and deep contestation over the idea of citizenship. My focus here is on a very short time span – four years, 2014–18 – and covers all three dimensions of citizenship, viz. legal status, rights, and identity. In each section thus organised, I will briefly recapitulate the main arguments relating to each of these dimensions in the book, before discussing the contemporary challenges of citizenship.

Status

Citizenship and Its Discontents documented a subtle shift in India from the more inclusive principle of legal citizenship articulated in the Constitution to a less inclusive conception: from a *jus soli* or birth-based to an increasingly, if covertly, *jus sanguinis* or descent-based principle. It showed how, though the country had in its Constitution adopted the *jus soli* principle, the tension between it and *jus sanguinis* has been present (if dormant) since the founding of the republic; and how the laws, rules, and jurisprudence on citizenship have come to be increasingly if subtly inflected by religion.

In the aftermath of the Partition and the gigantic scale of the movement of people across the newly defined borders of India and Pakistan, the Constituent Assembly defined the term in Articles 5–11 of the Constitution only for the immediate purpose of determining, for those extraordinary times, the citizenship of people moving across borders. The task of formulating a law of citizenship for ordinary times was left to the Indian Parliament, which passed the Citizenship Act in 1955.

Despite being limited to a formulation of the principles for people affected by the Partition, the articles on citizenship in the Constitution witnessed heated exchanges in the Constituent Assembly. The central question was whether the basis of Indian citizenship should be an individual's birth on the soil of the country – *jus soli* citizenship; or an individual's descent, or the citizenship of their parents – *jus sanguinis* citizenship. The Assembly settled on the first as a form of "enlightened, modern, civilised" and democratic citizenship, as against the second, which it said was "an idea of racial citizenship". This was a progressive decision, in keeping with the inclusive character of the independence movement. The Citizenship Act of 1955 incorporated both these conceptions, providing for citizenship by birth, in addition to other modes of acquiring citizenship by descent, naturalisation, and registration. An illegal immigrant was defined as a foreigner who entered India without valid travel documents, or a foreigner who remained in India beyond the time limit stated in travel documents.

From the 1980s onwards, the legal and constitutional conception of the Indian citizen started to undergo a subtle transformation, in response to political developments, through amendments to the Citizenship Act. The latest in a series of such amendments is the Citizenship (Amendment) Bill, introduced in Parliament in July 2016, and presently under consideration by a Joint Parliamentary Committee (JPC). If passed, this could culminate in a fundamental metamorphosis, entrenching the displacement of the principle of *jus soli* in favour of *jus sanguinis,* and thereby also entrenching a majoritarian and exclusionary conception of citizenship, replacing the existing, albeit already weakened, pluralist and inclusive conception.

The present amendment consolidates a trend that began with the Citizenship (Amendment) Bill, 1985, which amended the provisions pertaining to naturalisation. This gave legal expression to the Assam Accord between the Rajiv Gandhi government and the Assamese students' organisations that had led the agitation against the enfranchisement of migrants from Bangladesh. The accord was entered into in 1985, after the agitation led to the Nellie Massacre during the election of 1983. The enfranchisement of migrants was widely attributed to the Congress. The common perception was that all Bangladeshi immigrants were Muslims, and the Congress party was seen as the prime beneficiary of their votes. The accord put in place measures for the detection of foreigners and their deletion from the electoral rolls.

The 1985 amendment to the Citizenship Act that followed the accord introduced a new section titled "Special provisions as to citizenship of persons covered by the Assam Accord". Seeking to allay anxieties about migrants who had come in from Bangladesh after the 1971 war, this section created categories of eligibility for citizenship based on the year in which a person had migrated to India. All those who came before 1966 were declared citizens; those who came between 1966 and 1971 were struck off the electoral rolls and asked to wait ten years before applying for citizenship; and those who came after 1971 were deemed illegal immigrants. An amendment to the Citizenship Act that came into effect in 2004 provided that, even if born on Indian soil, a person who at the time of her birth had an illegal migrant as either of her two parents would not be eligible for citizenship by birth. Since most of the migrants from Bangladesh were Muslims, this covertly introduced a religion-based exception to the principle of citizenship by birth, undermining and making conditional the principle of *jus soli*. These provisions were a response to the political situation in Assam – where the anti-migrant sentiment was at fever pitch – but contained the seeds of the politicisation and incipient communalisation of the issue of migrants.

The present Bill, introduced in 2016, signifies a pronounced deviation from the religion-neutral conception of citizenship contained in the law and the Constitution.[1] While some elements of religious difference had, as mentioned above, been covertly smuggled in earlier, this Bill seeks to do so overtly. It provides that Hindus, Sikhs, Buddhists, Jains, Parsis (Zoroastrians), and Christians from Afghanistan, Bangladesh, and Pakistan, deemed "persons belonging to minority communities", "shall not be treated as illegal migrants for purposes of this Act", and, as such, will be eligible for citizenship after six years of residence in India, as opposed to the earlier requirement of twelve years.[2] In other words, those belonging to six religions from three countries are no longer to be described as illegal migrants and are therefore candidates for fast-tracked citizenship. The implication is that Muslims from these countries will continue to be treated as illegal immigrants and not be eligible for the same relaxation.

The ostensible ground for the exclusion of Muslims is that they are not minorities in these three countries. The Bill does not tell us why India is suddenly consumed by anxiety for the minorities of neighbouring countries, particularly when it is not visibly consumed by such concerns over its own. The Statement of Objects and Reasons that prefaces the Bill offers no rationale for the amendment other than stating that these people are denied the "opportunities and advantages" that only citizens of India can presently enjoy. The precise nature of these opportunities and advantages remains unspecified.

Two other recent legislative amendments offer suggestive pointers. In 2015, the Passport (Entry into India) Rules, 1950, and the Orders under the Foreigners Act, 1946, were amended to exempt these very same religious groups from the requirement of

[1] This section draws substantially on Jayal, "The 2016 Citizenship Amendment Bill".

[2] The Citizenship (Amendment) Bill, 2016, Bill No. 172 of 2016, https://www.prsindia.org/sites/default/files/bill_files/Citizenship_%28A%29_bill%2C_2016_0.pdf

holding valid passports and visas, and consequently exempt them from being prosecuted or deported. Both these amendments refer to "persons belonging to minority communities in Bangladesh and Pakistan" – Afghanistan was not included then – "who were compelled to seek shelter in India due to religious persecution or fear of religious persecution". If indeed the official concern is about religious persecution, it is puzzling why India forbore from extending similar hospitality to the Ahmadi or Rohingya Muslims, both persecuted sects in Pakistan and Myanmar respectively.

The Bill's gradual dilution of the principle of *jus soli* and increased recognition of elements of *jus sanguinis* based on religious identity were also presaged in another intervention of 2004. On the western border of India, the presence of another set of refugees – low caste but Hindu – from Pakistan triggered the formulation of rules (appended to the Citizenship Act) that make explicit mention of their religious identity, and also make it possible for the law, and the administration of it, to adopt a more benign approach toward them, precisely because they are seen as members of a vulnerable minority in the country of their origin. Till 2004, the religious identity of the migrants had only been implicitly signalled in the Citizenship Act. It was never explicitly mentioned. Now, the amendment to the Citizenship Rules dispenses with coyness. The language of "illegal migrants" has been dropped for these migrants, now officially described as "minority Hindus with Pakistan citizenship". These "minority Hindus with Pakistani citizenship" have been excluded from the definition of illegal immigrants. What is striking is that, even as the government has inscribed their religious identity into the rules, the migrants themselves repudiate all arguments of blood and belonging. In my fieldwork, I found that their understanding of citizenship has little to do with identity or affect; it is entirely about the social rights to which, in their view, citizenship holds the key: from electricity connections to admission in government schools, from caste certificates to access to subsidised food. Today, legislative initiatives are proposing the incorporation of groups like these based solely on their religious identity.

The proposed Citizenship Amendment Bill, 2016, is meant to fulfil an electoral promise, made by the ruling BJP in its election campaign in Assam in 2016, to "free" the state from illegal Bangladeshi migrants – no religion mentioned – by evicting and deporting them. It also promised to give Indian citizenship to all Bangladeshi Hindu immigrants if it won the election. After its election victory, the BJP refugee cell in Assam began to step up its demand for expediting amendments to the Citizenship Act in favour of Hindu refugees, and hence this amendment.

The twist in the tail, however, is that the move has angered many in Assam, including the BJP's own political allies, because they view the amendment as a violation of the Assam Accord, which treated *all those* who entered the state after 1971, regardless of their religious identity, as illegal immigrants. They are unwilling to accept the transformation of even Hindu migrants into legitimate citizens for fear of more in-migration and more claims on diminishing employment opportunities. The JPC, appointed in 2016, visited Assam in May 2018 and was petitioned by hundreds of organisations agitating against the Bill, expressing not only the secular constitutionalist objection of introducing religion-based citizenship provisions, but also the fear of both Assamese speakers as well as indigenous tribal communities of becoming minorities in their own land. Once again, the *difference* of linguistic and ethnic identity trumps *shared* religious identity.

Whatever the ultimate fate of the amendment, its potential for long-term damage lies in its contravention of constitutional provisions. The right to equality in Article 14 of the Indian Constitution,[3] for instance, is available even to foreigners who happen to be within

[3] Article 14: "The State shall not deny to any person equality before the law or the equal protection of the laws within the territory of India." See Constitution of India 1950, https://www.india.gov.in/sites/upload_files/npi/files/coi_part_full.pdf

the territory of India, and differential treatment to individuals on the basis of their religious faith contravenes it. More egregiously, the construction of Hindus as the natural and normal citizens of India is not just a debasement of the idea of India that joined several million people together in their struggle against imperial rule, it is also a transgression of the universalist and inclusive conception of citizenship contained in the Indian Constitution. An invidious distinction based exclusively on religion is, by this legislation, introduced into the law on citizenship, with provisions akin to Israel's Law of Return policy, and an open undermining of the *jus soli* principle on which the founding fathers based Indian citizenship.[4]

Another instance, albeit political rather than legal, of the displacement of the *jus soli* conception by *jus sanguinis* is the enthusiasm of successive Indian governments since the 1990s to accord a weak form of dual citizenship to the wealthy Indian diaspora. The mutual attraction of the Prime Minister and the diaspora was reflected, early in his tenure, in the organisation of massively well-attended events – usually held in big-capacity venues like Madison Square Garden or Wembley Stadium – from the US and the UK to France, Australia, and Dubai, that have successfully reached out in rock star fashion to swooning diasporic audiences. On his second visit to California, in September 2015, Prime Minister Modi enumerated the achievements of his government and asked the audience: "Today, after 16 months [in office], I want a certification from you. Have I kept the promise? Have I kept the promise? Am I working day and night? Am I doing it for the country? The responsibility you have given me, and the promise that I have made, I'm working on it."[5] Accountability to

[4] Viewing every Jew in the world as a potential citizen of the country, Israel's Law of Return (1950) gives every Jew, and her family members upto a third generation, the right to come to Israel as an immigrant. Shachar, "Citizenship and Membership".

[5] Prime Minister Narendra Modi's speech at San Jose, California, 27 September 2015, http://www.siliconvalleyoneworld.com/2015/09/30/modi-speaks-in-san-jose-the-indian-prime-minister-in-his-own-words/

the voter was trumped by accountability to the diaspora, which had of course contributed enormously to the Modi campaign, including monetarily. In concrete terms, members of the diaspora have been given the facility of lifelong visas and there is even an attempt to confer voting rights on them. In August 2017 the government approved a proposal to implement voting rights for Non-Resident Indians, even as Modi announced at several diaspora functions that he hopes to institute more investment and ownership rights for Persons of Indian Origin. "There is no question that this is a consolidated and viable vote-bank for us", a senior party official said.[6]

On the legal dimension of citizenship, thus, the movement towards the *jus sanguinis* regime has been hardened and consolidated. This is reflected as much in the ever more assiduous courting of the Indian diaspora, as in the successful electoral campaign of the BJP in the Assam Assembly elections of May 2016.

In these elections the BJP and its allies successfully channelled long-held sentiments of nativism against the Bangladeshi "outsider" by emphasising the religious identity of the latter, and adopting as its main poll plank the political rhetoric of sons-of-the-soil. The party's Chief Minister is the very person who had, as a student leader, filed the historic writ petition (*Sarbananda Sonowal vs Union of India*) in the Supreme Court, against the IMDT Act, sponsored by the Congress party, which had the purported objective of identifying and repatriating illegal immigrants to Bangladesh but which was highly suspect as it made it virtually impossible to actually do so.

Along with the Citizenship Amendment Bill (CAB), the National Register of Citizens (NRC) – initially created during the first Census of independent India in 1951[7] – specifically for Assam

[6] Haider, "Mr. Modi's Diaspower".

[7] https://timesofindia.indiatimes.com/city/guwahati/five-things-to-know-about-assams-national-register-of-citizens/articleshow/65207192.cms, accessed 11 October 2018.

also got embroiled in the game of electoral politics. The proposal to update the NRC had been intermittently revived in subsequent years but was taken up in right earnest only after a Supreme Court ruling in 2014 ordering that it be updated in a time-bound manner. Tens of millions of residents of Assam were required to submit documents to prove their citizenship, in other words to prove that they were not illegal Bangladeshi migrants. Large numbers of people had been pronounced "D-voters" (Doubtful Voters, who did not figure in the electoral rolls prepared before the 1971 influx). Various processes, flawed in varying degrees, were put in motion – from the "family tree verification" process to the initial rejection of Gram Panchayat certificates, mostly affecting women who had married and changed residence. It was shown in careful detail that "illegal" migrants were more likely to be in possession of "documentary citizenship" – papers like ration cards and voter cards – certifying their citizenship, while natives and their descendants might well have no documentation at all.[8] In a society in which the poor typically have few if any documents, this irony is not surprising.

When the much anticipated final draft list of the NRC was published on 30 July 2018, only about 58 per cent of those who had submitted documents found their names on it. In many families, some members were excluded while others were included. Women were particularly badly hit. Another round of submission of documents, towards appeals for revision and rectification, began. In the meantime, the NRC has become the new bogeyman of Indian politics. As BJP leaders clamour for its implementation in all Indian states,[9] especially West Bengal where the issue has some resonance on the ground, the BJP President Amit Shah has termed the four million people left out of the list "termites" and

[8] Sadiq, *Paper Citizens.*

[9] The list includes BJP MPs and MLAs, the Governor of Assam, a BJP national vice-president, and many others.

"illegal infiltrators" who must be disenfranchised and deported.[10] This was of course one of Modi's campaign promises in the Bengal and Assam Assembly elections of 2015 and 2016, respectively, where he made the distinction between Hindu refugees who had nowhere else to go and would have to be accommodated, and Muslim refugees who were illegal and worthy of deportation.[11] The "infiltrator" has become a metonym for the Muslim and feeds the xenophobia that provides a cover for the yearning to get rid of even Indian Muslims. However, given that they cannot be deported without the specific agreement of Bangladesh, and given the difficulty of obtaining such an agreement, the process could end up not merely disenfranchising and robbing millions of even their notional citizenship, but rendering them stateless and rights-less, on a par with the Rohingyas.

The one attribute that distinguishes the stateless and the rights-less is what Hannah Arendt eloquently described as the right to have rights.[12] This is indeed a defining characteristic of citizenship and takes me directly to my second citizenship lens, Rights.

Rights

The focus of *Citizenship and Its Discontents* was on social and economic rights chiefly because, other than during the Emergency of 1975–7, citizens of independent India had not been formally deprived of their civil and political rights. The conditions that made the enjoyment of these rights meaningful may have been lacking, but the rights themselves were for the most part legally available.

[10] https://indianexpress.com/article/india/amit-shah-100-crore-infiltrators-entered-country-eating-it-like-termites-5371011/ & https://www.hindustantimes.com/india-news/bangladeshi-migrants-are-termites-will-be-removed-from-voter-list-says-amit-shah/story-Z8BAAJiNd5MVa2Kr0bt6iJ.html, accessed 11 October 2018.

[11] https://www.ndtv.com/elections-news/come-may-16-bangladeshi-immigrants-must-pack-up-narendra-modi-559164, accessed 11 October 2018.

[12] Arendt, "The Decline of the Nation-State".

Today, regrettably, that is no longer true and civil and political rights, as much as social and economic rights, stand imperilled.

Freedom of speech and expression, as well as academic and artistic freedom, have become vulnerable to threats by vigilante censors and troll armies on social media. Journalists and rationalists have either been assassinated or receive open threats of extermination on Twitter.[13] Attempts have been made to muzzle civil society – especially international organisations like Greenpeace, Amnesty International, and the Ford Foundation – by the use of regulations governing foreign funding or tax laws. Greenpeace was charged in 2013 by the previous Congress-led United Progressive Alliance (UPA) government with obstructing development in India, primarily because it was mobilising protest against the nuclear reactor in Kudankulam in Tamil Nadu, but also because it was leading protests against thermal power, coal, and aluminium mining across India. In April 2015 the BJP government charged Greenpeace with financial violations of the Foreign Contribution Regulation Act, blocked all its bank accounts, and suspended its licence to receive foreign donations. The High Court gave it interim relief in May 2015, allowing domestic accounts to function for the operational costs of the organisation. But just a day before the scheduled hearing in court, the MHA cancelled the registration of Greenpeace India.[14]

Similarly, colonial laws on defamation and sedition have been liberally deployed to silence voices of dissent as well as of student resistance. In combination with vigilante censorship, these laws have been used to intimidate publishers to make them withdraw from publication anything that offends the all too easily hurt and

[13] These include the killings of the "rationalist" writers Narendra Dabholkar in 2013 and M.M. Kalburgi in 2015; as also of the Leftist activist Govind Pansare in 2014 and the journalist Gauri Lankesh in 2017.

[14] "Centre cancels Greenpeace India's FCRA registration", *The Indian Express*, 4 September 2015, https://indianexpress.com/article/india/india-others/greenpeace-indias-fcra-registration-cancelled-govt/, accessed 12 October 2018.

offended sentiments of the majority. In two of the most well-known examples of vigilante censorship, Rashtriya Swayamsevak Sangh (RSS) functionary, Dina Nath Batra, and his Shiksha Bachao Andolan Samiti ("Save Education" Movement) brought two leading publishers to their knees. One agreed to pulp Wendy Doniger's book *The Hindus: An Alternative History* in an out-of-court settlement with Batra; another stopped the release, at the very last minute, of an academic work on communalism and sexual violence in Gujarat.[15] That such incidents should lead to self-censorship and the unwillingness of publishers to take risks, and scholars to express dissenting opinions, is hardly surprising.

As far as the rights of social citizenship are concerned, India has a long history, dating back almost a century, of honourable – but largely unsuccessful – attempts at incorporating social and economic rights. In the early decades after independence, the resources available for redistribution were too small to afford such rights. Curiously, it was in the context of the economic reforms of the early noughties that a veritable explosion of rights occurred – to information, to work, to education, and to food security. The irony that the language of rights emerged in the context of weakened class politics can be explained by the fact that the social product was now larger.

It was doubly ironic that the acknowledgement by the state of its ability and willingness to help the poor happened to coincide with the introduction of new systems of public management. In keeping with the global trend of New Public Management, it was around this time that the responsibility for delivering welfare services was distributed amongst a range of non-state agencies and NGOs. Citizens now had more rights than ever before. However,

[15] Megha Kumar, *Communalism and Sexual Violence: Ahmedabad Since 1969*. The book was later published by Tulika Books, New Delhi, in 2017. Here is a brief account of the controversy: https://www.livemint.com/Leisure/z4QMri42Jp9vQqHR3mgsuN/The-book-will-come-out-one-way-or-another-Megha-Kumar.html

while the addressee of the rights claim would be the state, its withdrawal from the delivery of the services and their provision by non-state agencies created an ambiguity about who could or would be held responsible for the provision of the right. In relation to these non-state agencies, the citizen was rendered a user or consumer of services rather than a rights-bearing citizen. The subtle change in the vocabulary was not unimportant as it signalled a move away from the language of citizenship.

Further, the celebration of this accretion of social rights was, in the decade between 2010 and 2014, by no means universal. There was resistance from the middle classes recently empowered by the economic reforms: they did not avow the civic solidarity that usually underwrites redistributive social policy. This civic parsimony formed a central plank of the BJP's electoral campaign, pitting aspirations against welfare and positing the promise of empowerment over entitlement. Poor voters, it claimed, were fed up with "handouts" and aspired to real opportunities for economic mobility, for which the incoming government promised an ambitious target of job creation.

It was this philosophy that underpinned the Prime Minister's attacks, both in the election campaign as well as in his first year in office, on the MGNREGA – the flagship welfare programme of the UPA government for rural employment generation.[16] He mocked it as a programme in which poor people dug ditches. However, in an unexpected about-turn a year later, in response to an opposition jibe that he was running a government for wealthy capitalists, he defended an expanded budgetary allocation for the programme.

Notwithstanding this, the privileging of empowerment over entitlement resonated with what has been called "productivist welfare capitalism" in the East Asian context, an instrumental conception in which social policy and basic social provisioning

[16] MGNREGA: Mahatma Gandhi National Rural Employment Generation Act (2005).

are governed by the overriding objective of making the citizen workforce productive, rather than any notion of enhancing capabilities or human flourishing. Modi's fascination with the East Asian model of development has been frequently aired, most recently in a speech at an investors' summit in October 2018. Here, he recalled that when, in his early years as Chief Minister of the State of Gujarat, he was asked about his vision for the State, he had said his "idol" for the development of Gujarat was South Korea rather than the United Kingdom or the United States.[17] It is not insignificant that this pronouncement was made at an investors' summit in Dehradun, the capital city of the small BJP-ruled hill state of Uttarakhand. Such summits have been organised in the capitals of many states under BJP rule and could be interpreted as an attempt by the Modi-led BJP to walk a tightrope: catering simultaneously to corporate India, which finances elections, as well as to the vast masses of the poor, whose votes actually count.

Since the political need for populist welfare became apparent, a slew of new "schemes" for development and welfare were launched. A senior member of the opposition claimed that twenty-three of the new government's schemes were essentially programmes launched by the previous government, repackaged and renamed. The immediate response from the spokespersons of the ruling party was not to deny it but rather to argue that, be that as it may, they were now being better implemented.[18] A fact-checking website showed that the claim was true of nineteen out of twenty-three schemes.[19] Should this continuity be interpreted to suggest that the project of social citizenship is being advanced? Does the fact that MGNREGA got its highest ever allocation from the present government indicate that there has been a rethinking or even reversal of the

[17] "Wanted to turn Gujarat into South Korea When I was Chief Minister: PM", https://www.ndtv.com/india-news/pm-narendra-modi-wanted-to-turn-gujarat-into-south-korea-when-i-was-chief-minister-1928265, accessed 12 October 2018.

[18] Daga and Mohanty, "Modi May Have Repackaged 23 UPA Schemes".

[19] http://factchecker.in/?s=19+out+of+23+schemes. Accessed 12 October 2018.

empowerment versus entitlement equation? Or is this apparent abandonment of the empowerment framework simply a way of deflecting scrutiny from the government's failure to create jobs?[20]

It would be a mistake to think that the government has altogether abandoned its plank of "empowerment" in favour of "entitlement". Most of its social security schemes are designed to ensure that beneficiaries pay, however small or token an amount or premium, instead of receiving free sops. The JAM programme (a prime example of this Prime Minister's penchant for acronymistic governance) brings together three distinct components: the Jan Dhan Yojana, Aadhaar, and Mobile. The Jan Dhan is the government's fillip to financial inclusion, a programme that enables the opening of bank accounts for the poor, even if there is no money in them – as indeed there was not in 58 per cent of these accounts.[21] These accounts are linked to Aadhaar, the unique biometric digital identity, and also to the mobile telephone number of the individual. This "JAM trinity" was supposed to facilitate direct cash transfers, which would replace the in-kind entitlements previously given.

Under the Jan Dhan Yojana, a large number – six million between 2014 and 2016 – of mostly zero-balance bank accounts were indeed opened. A journalistic investigation using the Right to Information subsequently revealed that small sums ranging from one to five rupees had, unknown to the account holders, been deposited in many of these accounts in public sector banks.[22] The

[20] Job creation has been one of the biggest challenges faced by this government, and arguably its single biggest failure. The chosen method of escaping accountability on this has been the sponsorship of creative experiments with data collection methods. Cf. Kazmin, "Dodgy Data".

[21] This is according to the government's own figures for 2015, though zero-balance accounts miraculously decreased, under slightly suspicious circumstances, the following year.

[22] "The One-Rupee Trick: How banks cut their zero-balance Jan Dhan accounts", *The Indian Express*, 13 September 2016, https://indianexpress.com/article/business/banking-and-finance/how-banks-cut-their-zero-balance-jan-dhan-accounts-one-rupee-trick-3028190/, accessed 10 October 2018.

money was deposited by mid-level bank officials, often diverted from the branch's entertainment allowance, maintenance allowance, canteen allowance, bank charges for online transfers, and so forth. Some officials admitted to having been under "pressure" to show that zero-balance accounts were declining in number. One official said: "There was a perception that so many zero-balance accounts means no one is using them, so there was pressure on us to change that."[23] The number of zero-balance accounts thus declined from 8.5 million in August 2014 to 5.8 million two years later, with the government's initiative of financial inclusion by questionable methods getting a positive spin.

Schemes for insurance and pensions are also based on contributions and designed so as to automatically debit the Jan Dhan Account. The jobless poor are clearly not in a position to deposit money into their Jan Dhan accounts, but the rules specify that the benefits of the insurance and pension plans will cease if there is insufficient money in the bank account to keep the plan going. Social security is therefore offered only to those who earn sufficient wages to be able to make deposits. For the really poor working in the unorganised sector, it remains eyewash. The philosophy of welfare underlying these initiatives represents a decisive turning back on rights-based programmes to those that are linked to earnings and contributions.

Another claim on behalf of the new modes for the delivery of welfare was that they would resolve all problems of leakages by ensuring effective delivery in two ways: first, through Direct Benefit Transfers (DBT), i.e. cash transfers paid into the Jan Dhan Accounts of the poor; and second, through the use of the biometric identity, Aadhaar. In the case of food, the first implied a shift from the earlier system of Public Distribution System (PDS) ration cards for the poor, with which they could access subsidised food at Fair Price Shops. The new system requires them to draw money paid

[23] Ibid.

by the government into their bank account and purchase food from the PDS. Studies of the pilots have shown that this has not been working too well. People are forced to spend more time travelling to banks (sometimes multiple times) to check on whether the funds have been received, then to the market to purchase food at a considerably higher price than the subsidised rations they previously got. Worst of all, there is a punitive sanction: if a household does not purchase rice from the PDS, it is threatened with discontinuation of the DBT subsidy.

A study undertaken for the government think tank Niti Aayog, of the three Union Territories (Delhi, Pondicherry, and Dadra and Nagar Haveli) where the pilot was conducted, instantiated the difficulties with the operation of this scheme. It found that "On average, it costs beneficiaries more (in time and money) to travel to banks (to access cash) and markets (to use cash) than in collecting food rations."[24] People also found the cash inadequate for accessing the same amount of food as they would have got through the PDS, with the majority preferring the old system of ration shops to the new system of cash transfers.[25] Another survey of a more recent pilot in Jharkhand showed 97 per cent of citizens opposing it, saying that the money did not come into the bank account on time; that it was often not clear which family member's Jan Dhan account would be credited with the household's cash subsidy, so that people were having to run to different banks several times – sometimes for a week – to find out whether the money had arrived and if so in whose account; and that the price of rice was Rs 32 per kg, as opposed to Re 1 per kg under the old system.[26]

The second strategy for improving delivery was digitisation and the seeding of Aadhaar (the Unique Identity) with ration cards. In Jharkhand, the ration cards of those who could not "seed" their Aadhaar numbers were simply cancelled. The consequence: on the

[24] Muralidharan, *et al.*, "Direct Benefits Transfer in Food", p. 5.

[25] Ibid.

[26] Aggarwal, "Direct Benefit Transfer".

one hand, the government claimed credit in Parliament for having saved vast amounts of public money by weeding out fake cards; on the other, the mass exclusion of the very poor and multiple starvation deaths.[27] Those who did not or could not meet the requirement of seeding came to be denied rations in the PDS. In other words, you could possess both forms of identity, but unless they had been linked, benefits were denied.[28] It was only after the death of an eleven-year-old girl whose family had stopped receiving rations – merely because their ration card was not linked to Aadhaar – that the Food Minister of the State acknowledged that the policy of "no Aadhaar, no rations" was flawed and had excluded the most vulnerable.[29]

A legal challenge to the Aadhaar project itself was awaiting a Supreme Court verdict at this time. It has now been decided in a way that satisfies the middle classes – who were resentful of the requirement of linking Aadhaar with their phone numbers and bank accounts – but keeps the poor vulnerable. The apex court has ruled that Aadhaar will remain mandatory for social service delivery.[30] This will require the seeding and authentication of Aadhaar for every new welfare scheme, and the discontinuation of benefits to those who have not had it done. In some cases, such as for those registered under the employment guarantee scheme, this entails "double seeding", such as the linking of both bank account and job card under the Aadhaar Payments Bridge System.[31]

[27] Drèze, *et al.*, "Aadhaar and Food Security in Jharkhand", 50–9.

[28] The Supreme Court had not finally pronounced on the validity of making this form of identity mandatory even as, in the meantime, government officials virtually coerced people into obtaining it by denying access to almost every public (and some private, like funerals) services without proof of ABBA (Aadhaar Based Biometric Identification).

[29] https://www.telegraphindia.com/states/jharkhand/girl-death-corners-govt/cid/1343094?ref=search-page, accessed 12 October 2018.

[30] https://www.livemint.com/Companies/egjWCYZXFLH6OTVAnSGw6N/How-Supreme-Courts-Aadhaar-order-affects-you.html, accessed 12 October 2018.

[31] Drèze, "Ill Fares Aadhaar".

The obsession with technology as the pre-eminent mode of service delivery has, even if in a small number of cases, resulted in the denial of the right to life – whether due to hunger or the inability to access emergency health care. The extent of the rightlessness of the poor is only underscored by the jettisoning of the rights-based approach in favour of one that expects people to make contributions, however modest, to their own social security. Not only are vast numbers of the unemployed unable to protect themselves, even those who are employed frequently cannot afford such contributions. The LPG subsidy for women in poor households is a prime example of this flawed system.[32]

The continuity with the earlier rights-based approach is that the enjoyment of welfare provisioning remains in line with what T.H. Marshall famously called "class abatement".[33] This effectively means that the enjoyment of welfare is conditional upon the forsaking of equal civic status, and on one's placement in official categories like BPL. If special groups alone can enjoy special rights, the benefits of social welfare stand effectively severed from the status of citizenship.

To the extent that welfare provisioning is not universal, it is detached from the equality of citizenship that obtains in the case of, say, the civil and political rights of citizenship. Those who are entitled to welfare, by virtue of their poverty or lower incomes, are also formally citizens entitled to civil and political rights. However, they have to belong to especially denominated categories in order to enjoy the additional provisioning of welfare, which is contingent upon their belonging to groups designated as especially

[32] The Prime Minister's much-vaunted scheme for providing LPG cylinders at subsidised rates to women in poor households was a terrific idea to save women both the drudgery and the toxic emissions from cooking stoves using sticks and twigs or kerosene for fuel. The reality: few households have come back for refills because they have not been able to pay back the loan they received from the oil marketing companies for buying the gas stove in the first place, much less to afford the refill: https://www.ndtv.com/india-news/ahead-of-polls-loan-recovery-in-pradhan-mantri-ujjwala-yojana-deferred-1827989 24 March 2018, accessed 10 October 2018.

[33] Marshall, *Citizenship and Social Class.*

deserving. On the one hand, by making them visible and legible to the state, this strategy furthers the goal of inclusion and lends substance to their notionally equal civic status. On the other, it stigmatises them as well as the welfare services to which they are entitled. In Marshall's terms, such strategies work to abate "the nuisance of poverty".

For the enjoyment of substantive citizenship, then, those who are disadvantaged require markers of citizenship, the signs of belonging in boxes labelled "Poor" or "Dalit". At the same time, the markers themselves stigmatise their citizenship, rendering it of less consequence than the real citizenship of the unmarked citizen. For instance, while the Aadhaar marker, being technically universal in application, pretends to treat all citizens equally, it is a fact that the goods for which it is mandatory, such as food or cooking gas subsidies, are not those to which the otherwise unmarked citizen aspires.

There is, however, an important discontinuity as well. Under the rights-based approach, people's eligibility for welfare was determined simply by their being marked as belonging to a particular disadvantage box (SC/ST/BPL). Now, the information required includes biometrics like fingerprints and iris scans, which frequently do not work, and which would violate their privacy if they were considered deserving of such a luxury. The inability to provide biometric proof of this marker of identity can be – as we have seen – the difference between life and death.

This imbrication of rights with identities is not unique to India, but the particular form it takes is often aligned to not just the attribution of rights but also to their violation. Which takes us to my third lens on citizenship: identity.

Identity

The opening discussion of legal status signalled the fact that the dimension of identity has witnessed the most substantial reconfiguration of citizenship in recent times. The dramatic increase in incidents of vigilante violence against Muslims and Dalits, and the impunity enjoyed by the perpetrators of such violence, signify a systematic political and ideological attempt to render these groups second-class citizens.

Immediately after the BJP government assumed office, the social issue that acquired prominence was "Love Jihad", the label used for Muslim men marrying Hindu women, suggesting that Muslim men make false professions of love to Hindu women while their intent is to convert them to Islam.[34] Cases in which Muslim men, suspected of love jihad, were assaulted or killed, persist. Another initiative, which seems to have petered out after an aggressive beginning in 2014, is the "Ghar Wapsi" (Homecoming) programme, under which events were organised by the RSS and the Vishva Hindu Parishad (VHP) to convert Muslims and Christians to Hinduism.[35]

Violence against Muslims and Dalits has made these two sections of Indian society particularly vulnerable. It would be sufficient for our purposes here to briefly discuss just two landmark cases. First, in September 2015 an ironsmith named Mohammad Akhlaq was killed on suspicion of killing and consuming a cow. He was lynched by a mob in a small town in UP, where his family had lived amicably with its Hindu neighbours for four generations. Ruling party legislators raised the pitch by asking for his family to be prosecuted,[36] thus deflecting public attention from the

[34] A BJP MP who is now the Chief Minister of India's largest state made the claim, in 2014, that "love jihad" was an international conspiracy against India: http://www.wsj.com/articles/hindu-activists-in-india-warn-women-to-beware-of-love-jihad-1409874089, accessed 10 October 2018.

[35] http://www.thehindu.com/news/national/other-states/ghar-wapsi-to-continue-till-conversions-are-banned-adityanath/article6929001.ece 24 February 2015, accessed 10 October 2018.

[36] http://indianexpress.com/article/india/india-news-india/dadri-lynching-sanjeev-balyan-mahapanchayat-bishada-village-2838509/ 7 June 2016, accessed 10 October 2018.

barbarism of the murder – from the question of who killed Akhlaq to the question of what he was eating.[37] The victim was reinvented as the aggressor, and a police case filed against Akhlaq's wife and mother for slaughtering a cow.

Second, in July 2016, in Una town in Gujarat, four young Dalit men were stripped, paraded on the streets, and beaten up by a group of "Gau Rakshaks" (Cow Protectors) for skinning a dead cow. A video of the victims, some of them tied to a car, being attacked with iron rods and sticks, was widely circulated on social media. This chilling incident provoked a huge protest, with Dalit groups alleging police complicity in the act.[38] The most significant challenge – some called it India's Rosa Parks moment – thrown by the protesters was to boycott the collection of carcasses of fallen cows, an occupation traditionally associated with Dalit castes. "So we decided to stop doing it to teach them a lesson. The *gau rakshaks* beat us because they think the cow is their mother. Well, then, they should take care of her and pick up her carcass when she dies."[39] Violence against Dalits has been rising steadily, going up 44 per cent since 2014, according to official statistics.

Subsequent months have seen the mushrooming of hundreds of Gau Rakshak Dals (Cow Protection Groups) especially in states ruled by the BJP. They either extort money from the owners of cattle or kill them on the pretext of "saving" or "rescuing" the cows from slaughter. The targets of these vigilante groups are people

[37] It was sent to a forensic lab for testing: when it tested as mutton, it was sent to another forensic laboratory, which determined it to be beef. In the state of UP, cow slaughter is a crime but eating beef is not.

[38] Protests led by Una Ladat Samiti (an umbrella organisation of twenty Dalit organisations) even turned violent with highway blockades and the torching of public buses. Of potentially even greater significance from a political perspective was the fact that Muslim activists of the Jamiat-e-Ulema-e-Hind Gujarat joined Dalits in this protest in Ahmedabad.

[39] http://scroll.in/article/812329/your-mother-you-take-care-of-it-meet-the-dalits-behind-gujarats-stirring-cow-carcass-protests, 23 July 2016, accessed 10 October 2018.

who deal commercially with cattle, cowhide, or other byproducts of cows, such as textiles and tennis racquet strings. Gau Rakshak Dal vigilantes typically intercept trucks transporting cattle or raid slaughterhouses, and either extort money from the owners or kill them. They then post photographs of the cattle and themselves, posing with guns and bloodied limbs, on social media. Though buffaloes are neither sacred nor covered by laws on cow slaughter, owners and transporters of buffaloes are intimidated by citing laws against cruelty to animals, and bribes are forcibly extracted from them.[40]

Though carried out in the name of the Hindu reverence for the cow, such vigilantism is clearly aimed at the economic disenfranchisement of Dalits and Muslims. While the beef production and export business is dominated by Muslims, the skinning of cows for leather is traditionally work done by Dalits, thousands of whom work in slaughterhouses, leather factories, and tanneries, though the owners of tanneries and traders in cowhide are generally upper caste. India has been the world's largest exporter of beef (including buffalo meat). These activities led to a sharp drop in cow prices and a substantial decline in buffalo meat export from India, down by about US$ 700 million.[41] India also exports leather and leather goods worth approximately US$ 6 billion. Both these have declined and damaged the economy. However, neither the resulting loss of livelihoods nor the decline in revenue from exports seems to have caused any great concern in the ruling establishment.[42]

[40] Because of the Hindu belief in the sacredness of cows, many states have long had laws banning cow slaughter. Only the seven states of the north-east have no ban; a handful of states allow cow slaughter with conditions; most others have stringent laws prohibiting it. However, the trade in cow leather is mostly from fallen cows, and beef exports are mainly of buffalo meat.

[41] From US$ 4781 million to US$ 4068 million, mostly as orders from China, are now going to Brazil.

[42] The Prime Minister made a statement condemning the attempts of "a handful of opportunistic people who in the name of cow protection . . . poison social

Unconnected to cows, violence against Muslims and Dalits has also been on the rise. In 2017, a teenaged boy, Junaid Khan, returning home after shopping for Eid in Delhi, was barbarically lynched on a train. A few months later, a man in Rajasthan hacked and then set on fire a migrant worker from Bengal who he suspected was in a relationship with a Hindu woman. He videotaped the murder as well as his own speech justifying it and circulated both on the social media. The most recent horror was the gang rape, repeated over a whole week, and followed by the murder of a little Muslim girl in Kathua in Kashmir.

Today, thus, not for the first time but in an accelerated, even everyday form, violence is being systematically visited on particular groups whose position in Indian society is on all parameters deeply inequitable. Vigilante violence or violence by lynch mobs – with more than a hint of state protection[43] – is being disproportionately visited on groups that are vulnerable on account of multiple, often intersecting inequalities of class, caste, religion, tribe, gender. The normalisation of this type of violence is becoming almost a defining feature of identity-based inequality, such that to be different and unequal is not just to lack well-being but to be subjected, over and above that lack, to violence and/or oppression that is no longer episodic and which finds public justification.

---

harmony." He claimed that 80 per cent of *gau rakshaks* were this type of "fake cow protectors", and that it was not acceptable to kill people in the name of the cow, but his statement was promptly rebutted by the RSS, which averred its own espousal of "the cause of gau raksha". "PM Narendra Modi's remark that 80 per cent gau rakshaks are fake should have been avoided: RSS", *The Indian Express*, 9 August 2016, http://indianexpress.com/article/india/india-news-india/narendra-modi-fake-gau-rakshak-rss-beef-ban-cow-slaughter-gujarat-dalit-thrashing-2962750/, accessed 10 October 2018.

[43] Union Minister for Civil Aviation Jayant Sinha actually felicitated a group of men in his constituency who had been accused of mob lynching and released on bail: https://timesofindia.indiatimes.com/india/union-minister-jayant-sinha-garlands-8-lynching-convicts-faces-opposition-flak/articleshow/64901863.cms, accessed 12 October 2018.

From Akhlaq to Junaid and from Una to Kathua, we are seeing a pattern of violence targeted against particular groups – Muslims, Dalits, and women belonging to these groups; and such violence is increasingly getting normalised. The impunity enjoyed by the perpetrators of such violence is also a function of inequality. Official figures compiled by the National Crime Records Bureau, for instance, tell us that although violence against Dalits is up 44 per cent since 2014, a 90 per cent charge-sheeting rate yields a conviction rate of barely 20 per cent. If we consider only cow-related "hate crimes", 100 per cent of the victims in 2018 were Muslim; 61 per cent in 2017 were Muslim; and, in 2016, 43 per cent Muslim and 34 per cent Dalit.[44] The burdens of identity are clearly intolerable and diminish citizenship.

Recent data on citizen perceptions provide further evidence of the huge social distance between these vulnerable groups and the rest of the population. The report of the first Lokniti-Azim Premji University survey of four States – Gujarat, Haryana, Odisha, and Karnataka – found that half the Hindus in Odisha and Haryana saw Muslims as the most violent community.[45] The second report surveyed another eight States and found strong public support for majoritarian nationalism, e.g. favouring a State ban on the consumption of beef.[46] Both reports testify to the fact that personal friendships across castes and religious communities are weak. Significantly, the States where the social distance between upper castes and Other Backward Classes (OBCs), on the one hand, and Dalits on the other, is the highest – Bihar and Rajasthan – are also the States where caste violence is more prevalent.

The normalisation of patterned violence is now pervasive, and recent writings have demonstrated the role of Hindu nationalist

[44] http://lynch.factchecker.in

[45] Centre for the Study of Developing Societies and Azim Premji University, *Society and Politics Between Elections*.

[46] Ibid.

ideology and mobilisation in facilitating it.[47] Physically and discursively, they have rendered violence a legitimate means to a variety of goals – avenging dishonour to women, the nation, the cow, or indeed any other purpose that has been unilaterally determined to be morally right or culturally superior. Violence then is no longer pathological; it has become normalised as an acceptable and justifiable way of pursuing the social and political objective of using fear and intimidation to entrench power over the powerless.

Conclusion

Through this limited and illustrative survey of the landscape of citizenship in present-day India, I have sought to argue that the legal status of equal citizenship is under challenge by a legislative amendment that seeks to introduce explicit religious difference into the religion-neutral law of citizenship; that the rights of social citizenship are being compromised by a shift from a rights-based approach to a contributory approach to welfare, and by the punishing requirement of a digital identity; and, finally, that the inclusionary provisions of the constitution, providing equal citizenship to members of diverse social and religious groups, are being undermined by acts of routinised violence, executed with impunity, against minorities and lower castes. The philosophy of citizenship today is of creating second-class citizens based on caste and religious identity, and implicitly keeping the poor as the lesser citizens they have always been.

[47] Cf. Basu, *Violent Conjunctures in Democratic India*; Pai and Kumar, *Everyday Communalism*.

PART III

ANTINOMIES

5

A False Dichotomy? The Unresolved Tension Between Universal and Differentiated Citizenship in India

Universal and Group-Differentiated Citizenship: Theoretical Issues

. . . any electoral representation in India would be doomed to mischievous failure which aimed at granting a personal enfranchisement, regardless of the beliefs and traditions of the communities composing the population of this continent.

– Viceroy Minto responding to the Muslim demand for Special Electorates[1]

This statement, made more than a hundred years ago, implicitly acknowledges one of the most important and enduring disputes in India across the twentieth century: between universal and group-differentiated conceptions of citizenship. This is admittedly an anachronistic term, for "differentiated citizenship" was obviously not the phrase used to describe the legal and political forms of accommodating diversity improvised for early-twentieth-century India. The term is of more recent origin, used by political theorists to signal their discomfort with universalist notions of citizenship which entail the recognition of individuals as constitutive units of the polity, and as bearers of equal rights without any consideration of inequalities in their wealth,

[1] Wolpert, *Morley and India*, 189.

social status, or identity. However, it is widely recognised that the presence of inequalities, especially those based in group identity, and marked by the discrimination or disadvantages that attach to belonging to particular social groups, can result in a lack of voice and participation in the polity for those within such groups. In these circumstances, the language of common and even equal citizenship renders invisible the many inequalities that lie concealed beneath the mask of formal equality and obscures the inadequacies of liberal neutrality as state policy.

Group-differentiated citizenship (GDC) has become a widely accepted strategy to assuage this discomfort with liberal, homogenising, difference-blind accounts of citizenship.[2] In Iris Marion Young's definitive formulation of the basic principle of differentiated citizenship, "a democratic public, however that is constituted, should provide mechanisms for the effective representation and recognition of the distinct voices and perspectives of those of its constituent groups that are oppressed or disadvantaged within it."[3] Young specified oppression as including exploitation, marginalisation, powerlessness, cultural imperialism, and vulnerability to violence motivated by hatred and fear. Though she explicitly included poor and working-class people, she also argued that such groups are defined by their "comprehensive identities and ways of life" rather than by any particular position or interest.[4] In contemporary politics, identity differences have often been regarded as the most suitable basis for claims to group-differentiated citizenship, which finds institutional expression in many familiar forms: rights

[2] Young, "Polity and Group Difference"; Kymlicka and Norman, "Return of the Citizen"; Carens, *Culture, Citizenship*.

[3] Young, "Polity and Group Difference", 188–9.

[4] Ibid., 199. In the American context, these criteria yielded the following plausible candidates for differentiated citizenship: "women, blacks, Native Americans, Chicanos, Puerto Ricans and other Spanish-speaking Americans, Asian Americans, gay men, lesbians, working-class people, poor people, old people, and mentally and physically disabled people." Young, "Polity and Group Difference", 195.

to guaranteed representation in institutions of governance, minority rights, language rights, affirmative action, and, of course, various modes of symbolic recognition.

Advocates of differentiated citizenship do, however, recognise a range of legitimate anxieties associated with it. The first type of anxiety has to do with the implications of GDC for the quality of citizenship in the polity as a whole. To the extent that differentiated citizenship speaks to the dimension of citizenship as status (or "thin" citizenship) rather than citizenship as practice ("thick" citizenship), and the first is logically prior to the second, differentiated citizenship does not provide an account of how status might translate into practice, which arguably requires the recognition of "transcendent political considerations" of a common and even universal purpose.[5] If "all is particularity", as Ronald Beiner puts it, where, in the absence of a civic community, might citizenship be located or practised?[6]

GDC may also postpone, perhaps indefinitely, the possibility of articulating a shared common purpose for the polity as a whole, given its propensity to provide institutional incentives that may contribute to the entrenchment of identities, to their reinforcement and hardening. High levels of differentiated citizenship are therefore associated with the fear of weakening social cohesion and integration. In an extreme form, where minorities are territorially concentrated, they may even spawn demands for secession and self-governing states.[7] Indeed, differentiated citizenship may itself bring into existence new categories of disadvantaged citizens, making members of the majority community, or even sub-groups within minorities, apprehensive that certain minority rights may make them second-class citizens.[8] As such, there is the challenge of designing institutions and policy instruments

[5] Meyer, "The Politics of Differentiated Citizenship", 76–7.

[6] Beiner, *Theorizing Citizenship*, 10.

[7] Kymlicka and Norman, "Citizenship in Culturally Diverse Societies", 39–40.

[8] Ibid., 32.

that would most effectively further the objectives of GDC while avoiding these pitfalls.

A second type of concern relates to the proper determination of which groups should receive differentiated citizenship rights. This could imply making judgements not only about which groups are disadvantaged or oppressed, but also about what, in a particular context, qualifies as oppression or disadvantage: distinguishing clearly, in Kymlicka's words, "the reality of inequality and the oppression and stigmatization it fosters . . . from the perception of unequal status."[9] Since GDC is assumed not to encompass all inequalities that are morally objectionable but only those rooted in, *pace* Young, comprehensive identities and ways of life, there is a need also to provide reasons for why such difference-based inequalities should be redressed through differentiated rights of citizenship while non-difference-based inequalities do not demand similar attention.

This chapter makes the claim that the Indian experience – beginning over a hundred years ago, but especially in its post-colonial constitutional form – may be usefully interpreted in this frame. Not only do India's experiments with quotas (locally referred to as "reservations") anticipate the idea of GDC and represent it empirically, they also powerfully illustrate many of the complexities and contradictions inherent in the concept, expressed in the preceding paragraphs as concerns. For instance, the question of whether differentiated citizenship strategies should address only difference-based inequalities is of particular interest in the Indian context where the two types of inequalities – cultural and symbolic on the one hand, and material on the other – tend to overlap. There are concerns also about how to balance competing claims to recognition through the nitty-gritty of formulating appropriate criteria to adjudicate competing claims to differentiated citizenship.

[9] Ibid.

The next section prefaces a substantive discussion of the more recent challenges of GDC in India, and their normative and political implications, with a quick survey of the major institutional practices and political arguments for what could be described as GDC before 1947, and a brief account of the constitutional consensus.

Colonial Institutional Innovations and Political Arguments for GDC

In post-colonial India, the idea that representation should be differentiated by social groups is clearly framed by the trope of equality. There is an obviously different form of governmentality at work in the articulation of the same idea in colonial times, when it is simply a technique for the more effective management of an empire. The assumption underlying separate representation was the conviction that the intensity of group differences in India precluded any possibility of commonality and the task of colonial governance was therefore to "manage" these differences by allowing each group to have its point of view represented "by the mouth of some member specially acquainted with them" – as a government despatch of 1892 stated.[10]

As early as the 1880s, Punjab experimented with separate electorates in local government and communal representation in the bureaucracy, the apparent purpose of these – eventually unsuccessful – policies being to prevent violence between Hindus

[10] At this time, the phrase "classes, races, and interests" (from the Aitchison Commission Report on the Public Services) gained widespread currency. In the debate leading to the Indian Councils Act of 1892, a government despatch claimed that "Representation of such a community upon such a scale as the Act permits can only be secured by providing that each important class shall have at least the opportunity of making its views known in the Council *by the mouth of some member specially acquainted with them*". Banerjee, *Indian Constitutional Documents*, 298 (emphasis added).

and Muslims, and to secure the loyalty and quiescence of what was perceived to be an inconveniently combative Muslim minority.[11] At the national level, it was in the Indian Councils Act of 1909 that the principle of separate electorates for elections to the provincial legislatures was first recognised.[12]

The crystallisation of official discourse on issues of representation was not an uncontested process. There was disputation within the political establishment in Britain and in India on every aspect of institutional reform – the enhancement of non-official representation; whether this was to be done through election or nomination; and, most importantly, how different groups were to be represented. Some members of Lord Morley's Council of India supported the creation of electoral colleges based on "race, caste or religion" across India, and separate representation for Muslims.[13] The need for separate representation was usually justified with reference to attributes of "backwardness" of the community in question, a category that has endured in public policy until the present day.

Initially, colonial policies of differentiation did not explicitly frame issues of representation as questions of citizenship, but over time there does appear to have been a clear official recognition of the relationship between citizenship and differential representative entitlements.[14] By the 1920s, there was an explicit recognition

[11] Barrier, "The Punjab Government".

[12] https:// www. constitutionofindia.net/ historical_constitutions/ indian_councils_act__1909_1st%20January%201909

[13] Wolpert, *Morley and India*, 141.

[14] Morley hailed the "didactic value" of representative institutions for training Indians in "habits of political responsibility". Wolpert, *Morley and India*, 159. The 1908 Royal Proclamation drafted by him announced that measures were planned to satisfy the claim of "equality of citizenship, and a greater share in legislation and government". Ibid., 152. Minto's famous assurance to the 1906 deputation demanding separate electorates for Muslims forcefully articulated the position that group representation, rather than individual franchise, was the way forward: "any electoral representation in India would be doomed to mischievous failure which aimed at granting a *personal enfranchisement*, regardless of the beliefs and traditions of the communities composing the population . . .". Ibid., 189.

of the adverse implications of separate electorates for a common citizenship.[15] The Montagu report that resulted in the Act of 1919 affirmed that "The history of self-government among the nations who developed it . . . is decisively against the admission by the State of any divided allegiance; against the State's arranging its members in any way which encourages them to think of themselves primarily as citizens of any smaller unit than itself."[16] The Statutory (Simon) Commission likewise pronounced separate electorates to be "an undoubted obstacle in the way of the growth of a sense of common citizenship."[17]

The most radical political claim to GDC in colonial India was indisputably that which, beginning with the demand for separate electorates, culminated in the demand for the separate state of Pakistan. There were, however, other claimants also, and in the two decades before independence there was a cornucopia of rival and competing conceptions of citizenship. These may be usefully distinguished in terms of the two umbrella categories of universal and differentiated citizenship, recognising that the category of the universal is itself differentiated.

[15] The Congress, in its Lahore session of 1909, expressed its strong disapproval of the creation of separate electorates on the basis of religion. Morley's friend Gokhale, however, took a pragmatic view, arguing that "unless by special separate treatment soreness in minds of minorities is removed real union will be retarded". Ibid., 196. As one historian puts it, "separate electorates put a formal seal of approval on the institutionalised conception of Muslim political identity and contributed to the forging of communitarian identities that were, both in conception and articulation, profoundly divisive and inherently conflict-oriented." Hasan, "The Myth of Unity", 193.

[16] Ibid., 200.

[17] Ibid. It is not surprising that, in the first official recognition of the Depressed Classes as a distinct and disadvantaged group, the Government of India Act of 1919 chose to give this group representation in the form of non-official nominated members in the Central Legislative Assembly as well as the Provincial Legislatures. "Depressed Classes" was the name by which the "untouchable" castes were then known. Gandhi subsequently gave them the name "Harijan" (People of God), but both of these usages have now been overridden by the two currently dominant: the official category "Scheduled Castes" and the political category "Dalit" (the oppressed).

There can be little dispute about the description of the Congress as articulating a broadly universal conception of citizenship, and the classic statement of the universalist model is arguably the report of the Motilal Nehru Committee (for the All-Parties Conference) which recommended universal adult franchise and the complete dissociation of state and religion.[18] Within the Congress, in the years that followed, it was the Nehruvian strand alone that was consistently universalist in the classical liberal-individualist sense of the term. There were other, weaker forms of universalism in the Congress party, which sought merely to accommodate and even assimilate differences within it. Gandhi's acknowledgement of communities, for instance, and his simultaneous recognition of the territoriality of the Indian nation, made it possible for him to argue for a universalist citizenship that included all who inhabited the land. As far as disadvantaged groups were concerned, however, Gandhi argued that the "protection of neglected classes should not be carried to an extent which will harm them and harm the country."[19]

In this period, two other conceptions of citizenship can be designated as broadly universalist: those advanced by Hindu nationalism and by the women's movement. The proposition that the Hindu nationalist conception, scripted by the leaders of the Hindu Mahasabha (Hindu Association) and the Rashtriya Swayamsevak Sangh (National Volunteer Organisation; RSS), should be seen as a distinct sub-category of universalist citizenship may seem puzzling. Hindu majoritarian ideology would seem to belong, almost self-evidently and even perversely, to the category of GDC, as citizenship is anchored to identity, and the aspiration is to create classes of citizens in which Hindus occupy pride of place. On the other hand, its very majoritarianism pushes it aspirationally

[18] The Nehru Committee Report rejected separate electorates but did propose their replacement by reserving legislative seats for Muslims in provinces in which they were in a minority.

[19] Gandhi, "Answers to Questions", 119.

in the direction of a proto-universalism and this is why I propose here that it may be useful to think of Hindutva as a distinctive, exclusionary, version of the universalist argument, a descriptive – as opposed to substantive – form of universalism.[20] The strategies to achieve this complete synonymy between nation and religion vary across the proponents of Hindutva, ranging from the elimination of minorities to their reconversion and assimilation.[21]

After its separation from the Congress party in the late 1930s,[22] the Hindu Mahasabha came to be led by V.D. Savarkar, who coined the word Hindutva and defined it in terms of the geographical unity of the Indian nation and its association with territory, race, and culture, with religion being ostensibly only one component of culture. Savarkar cleverly asserted commonality with Muslims in terms of their inheritance of Hindu blood "almost unaffected by an alien adulteration". Without explicitly stating that religion trumped all other features of potential belonging, he pointed to the extra-territorial locus of the affiliation of non-Hindus, arguing that they could not be Hindus only because for them their alien Holy Land (Punyabhu) was above their Fatherland (Pitribhu).[23]

[20] Hindutva: lit., "Hinduness". The term is used to describe the ideology of the organisations that advocate a Hindu nation.

[21] Lal Chand, in Jaffrelot, *Hindu Nationalism*, 49.

[22] The Hindu Mahasabha started as a group within the Congress party, anchored by Lajpat Rai and M.M. Malaviya, who asserted the need for Hindus and Muslims to be on terms of love and goodwill, distanced themselves from talk of a Hindu Raj, and commented on incidents of communal violence in the language of pain and despair rather than aggression and violence.

[23] "Ye, who by race, by blood, by culture, by nationality, possess almost all the essentials of Hindutva and had been forcibly snatched out of our ancestral home by the hand of violence – ye, have only to render whole-hearted love to our common Mother and recognize her not only as Fatherland (Pitribhu) but even as a Holyland (Punyabhu); and ye would be most welcome to the Hindu fold." Savarkar, *Essentials of Hindutva*, 43. And again: "The majority of the Indian Mohammedans may, if free from the prejudices born of ignorance, come to love our land as their fatherland, as the patriotic and noble-minded amongst them have always been doing . . . We have tried to determine the essentials of Hindutva and in doing so we have discovered

While Savarkar professed the principle that religious minorities should enjoy equal formal rights of citizenship, M.S. Golwalkar – who, starting in 1940, headed the RSS for more than thirty years – argued that non-Hindus who did not "respect and revere" the Hindu religion and adopt its culture and language could stay in the country in subordination but "claiming nothing, deserving no privileges, far less any preferential treatment, not even citizen's rights."[24] For Golwalkar, minorities needed to be made Hindus not by persuasion but by coercion, and under threat of violence if necessary.

These two versions of the universalist argument – the national-civic argument of modernists like Nehru, and the national-ethnic argument of Hindu nationalism – are quite fundamentally opposed to each other.[25] The first form of universalism is identity-neutral, accommodative of difference, and appreciative of diversity, though it could be vulnerable to the criticism of representing the view of dominant religious and caste groups. Counterposed to this is the rival Hindutva form of universalism that views the "other" as actually a part of the "self" – a part that has been separated (by conversion) and misled into owing allegiance to a holy land beyond the land of the Hindus, but may be readmitted on condition that it agrees to forsake its otherness. This is an argument that seeks to universalise through homogenisation.[26] It projects majoritarianism

---

that the Bohras and such other Mohammedan or Christian communities possess all the essential qualifications of Hindutva but one, and that is that they do not look upon India as their Holyland." Savarkar, in Jaffrelot, *Hindu Nationalism*, 94–5.

[24] Golwalkar, quoted in Basu, *et al.*, *Khaki Shorts*, 26–7.

[25] In Kymlicka's terms, these could be described as versions of liberal and illiberal nationalism. Kymlicka, "Introduction: An Emerging Consensus", 145–6.

[26] "Political *sangathan* [organisation] may have been legitimised through the language of internal reform, but its clear purpose was to create, strengthen, and consolidate the idea of a distinct nationwide imagined community of Hindus whose interests had to be articulated in the political sphere of Indian nationalism, but which could also be constituted as a distinct communalised public sphere in its own right. This agenda was very different from that of the anti-sectarian tendencies of

into universalism through the systematic elimination, or by the incorporation, of difference. Being intolerant of difference, it would have us either absorb or banish diversity. The distinction between the two forms of universalism is that while the first accepts the coexistence of diversity within a pluralist framework, the second wishes to devour or eliminate it in an aspirational mono-national and mono-cultural state. Though Hindutva clearly makes a claim based on a particular identity, it is the claim of a dominant group, and not one based in disadvantage or oppression. If it argues for differentiated citizenship, it does so by marrying this identity with the idea of universalism, such that differentiation creates an exclusion from the Hindu universal.

This projection of the particular as the universal is also evident in the views of Hindu organisations towards the claims of lower castes, before as well as after 1947. It has been argued that the upper-caste orientation of Hindu nationalist organisations, and the RSS in particular, stemmed from the latter's Maharashtrian origins, and the fear of Dalit assertiveness in that region.[27] The organic vision of the Hindu Rashtra (Hindu nation) refuses to recognise the need for special rights for groups. Hindutva differentiates between Hindus and non-Hindus but refuses to acknowledge claims of differentiation from other Hindu groups. If it is intolerant of Muslim claims to personal law, it has historically also opposed sectional claims from within the Hindu fold for quotas in public service, though political expediency has encouraged it to make some concessions to this in recent times.[28] In general, the

---

the national movement, but the two often shared the same public space and sphere of organisation." Bhatt, *Hindu Nationalism*, 76.

[27] Basu, *et al.*, *Khaki Shorts*, 10. The term Dalit – lit. "the oppressed" – refers to the former untouchable castes, known as the Depressed Classes in colonial times (see fn.6). The contemporary official label is Scheduled Castes, due to the Schedule of the constitution in which they are listed for purposes of identifying eligibility for quotas; the preferred self-description of these groups is the political label Dalit.

[28] The RSS was vocally hostile to the announcement of the implementation of

approach of the nationalist Bharatiya Janata Party (BJP) has been to encourage groups like the Other Backward Classes (OBCs) to see themselves as Hindus first, and has viewed itself – *vis-à-vis* the undifferentiated Hindu community – as an assimilative and absorptive entity, much like the Congress did historically, though with a wider section of social groups.[29]

The other, quintessentially liberal, assertion of universal citizenship was contained in the claims advanced by women's organisations, in the early years of the twentieth century, for universal adult franchise and equal political status. The first women's delegation to the Secretary of State and the Viceroy (Montagu and Chelmsford) in 1917 asked the colonial government to give women the vote and thereby grant them the status of "people".[30] Their demand for absolute political equality led them to reject preferential treatment. A strident language of universal citizenship, and resentment at being treated as a "reservable" category rather than as equal, pervades the documents that emanated from

---

the Mandal Commission Report, even proposing a gradual reduction in the quotas for Scheduled Castes. The BJP, initially opposing caste quotas, eventually capitulated to what it saw as a political necessity to attract the Other Backward Classes (OBC) vote, and to please its partners in the National Democratic Alliance. Jaffrelot, *Hindu Nationalism*, 256–7.

[29] Nehruvian universalism also, it could be argued, recognised the interests of disadvantaged caste and tribal groups as deserving (even if temporarily) special provision, but was not equally sympathetic to the claims of, say, the groups today known as the Other Backward Classes.

[30] Forbes, *Women in Modern India*, 92. The following year, Sarojini Naidu – who had led that delegation – argued eloquently at the Congress session for the rational, scientific, and political soundness of enfranchising women. She simultaneously reassured her audience – which passed the resolution by a resounding three-fourths majority – that this was no transgression of tradition and that women would not, by participating in politics, become less feminine! Her views were echoed by other women leaders, such as Saraladevi Chaudhurani, who defined the sphere of women as including politics and "comradeship with men in the rough and tumble of life". Ibid., 94.

women's organisations through the 1930s.[31] In 1933, the All India Women's Conference repudiated both separate electorates and reserved seats thus: "We look upon nominations, reservation of seats, and co-option in any sphere of activity as a pernicious and humiliating system which must run counter to all real progress. However impartially carried out it must, by its very nature, engender an inferiority complex amongst those for whom it caters, a contingency to be avoided at all costs . . ."[32] Ironically, the claims of women to universal citizenship were repeatedly rebuffed and in fact women were treated as deserving of differentiated policy. Coaxed – by the government, the nationalist leadership, and their friends in the British suffragist movement – the leaders of the women's movement eventually accepted reservations as the first step towards social reform, and small numbers of women entered the provincial legislative assemblies.[33]

[31] Women's demands for enfranchisement were strongly influenced by the ideas of the British suffragists, many of whom were in touch with the women's movement in India. Eleanor Rathbone actually disagreed with the Indian women's insistence on universal adult franchise and suggested to Indian women colleagues that they accept reservations to take forward the project of social reform. The denial of the franchise on the grounds that it was "premature" triggered angry activity and depositions before many official committees in England as well as in India. Even as they claimed to speak on behalf of all Indian women, British officials dismissed them as elite exceptions to the vast majority of women in India – stereotypically characterised as veiled, uneducated, and ignorant – and therefore representing only their own limited class.

[32] Dhanda, *Reservations for Women*, 5.

[33] Where women leaders demanded a proportion of 1:5 female to male voters, the White Paper of 1933 recommended an increase from the existing 1:20 to 1:10. The apparently widely shared understanding that women themselves dropped their political demands out of deference to Gandhi has been variously represented. Singer, "*A Constituency Suitable*", 36. In Radha Kumar's characterisation, "Gandhian feminism which developed in the 1920s became majority feminism in the 1930s." Kumar, *History of Doing*, 67. Chatterjee's argument (in Chatterjee, "The Nationalist Resolution"), for a somewhat earlier period, that nationalism domesticated the issue of women by confining it to the home and refusing to make it a matter of political

Against their wishes, then, women came to be treated – like Muslims – as a discrete constituency. Both Muslims and women received the right to vote in separate Muslim-only and women-only constituencies, respectively, with Muslim women finding themselves under considerable pressure from the Muslim League to support community candidates and disavow gender affiliations. The Indian National Congress likewise supported only those women who contested reserved seats, with even Nehru using nationalism to trump women's demands.[34] Gandhi had, in any case, enjoined women to fight alongside men against the greatest common enemy, British rule, the removal of which would bring with it the right to vote among all other rights.

Women's claims to universal citizenship were curiously premised on the idea of separate spheres – "separate goals, separate destinies" – for men and women.[35] Citizenship was viewed as belonging to the public sphere to which women would, through their enfranchisement, bring the values and virtues of the private sphere, without in any way threatening men's exercise of their functions and civic duties. The public sphere was presented as a domain where rights were exercised, while the private sphere was represented as a domain of responsibilities towards families and children, with women's responsibilities in the private sphere also entailing their role as mothers of the nation, imparting civic education to their children.

negotiation with the state, is implicitly echoed in Forbes' view that prominent nationalists preferred that women busy themselves with issues of civil rights and franchise instead of engaging in culturally disloyal discussions on patriarchy and subordination. Indeed, Lord Montagu actually expressed his reluctance to offend (male) nationalists on religious grounds by conceding the demands of women. Forbes, *Women in Modern India*, 99. In one way or another, women were encouraged into, and largely accepted, political quiescence.

[34] In the 1937 elections to the provincial assemblies, four million women voters were enfranchised, though only a quarter of them actually voted – and about sixty women contested elections from reserved constituencies. Singer, "*A Constituency Suitable*", 39–45.

[35] Naidu, quoted in Forbes, *Women in Modern India*, 94.

The two – albeit very different – forms of universalism discussed above contrast sharply with claims to GDC before independence, the strongest being the Muslim minority's claim, which eventually culminated in the demand for the separate state of Pakistan. The focus here will be on the other strong argument for differentiated citizenship, Ambedkar's demand for separate electorates for the Depressed Classes.[36] The colonial state was on the whole less receptive to this demand.[37] The reason was that it had already generated new fears among the (mostly upper-caste Hindu) nationalists, since these groups represented between 15 and 20 per cent of the population, not a proportion to be dismissed lightly in the electoral arithmetic.[38] Gandhi's fierce opposition to this proposal is well known, leading to the compromise formula arrived at in the Poona Pact of 1932, by which Hindus and the Depressed Classes were kept in the same electorates, with a proportion of seats reserved in the assemblies for Depressed Class candidates. This was of course an important part of the template provided in late 1946 to the Constituent Assembly.

Ambedkar was also a modernist, and there are intriguing shifts in his position over time and in response to political imperatives. In the 1920s, for instance, he was far from convinced about the merits of separate electorates and supported adult franchise as an antidote to these.[39] He recognised that such electorates had the merit of representing particular groups but feared their divisive potential and cited the example of many countries in which diversity was accommodated within the framework of a common

[36] Born into a family of untouchables, B.R. Ambedkar overcame tremendous odds to become a lawyer (obtaining qualifications in law at Columbia University and in economics at the University of London); the most powerfully articulate and influential leader of the Depressed Classes in colonial India; and Chairman of the Drafting Committee of the Indian Constitution.

[37] Zeliott, "Gandhi and Ambedkar", 90.

[38] This was particularly the case in Bengal and the Punjab, in both of which the Hindu and Muslim populations were fairly evenly balanced in terms of numbers.

[39] Rodrigues, *The Essential Writings of B.R. Ambedkar*, 66.

government.[40] On the question of whether there were separate interests that needed to be separately represented, Ambedkar argued that many important issues in the secular domain – such as taxation, education, land tenure, social insurance, the role of the state in the economy, and so on – could hardly be said to be issues which concerned one community alone.[41] There can therefore be *special concerns* but not *special interests*. It is this incipient idea of special concerns that found reflection, some decades later, in the deliberations of the Constituent Assembly over which he presided.

As a modernist and nation-builder, Ambedkar hoped for the annihilation of caste: "You cannot build anything on the foundations of caste. You cannot build up a nation, you cannot build up a morality. Anything that you will build on the foundations of caste will crack and will never be a whole."[42] But as a Dalit leader he fought hard for political safeguards for Dalits. These included the rights of equal citizenship along with adequate representation in the Cabinet, the bureaucracy, and of course the legislatures, with the right to elect their own representatives by adult suffrage, by separate electorates for the first ten years and thereafter by joint electorates and reserved seats.[43]

In retrospect, Ambedkar's advocacy of separate representation for the Depressed Classes sits oddly with his declared vision of a society from which caste would be completely abolished.[44] In fact, he oscillated between two quite distinct programmatic visions for Dalits: on the one hand, emphasising political organisation for the representation of Dalits in public institutions, and, on the other,

[40] Ibid., 85. The examples cited were Poland, Latvia, Estonia, Czechoslovakia, Austria.

[41] Ibid., 83.

[42] Ibid., 287–8.

[43] Ibid., 369–81.

[44] In a later phase, he was of the view that the "solvent" for caste was intermarriage. Ibid., 289.

advocating that Dalits convert to non-Hindu religions.[45] Although they ran in parallel, there appears to be a tension between them: one is a strategy for claiming rights in public institutions, and the second a strategy for opting out – to use Hirschman's terms,[46] strategies simultaneously of voice and of exit. His attempts at mobilising labour belonged to a completely distinct third category to which caste was clearly peripheral.

Finally, there were the claims of the Backward Classes. This phrase has been endowed with different meanings at different points in time, with the current meaning having been fixed as recently as 1985. The groups that we identify by the label OBCs today were recognised in the early 1900s in the princely states of Kolhapur (1902) and Mysore (1920s), as well as in the Bombay and Madras presidencies, which provided for reservations in public employment and education for "backward communities". These were defined as comprising all non-Brahmins, i.e. as also encompassing the groups that would today be described as Scheduled Castes and Scheduled Tribes.[47] The anti-Brahmin movement of the Justice Party in Madras resulted in the allocation of all public service appointments in a fixed proportion between various caste and religious groups, but the claims of the non-Brahmin castes at this time were not so much to reject caste as usurp caste power from the Brahmins. As such, it was a substantively different project to that of the Dalits, who were fighting discrimination and subordination; and a substantively similar one to that of the Muslims, in that the backward castes were also seeking a share in power through proportional representation in the legislatures and the administration.

[45] Jaffrelot, *Dr. Ambedkar*, 51.

[46] Hirschman, *Exit, Voice, and Loyalty*.

[47] The Scheduled Castes and Scheduled Tribes are those groups – belonging, respectively, to the former untouchable castes and the indigenous tribal communities – that are listed in a Schedule of the Constitution to authenticate their claims to special provisions such as quotas.

The fault lines do not change very much after 1947, though it is the groups whose interests are apparently neglected by the constitutional consensus, especially the backward castes, that become more assertive in the post-independence period.

The Constitutional Consensus of 1950

The Indian Constitution strove to strike a fine balance between the universal rights of citizenship and the need to make special provision for minorities and historically disadvantaged groups. The claim has been advanced that the Constituent Assembly (1947–9) was presciently anticipating the arguments of the political theorists of multiculturalism and GDC by at least a few decades. In fact, on this issue, the Constituent Assembly was working within the received template of colonial constitutionalism, revisiting and reshaping the various forms of group-differentiated representation that had been part of colonial discourse since the last decade of the nineteenth century and given institutional expression since the early years of the twentieth. As such, it was drawing upon the resources of antecedent institutional practices of differentiation, but providing normative justifications more appropriate to the new democratic context.

In a triumph of the Nehruvian version of universalist citizenship, the constitution of independent India defined citizenship in "national-civic" rather than "national-ethnic" terms,[48] even as national identity remained a rather fragile construct, a complex and, over time, increasingly fraught "national-civic-plural-ethnic" combination.[49] Privileging the conception of universal citizenship,

---

[48] Beiner, *Theorizing Citizenship*.

[49] Of course, the idea of a purely civic nationhood is a contested one. Rogers Smith, for instance, disagrees with the proposition that "political communities can be sustained by agreement on shared political principles alone". Smith, *Stories of Peoplehood*, 190. The amorphous quality of the Indian combination of "national-civic-plural-ethnic" may explain its fragility in the face of the first systematic attempt to

the Constitution consciously sought to accommodate the claims of historically disadvantaged groups on the grounds, variously, of *protection or compensation for disadvantage, rather than on the grounds that these were distinctive interests that needed special representation in the political system.*[50] As such, members of the Scheduled Castes and Scheduled Tribes were provided with reserved seats in joint electorates, and reservations in public institutions. These were not intended as a denial of equality; on the contrary, they were measures designed to promote *effective* equality. The normative justification was that equality of opportunity would be effectively denied to these groups as they could not, given their histories of marginalisation, compete on really equal terms, and hence required special guarantees in the form of reservations in legislatures and public employment as enabling background conditions for equality.

In respect of religious minorities, though separate electorates were decisively rejected, there was some recognition that the principle of equality is an insufficient guarantee for minorities who will, in the presence of a dominant majority, always be insecure in the enjoyment of their cultural rights. This resulted in guarantees for the freedom of religion, including the freedom to practice and propagate it, as well as separate personal laws for members of religious minorities. The question of women's representation was uncontentious as women members of the Constituent Assembly

---

give concrete shape to the nation, the project of Hindutva. It is arguably also reflected in the ironic but unmistakable resemblance between the qualities attributed to, on the one hand, the Congress party in the nationalist movement, and carried over into the Indian nation after independence, and, on the other, the features attributed to Hinduism. The adjectives employed (rightly or wrongly) to describe the Hindu religion – absorptive, assimilative, accommodative, eclectic, tolerant – were treated as accurate descriptions of society itself, and therefore as attributes of the "umbrella" nationalist party that claimed to represent all its members.

[50] There was also a conviction – perhaps nowhere better expressed than in the *locus classicus* of the unity-in-diversity approach, Jawaharlal Nehru's *Discovery of India* (1946) – that identities were retrograde phenomena which would surely be transcended by the alliance of science, reason, and economic development.

continued to oppose reservations for themselves as "an impediment to our growth and an insult to our very intelligence and capacity".[51]

In the case of the Scheduled Castes, despite the rhetoric of equality, there was a perceptible normative shift from representation to protection. By contrast, the mode of incorporation of the Scheduled Tribes into the Constitution expressed a strong continuity with the colonial discourse of protection, though there was an important difference in the way in which protection was conceived. The colonial discourse had infantilised tribal communities, seeking to isolate them with the stated objective of providing protection from the destructions of "civilization".[52] In post-independence India, protection did not imply isolationism, but the political recognition of the distinctive cultural identity, customs, and land laws of tribal communities.[53] Along with the argument that reservations would provide an opportunity for "improving" tribal communities, so enabling them to be better integrated into the national mainstream,[54] backwardness would be addressed through state-led developmentalism.

Separate personal laws and policies of compensatory discrimination were both, moreover, viewed as *interim* measures on the path to a society in which greater social equality and processes of secularisation would eventually lead to universalist norms of citizenship becoming firmly entrenched.

Though some members of the Constituent Assembly supported an educational qualification for political rights, the Sapru Committee and Ambedkar both argued forcefully that the suffrage itself would serve as an education, especially for the hitherto excluded "untouchables", and therefore no educational or property

[51] Quoted in John, "Reservations and the Women's Movement", 50.

[52] Corbridge, "Competing Inequalities", 182.

[53] This was in line with the Chotanagpur Improvement Society's memorandum to the Simon Commission asking for the political recognition of the distinctive cultural identity, customs, and land laws of tribal communities. Prakash, *Jharkhand*, chapter 2.

[54] Prakash, *Jharkhand*.

qualification was required.[55] Together with adult suffrage, the adoption of direct elections (and the concomitant rejection of separate electorates or proportional representation) was justified by the argument that they made possible the creation of a new national identity among Indians as a people, superseding parochial and caste identities.[56] Universal citizenship based on the political equality of individual citizens was the default position; GDC was a temporary deviation, justified not by the purpose of giving these groups a voice in legislation but for improving their condition of social and economic "backwardness" through a form of what has been called political affirmative action.[57]

The idea of "backwardness" finds explicit recognition, if not precise definition, in the Constitution of India, in which Articles 15 and 16, among others, provide an opportunity for special policy provisions to be made for socially and educationally backward classes of citizens. The ambiguity of meaning is reflected in Nehru

[55] The Sapru Committee was established in 1944 by the Standing Committee of the Non-Party Conference, in the wake of the collapse of talks between Gandhi and Jinnah on the communal question, to examine the question of minorities from a political and constitutional point of view. It came to these conclusions from rather different premises. The risk of enfranchising the entire adult population, it stated, should be taken to prevent the concentration of power in the hands of a powerful few. Hence, though the average voter's "judgment may be faulty, his reasoning inaccurate, and his support of a candidate not infrequently determined by considerations removed from a high sense of democracy, he is yet no better or worse than the average voter in many parts of Europe where adult franchise has been in force for some time." Quoted in Austin, *Working a Democratic Constitution*, 147.

[56] Three mechanisms of representation were proposed in the Constituent Assembly, any or all of which could qualify as (imperfect) forms of group-differentiated citizenship. Rochana Bajpai's work shows that separate electorates were opposed on grounds of universal citizenship and political equality, but most strongly on grounds of "national unity" and a common political community. Proportional representation was considered unsuited to an unlettered electorate and even viewed by some as an introduction of separate electorates by the back door. The consensus of the Assembly was on the third alternative, reservation of seats (quotas), and these were couched in the language of transition. Bajpai, "Minority Representation", 377.

[57] Ibid., 379.

stating in the Constituent Assembly that while he would like to put an end to all reservations, he realised that in the case of the Scheduled Castes it would not be desirable: "I try to look upon the problem not in the sense of religious minority but rather in the sense of helping backward groups in the country. I do not look at it from the religious point of view or the caste point of view, but from the point of view that a backward group ought to be helped and I am glad that this reservation will also be limited to ten years."[58]

The Indian Constitution contains a complementary, though often forgotten, vision of social citizenship, expressed in the welfare orientation of the state, which was given the primary responsibility for development. Though non-justiciable, the Directive Principles of State Policy provided the framework for a just and egalitarian society. They enjoined the state to promote welfare; minimise inequalities of income, status, and opportunities; ensure the right to work; prevent the concentration of wealth; provide free and compulsory education; and so on. It is interesting also that while the Fundamental Rights were formulated in a largely gender-neutral way, the visibility of women was greater in the Directive Principles, with several articles explicitly mentioning them – e.g. the right to equal pay for equal work, the right to an adequate livelihood, just and humane conditions of work, maternity relief, and, of course, the uniform civil code.

In sum, then, the Indian citizenship regime inaugurated in 1950 conceptualised the individual as the basic unit of citizenship, whose inclusion in the polity was on equal terms with every other citizen. Groups and cultural communities found recognition in the form of special compensatory provisions, but they were not in the first instance viewed as the locus of the primary membership of the individual; nor were they recognised as the

[58] *Constituent Assembly Debates*, vol. VIII, 26 May 1949, 8.92.45. https://www.constitutionofindia.net/constitution_assembly_debates/volume/8/1949-05-26

mandated mediators of group interests *vis-à-vis* the state. In terms of the substance of citizenship rights, these were interpreted comprehensively and expansively, even if the state capacity to provide them proved wanting.

Challenges to the Constitutional Consensus and the Dilemmas of GDC

The fragility of the constitutional consensus is signalled by the continuing tension in the Indian polity between universal and differentiated forms of citizenship. Two recent challenges in particular are notable. The first, from within the universalist stable, is the exclusionary universalism of Hindutva from the 1990s, expressed in grotesque violence against minorities and presenting a fundamental challenge to the universalistic conception of citizenship contained in the Constitution. The second is the challenge represented by the claims to GDC of the OBCs. There is, of course, a third challenge, which remains an outlier: the pending claim of the women's movement to a third of the seats in the legislatures. It is the second challenge that forms our substantive focus here.

It is ironic that the colonial state, with no pretensions to democracy, avowed (however instrumentally) the importance of *representing* different groups, while the Constitution of the free Indian republic spoke the paternalist language of *protection* and *backwardness*. Of these fuzzy, even implausible categories, the discourse of protection proved to be ephemeral, while the rather amorphous concept of backwardness has endured into the present as a category which, in its claim to just redress, implicitly aspires to the same status as categories such as oppression, marginalisation, or exploitation. Just redress, in turn, has acquired the form of microcosmic or descriptive representation in public institutions.[59]

[59] Microcosmic or descriptive representation entails representing proportionately – as, for example, in a legislature – the different sections of a population.

The constitutional – and indeed Ambedkarite – rejection of the idea that particular groups have special interests has thus been smuggled in through the back door. Disguising its instrumental quality, representation was presented by the colonial state as a state objective on the grounds that groups had special interests which could only be represented by people of those groups. The democratic state repudiated the idea of special interests but mirror representation (in which a representative assembly should mirror the social composition of the polity) gradually became the most important mechanism for redressing backwardness. Representation – including and especially through reservations – thus moved from being the goal to being the exclusive instrument of justice.

The Constitution allowed the State to make special provision for "the advancement of any socially and educationally backward classes of citizens", but did not specify how these classes would be identified. It has been persuasively argued that – along with the right to property and Parliament's right to amend the Constitution – this has proved to be one of the three most important sites of conflict between Parliament and the Supreme Court in independent India.[60]

The phrase "backward classes" had been in use for half a century already, though possessing different meanings at different points in time. The debates in the Constituent Assembly reflect this ambiguity, with some members using the phrase to encompass the section of the population between the highest castes and the scheduled castes; some as synonymous with the Scheduled Castes; others to refer to a stratum of non-untouchable Hindu castes; and yet others to refer to "all but Brahmins".[61] It seems to have been widely accepted that, despite its boundaries being "unclear and elastic",[62] the category of the Backward Classes included the

[60] Dhavan, *Reserved!*

[61] Ibid., 208ff.

[62] Béteille, *The Backward Classes*, 9.

SCs and the STs, with the OBCs being the amorphous residual. Ambedkar provided what was surely the most pragmatic definition, that a backward community was simply "a community that is backward *in the opinion of the Government*".[63]

It was left to the First Backward Classes Commission (1955) to wrestle with the definitional problem, and it elected to classify communities on the basis of their position in the caste hierarchy, literacy and educational standards, representation in government and industry, and economic backwardness. The Chairman of the Commission, Kaka Kalelkar, eventually distanced himself from the report, saying that "it would have been better if we could determine backwardness on principles other than caste." The government also decided that the caste criterion was objectionable and in any case would mean that the bulk of the population was backward, which was hardly useful.

Meanwhile, various court judgments had already indicated that while classes need not be only castes, castes definitely qualified as classes.[64] This was the perspective adopted by the Second Commission on Backward Classes (1978–80) – better known as the Mandal Commission by the name of its chairman, B.P. Mandal – which stated that "castes are the only readily and clearly recognisable and persistent collectivities."[65] Arguing that poverty is a direct outcome of social and educational backwardness, the Commission stated that "the substitution of caste by economic tests will amount to ignoring the genesis of social backwardness

[63] *Constituent Assembly Debates*, vol. VII, 702, 30 November 1948. 7.63.206. https://www.constitutionofindia.net/constitution_assembly_debates/volume/7/1948-11-30

[64] E.g. in *M.R. Balaji vs State of Mysore*, AIR 1963 SC 749, it was held that there ought to be a clear distinction between caste and class; in *P. Rajendran vs State of Madras*, AIR 1968 SC 1012 that a caste is also a class of citizens; and in *A. Periakaruppan vs. State of Tamil Nadu*, AIR 1973 SC 2310 that a caste has always been recognised as a class. Béteille, *The Backward Classes*, 9, 26.

[65] Government of India, *Report of the Backward Classes Commission*, 54.

in the Indian society."[66] In any case, the economic criterion was difficult to apply and was subject to change. The Mandal Commission therefore adopted a weighted ranking in which a total of twenty-two points were distributed unequally across factors of social, educational, and economic backwardness, such that indicators of social backwardness (including untouchability, stigma of low occupation, nomadism, etc.) would carry a weight three times higher than those of economic backwardness.[67] This was despite the acceptance by the Commission that the data available for determination of social backwardness was the 1931 Census.[68] While the Kalelkar Commission had, on this basis, come to the conclusion that one-third of India's population was backward, the Mandal Commission arrived at a proportion of just over half, i.e. 52 per cent.

One criterion of backwardness adopted by both these Commissions was the representation of groups in public services, leading to a curious situation where just one (and that not the most critical) criterion for determining backwardness became, through quotas in public employment, the supreme and complete mechanism to redress it. While the Mandal Commission Report also made recommendations about the need for structural remedies such

[66] Ibid., 4.

[67] Social indicators (e.g. groups considered backward by others; groups that are mainly dependent on manual labour for livelihood; groups in which 25 per cent women and 10 per cent men get married below 17 years; groups in which the female work participation rate is 25 per cent above the state average) got a weightage of 3 points each; educational indicators (e.g. groups in which the number of children between the ages of 5 and 15 years who never attended school is 25 per cent above the state average; where the proportion of matriculates is 25 per cent below the state average) a weightage of 2 points each; and economic indicators (e.g. the average value of family assets; the availability of drinking water at a distance greater than 0.5 km; consumption loans by households) a weightage of 1 point each. On a total score of 22, all castes that secured 11 points or 50 per cent were listed as socially and educationally backward.

[68] Government of India, *Report of the Backward Classes Commission*, 56.

as land reform, the report came to be identified with a single criterion, namely caste, and a singular policy instrument, namely reservations. The Commission stayed within the 50 per cent limit on quotas laid down by the Supreme Court and also refused to countenance any further differentiation by sub-group.

The announcement of the implementation of the Mandal Commission Report in 1990, as well as the extension of quotas to institutions of higher education in 2006 (popularly known as Mandal-II), were met with widespread agitation by young people of the upper castes who feared that additional quotas would deprive them of opportunities. Both were contested in the Supreme Court, leading to important judicial verdicts, and in both cases led to a confrontation with Parliament.

The judiciary has itself been internally divided on these cases, as is apparent from the fact that the nine-judge Supreme Court bench that decided the first Mandal case (*Indra Sawhney vs Union of India, 1992*) yielded seven different judgments. Three of these were in favour of using purely economic criteria to the exclusion of caste. The remaining four accepted caste so long as it was not the only criterion used. This incidentally was the judgment that introduced the idea of excluding "the creamy layer" from eligibility for reservations.[69] The five-judge Supreme Court bench that decided the OBC Education case in 2008 (*Ashok Kumar Thakur vs Union of India*) similarly produced four judgments.

It is striking that the major contentions – decided by the courts even if subsequently repudiated by Parliament – have been those relating to what would appear to be issues of detail in administrative practice: determining the creamy layer; quotas for promotion and their implication for accelerated seniority; and the carrying forward of unfilled vacancies. On each of these issues, the court's decision has been overturned by Parliament through a constitutional

[69] The "creamy layer" is a euphemism for the more privileged among the backward groups.

amendment. Thus, the 77th Constitution Amendment Act of 1995 overturned the court's injunction against quotas in promotions by accepting this injunction for OBCs but restoring such quotas for SCs and STs. Likewise, the 81st Constitution Amendment Act of 2000 made it possible to carry forward unfilled vacancies to subsequent years in a way that exempted them from the upper limit of 50 per cent reservations. Finally, there was the controversy over whether quotas in promotion did not give SC and ST officials an artificial seniority over other candidates, allowing them to compete for higher positions by claiming seniority over the latter, even though this seniority had, in the first place, been achieved by quotas in promotions. Here again the judiciary was overruled by the passage of the 85th Constitution Amendment Act, 2001. Additionally, there has been contention over whether certain categories of institutions – not funded by the state or run by minorities – are obliged to provide reservations. The 93rd Constitution Amendment Act of 2005 made this mandatory for all but minority institutions. With the exception of this last, it is worth noting that the major contentions over reservations in recent years have been about intra-bureaucratic careerist issues, which are obviously of great concern to those who have already accessed differentiated rights, but which could also have gate-keeping implications for the claims to the admission of new groups, such as the Most Backward Classes or even Dalit Christians. The latter are groups subject to many forms of discrimination, including untouchability. However, because the Indian Constitution does not recognise, for purposes of providing redress, Dalits belonging to non-Hindu religions, these groups are not eligible for quota provisions. The same limitation applies to Dalits among the Sikhs and even those who converted to Buddhism to escape Hindu caste oppression.

In the first section of this chapter, two sets of anxieties were identified that have worried political theorists, including advocates of GDC. To assess the normative and political implications of the Indian experience of GDC, let us now revisit these anxieties, though in reverse order. One set of anxieties was about the proper determination of the basis on which groups may be entitled to differentiated rights. In the Indian context, backwardness has been a distinctive motif and often the authoritative basis for claiming GDC. It has not been easy to specify the concept of backwardness in a way that presents it as a robust claim to justice, equivalent to the claims of oppression, marginalisation, and exploitation. The argument that backwardness must have two components – of disadvantage as well as of discrimination – has not found acceptance, evidently because this would limit the application of the concept only to the scheduled castes and tribes. Logically, backwardness should have to be measured in relation to something that is not backward, but it is not entirely clear how that benchmark may be determined. How further might we distinguish between what Kymlicka and Norman call the reality of oppression versus the perception of it?[70]

The definition of backwardness in the Mandal Commission Report appears to be overdetermined by ritual criteria, based on social and demographic data gathered a full fifty years before the Commission's deliberations. The Mandal Commission Report itself acknowledged that the social salience of caste has declined as its political consequence has increased, but nevertheless chose to base its understanding of social backwardness on the former. It is now an additional twenty-five years since that report was submitted, but it remains the definitive document on social justice in India. The wisdom of treating backwardness as a static category with an unchanging content has seldom been questioned, though it is surely reasonable to expect that the attributes of a community change over time, and that so arguably do the benchmarks by which backwardness is measured. The Supreme Court's requirement, in the Mandal decision of 1992, of revision based on empirical data has been ignored.

[70] Kymlicka and Norman, "Return of the Citizen".

The uniform solution of reservations for all claims, moreover, suggests that backwardness is assumed to have the same characteristics in every group, such that historical, locational, and social differences do not make for different forms of backwardness. But tribal backwardness is arguably very different from Muslim backwardness and would therefore appear to require rather different types of policy intervention. The arbitration of the competing claims of different groups would also seem to require a greater sensitivity to such variations.

As far as the question of determining the eligibility of particular groups in the most just manner is concerned, the Indian way of constructing GDC could also be seen as somewhat inconsistent. Claims to GDC are just that – claims of groups or collectivities rather than individuals. This was part of the reason for disallowing economic criteria, which were seen to introduce illegitimate, because individual-centric, considerations. However, the judicial introduction of the idea of the creamy layer has meant that individual/household-level criteria have in fact been admitted. This suggests an inconsistency, in that only groups (and not individuals) can make claims to inclusion, while only individuals (not groups) can be excluded.

The economic criterion moreover was unacceptable to the Mandal Commission because it was said to be difficult to measure and apply, and because it was fluid and changeable. Following the Supreme Court judgment on the creamy layer, this segment is identified by economic criteria, leading to a strange situation in which a criterion that is unacceptable for determining who should be included in the category of OBCs is also the singular criterion that is acceptable for determining who should be excluded from the same category.

Strategies of GDC are usually designed to capture and address one salient indicator of disadvantage. In India, likewise, legal and policy provisions have not adequately accounted for the complex and overlapping nature of social inequalities, and in particular the overlap between inherited symbolic or cultural disadvantages of caste or religious identity on the one hand, and economic disadvantage on the other. The way in which Mandal assigned weights clearly prioritised the social indicator of caste ranking. For the Scheduled Castes, the Scheduled Tribes, and the Muslims, who together account for close to 38 per cent of India's population, historical forms of social inequality coexist with, and are reinforced by, inequalities arising out of the sphere of production and economic activity. Multiple and mutually compounding forms of disadvantage suggest that the groups that need special attention may be those that are doubly disadvantaged – i.e. both culturally and in terms of their human development indicators. Some – e.g. poor Dalit or Muslim women – may be simultaneously disadvantaged in three ways, by gender, class, and caste/religion. Building in multiple types of disadvantage is a challenge for theories of GDC, which are typically grounded in a single indicator of disadvantage.

If the category of backwardness has not been sufficiently disaggregated and finessed, the strategy for redressing it has also remained unvarying and uniform, with descriptive representation being the goal, and reservations being the single policy instrument to achieve it. Feminist scholarship offers a useful distinction between descriptive and substantive representation, to consider the outcomes of quota-based approaches for disadvantaged groups.[71] An empirical study of women's representation in thirty-six countries came to the conclusion that "descriptive representation is severely limited as an avenue for providing substantive representation".[72]

[71] The distinction between descriptive and substantive representation is particularly developed in the literature on women's representation. The underlying concern is about the effectiveness of policies intended to provide guaranteed representation for women in, say, legislatures, whether through legislative quotas or party quotas. Does, for instance, the descriptive representation of women (DRW) result in their substantive representation (SRW) such that their influence on policy-making is visible and discernible in actual policy outcomes?

[72] Weldon, "Beyond Bodies", 1171.

Similarly, existing evidence about the participation of Dalit parliamentarians in India suggests that descriptive representation does not invariably translate into substantive representation.

Apart from being limited in this way, descriptive representation can also encourage unwarranted complacence. While the electoral success of leaders belonging to disadvantaged caste groups generates legitimate euphoria, their tenures in government often produce despondence at the lack of distributive outcomes for ordinary citizens belonging to those very groups. The successful political mobilisation not only of Dalits, but also of backward castes, over the last two decades has yielded rich results in that backward-caste parties have come to power in several states, and their numbers in Parliament have increased five-fold since the 1950s, reflected also in a higher representation in Cabinets. The concern, however, remains that while symbolic inequalities have begun to be more effectively addressed, the inequalities of poverty or unequal access to land resources have not. It is useful to bear in mind Nancy Fraser's caution – articulated in the context of feminism but with connotations beyond it – that in neo-liberal times governments often find symbolic political solutions less challenging than policies that call for the redistribution of power and material resources.[73]

One of the core issues in the first set of anxieties mentioned at the start was the concern that GDC for some groups may create tensions between these and other similarly situated groups, or resentment amongst groups that see these policies as working to their detriment. Despite the Mandal Commission's firm refusal to

[73] "The shift to a culturalised politics of recognition occurred at precisely the moment when neoliberalism was staging its spectacular comeback. Throughout this period, academic feminist theory was largely preoccupied with debates about 'difference' . . . tended to remain on the terrain of recognition, where subordination was construed as a problem of culture and dissociated from political economy. The effect was to leave us defenceless against free-market fundamentalism, which had meanwhile become hegemonic." Fraser, *Scales of Justice*, 106.

admit any sub-group differentiation, India's experiment with GDC has been an experience of increasing fragmentation and competing claims to limited resources. Andhra Pradesh has witnessed intense political conflict between the Malas and Madigas, who together account for 80 per cent of scheduled castes in that state. For decades now, the Madigas have been agitating against the larger share of the scheduled caste quota being appropriated by the Malas, and demanding a separate sub-quota for themselves.[74]

The concern that GDC may create institutional incentives for the invention of new identities of disadvantage is also illustrated by the violent agitation by the Gujjars in Rajasthan over the past few years, demanding that they be classified as Scheduled Tribes and eligible to a share of the Scheduled Tribe quota. This demand to be re-categorised as a social group that is ritually lower has perplexed many, for the Gujjars have long enjoyed OBC status. However, they have felt marginalised by the domination of a creamy layer among the OBCs, and in particular by the inclusion of the powerful Jats in the same category. On the other hand, their perception that another group, the Meenas, have by virtue of their Scheduled Tribe status experienced considerable mobility through state employment, has fuelled the Gujjars' agitation for what would be a ritual "downgrade", even if a secular "upgrade", to the status of Scheduled Tribe.

Above all, there is the question of whether the idea of GDC can accommodate the idea of a civic community. Is a civic community an aggregation of social groups, or should it provide a space for the performance of individual citizenship? In spite of recognising and even expanding the scope of GDC, India has manifestly found it hard to reconcile claims of cultural communities with the project of creating and nurturing a civic community. The future of the civic project, of an overarching conception of the common good putatively shared by all citizens, or even of a shared space in which

[74] Balagopal, "A Tangled Web".

such a common good may be determined through public reasoning and debate, remains fragile and uncertain.[75]

The principled necessity for differentiated forms of citizenship is, however, not undermined by these questions. In a diverse and complex world, it is scarcely possible to argue for a relentlessly uniform and universal conception of citizenship. The challenge is to identify the criteria by which different types of claims to differentiated citizenship can be arbitrated in a manner that is normatively just and satisfactory, and still leaves room for the practice of a universal conception of citizenship.

[75] It is possible to hazard a historical explanation for this, such that in nations where the national-civic was already formed and consolidated, differentiated citizenship may have provided a much needed, but not socially destabilising, corrective to the homogenising and uniformising definition of universal citizenship. By contrast, in a relatively young nation like India, where the project of constructing a national identity went hand in hand with the anti-colonial struggle, the idea of the national-civic was somewhat more fragile.

6

The Challenge of Human Development

Inclusion or Democratic Citizenship?

Introduction

Inclusion has become a hurrah word in contemporary political discourse – unquestionably an appealing sentiment, but arguably a somewhat weak and pallid political instrument. My intent in this chapter is to explore the possibilities contained in the idea of democratic citizenship as a potentially superior guarantor of human development than inclusion. I will shift back and forth between a theoretical and an empirical narrative, with the empirical parts focused on the Indian experience.

In the first part, I will briefly discuss the relationship of democracy with equality and human development. In the second, I will explore, theoretically and in relation to each other, two concepts – inclusion and citizenship – and suggest why citizenship may be preferred to inclusion for purposes of human development. The third part will dwell substantially on the experience of marginalised and excluded social groups in India, based on which I will, in the last section, urge a reconsideration – grounded in this experience but with broader implications – of the potential role of democracy and citizenship in human development.

Democracy, Development, and Human Development

It is instructive to revisit a once influential though now somewhat dated debate which characterised democracy and development as adversaries, and pointed to the developmental deficits induced by democracy. That debate was underwritten by the assumption that, in democratic polities, economic development is always and inevitably more difficult to accomplish; and the accompanying dogma that authoritarian systems of governance invariably yield superior developmental outcomes.

Notwithstanding its curious resilience in popular discourse, the democracy vs development debate came to be widely acknowledged as sterile. It was also famously inconclusive, with as many studies confirming the development-inhibiting role of democracy as did the opposite.[1] It was memorably the "Asian flu" of the mid-1990s, rather than some striking research finding, that dealt the deathblow to this debate.[2] This was not, however, a blow in favour of democracy, for while it brought into question the sustainability of the economic achievements that had once been so celebrated, it only rendered the democracy question irrelevant. There were, of course, all along, important dissenting voices, most notably those of Jean Drèze and Amartya Sen, arguing that democracy had not only an instrumental but also an intrinsic and constructive value in relation to the project of development.[3]

With respect to India, the thesis that democracy inhibits development appeared initially to possess empirical plausibility. Its normative implications, however, were always widely contested

[1] Przeworski and Limongi, "Political Regimes". There were, of course, other perspectives that did not share the premise of this binary, and reflected rather differently on the question of whether regime types actually have an exclusive, or even pre-eminent, role in determining developmental outcomes. These convincingly controverted the fundamental assumptions of that debate by identifying a range of factors other than regime type that were responsible for the success of the East Asian economies. Cf. Bardhan, "Symposium on Democracy".

[2] As Przeworski, *et al.*, subsequently wrote: "Albeit in omniscient retrospect, the entire controversy seems to have been much ado about nothing." Przeworski, *et al.*, *Democracy and Development*, 178.

[3] Drèze and Sen, *India: Economic Development*; Drèze and Sen, *India: Development and Participation*.

and sharply interrogated, examples being the widespread criticism of involuntary displacement and of human rights violations justified by developmental purposes, and executed without any heed to democratic protest. It was not long before sudden and surprising spurts in the economic growth rate in India established not only that the thesis was normatively flawed but also that it was *empirically* wrong. Economic development *qua* development disproved the dire predictions of soothsaying developmentalists – for democracy had not, as it turned out, inhibited economic development. Notwithstanding high rates of economic growth, however, democracy had equally clearly not enabled the benefits of this development to be more widely distributed, so as to improve human development indicators.

Is this disjuncture between democracy and human development a case of Indian exceptionalism, as is so much else about Indian democracy? Like South Africa, India belongs to the Medium Human Development category in the Human Development Report (HDR) for 2007/8. Though the HDR obviously does not relate its rankings to regime type, a quick back-of-the-envelope correlation reveals that the top twenty countries in the High Human Development Category are all robust democracies, for the most part democracies with strong welfarist traditions.[4]

At the other end of the scale are twenty-one countries listed in the Low Human Development category, topped by the most stable democracy in Africa, viz. Senegal.[5] Apart from a couple of others which could arguably qualify as democracies (Benin and Mali) most of the other countries in the Low Human Development category

[4] Singapore and South Korea, about which there may be some equivocation, stand at ranks 25 and 26 respectively. UNDP, *Human Development Report*, 234.

[5] Twenty-one countries are listed in the Low Human Development category – Senegal, Ethiopia, Nigeria, Tanzania, Guinea, Rwanda, Angola, Benin, Malawi, Zambia, Cote d'Ivoire, Burundi, Democratic Republic of Congo, Chad, Central African Republic, Mozambique, Mali, Niger, Guinea-Bissau, Burkina Faso and Sierra Leone. South Africa and India, at rank 121 and 128 respectively, are in the Medium Human Development category. Ibid., 236–7.

are non-democracies, quasi-dictatorships, or countries in the grip of civil war and deep ethnic conflict. Is it an accident that countries with High Human Development are almost always democratic, and countries at the bottom of the human development scale are almost always not? The relationship between democracy and human development clearly merits closer examination.

This begs, of course, the larger question of the relationship between democracy and social inequality. The tension between political equality, on the one hand, and social and economic equality, on the other, is an old and well-known one, with the enduring questions being: first, can democracy take root in a society marked by deep inequalities? And second, under what conditions can democracy produce a more egalitarian social and economic order? The difference between the two questions is in the placing of the analytical weight: thus, the first question seeks to discover the impact of inequality on democracy, while the second attempts to assess the impact of democracy on inequality. Which of these questions is asked will generally depend on the normative and even ideological preferences of the enquirer. I shall illustrate this ambivalence by quoting two social theorists – Alexis de Tocqueville and B.R. Ambedkar – whose best-known writings are separated by a hundred years.

The first question – under what conditions can democracy take root in a society marked by deep inequalities? – suggests that social equality has primacy, and is therefore identified as a necessary background condition for successful democratisation. Tocqueville, of course, credited America's relatively egalitarian society with having provided the necessary social and historical background for a flourishing democratic polity: "the social state of America is a very strange phenomenon. Men there are nearer equality in wealth and mental endowments, or, in other words, more nearly equally powerful, than in any other country of the world or in any other age of recorded history."[6] This was despite

[6] Tocqueville, *Democracy in America*, 56.

the fact that he noted with pessimism the inequality and exclusion that marked the condition of what he labelled the "two unlucky races" – native Indians and African slaves. Its obverse was the cautionary injunction of Dr B.R. Ambedkar who, at the adoption of India's Constitution, warned that India was

> going to enter into a life of contradictions. In politics we will have equality and in social and economic life we will have inequality. In politics we will be recognising the principle of one man one vote and one vote one value. In our social and economic life, we shall, by reason of our social and economic structure, continue to deny the principle of one man one value. How long shall we continue to live this life of contradictions? How long shall we continue to deny equality in our social and economic life? If we continue to deny it for long, we will do so only by putting our political democracy in peril. We must remove this contradiction at the earliest possible moment or else those who suffer from inequality will blow up the structure of political democracy which the Assembly has so laboriously built up.[7]

The second question – under what conditions can democracy be an effective mechanism to produce a more just and equal social and economic order? – clearly privileges political organisation, and so places on democracy itself the onus of creating a more egalitarian society. This instrumentalist view of democracy was expressed by Ambedkar when he described democracy as a form of government in which "revolutionary changes in the economic and social life of people are brought about without bloodshed", a vehicle that could take citizens towards a more egalitarian society. But here again, recall Tocqueville's contrarian warning that the poor, even in a democracy, will rarely exercise their vote to dispossess the wealthy.

[7] B.R. Ambedkar, *Constituent Assembly Debates*, 29 November 1949, https://www.constitutionofindia.net/constitution_assembly_debates/volume/11/1949-11-25, 11.165.325.

Both Tocqueville and Ambedkar recognised the potential role of social inequalities in undermining the egalitarian promise of democracy. For Tocqueville, the explanation for the success of America's democracy lay in its relatively egalitarian society, and the historical absence of a feudal social order. Ambedkar recognised that the deep social inequalities that marked Indian society would be a serious obstacle in the way of creating a robust democracy in which every citizen could enjoy substantive political equality. However, as the chief architect of the Constitution of a new republic, he hoped that social inequalities would be diminished over time, in and through the practice of democracy. Writing in a manifestly different context, Tocqueville was evidently less sanguine about the prospects of the poor using the resources of democracy to divest the rich of their power.

On the whole, it is the first way of formulating the question about the relationship between democracy in the political sphere and equality in social and economic life that has remained pre-eminent. It is clearly a question more challenging than the combined resources of several centuries of profound and original thinking have been able to answer satisfactorily. Let us therefore rephrase the question: instead of asking how to democratically produce a more equal society, perhaps we can try and explore the question of how to democratically produce a society with high levels of human development, as also a society in which levels of human development are not correlated with belonging to particular ethnic or religious groups, a society which is, in other words, more inclusive in every way.

This is especially relevant in the Indian context, where any discussion of inequality and the imperative of inclusion in relation to human development must frontally address two issues: it must, first, acknowledge and address the fact that the human development indicators of particular social groups are lower and that the inter-group distribution of human development strongly reflects social and cultural inequalities and axes of social exclusion. This relates to the relationship between human development and inclusion. And, second, it must acknowledge and address the phenomenon of cultural inequalities being reproduced as material inequalities in a society in which a constitutional democratic and political framework guarantees formal equality to all citizens. This refers to the relationship between human development and democracy.

The purpose of this rather extended introduction has been to argue the case for examining, through a focus on the Indian developmental experience, the relationship between human development, inclusion, and democracy, and to suggest that the idea of inclusion may be more usefully substituted by the idea of citizenship.

Inclusion or Citizenship?

Inclusion has a disconcerting propensity to get appropriated as a political, even rhetorical, slogan. In India, for instance, those uneasy with the hollowness of the hyperbolic narrative of India's emergence as an economic giant have begun to speak in terms of "inclusive growth". Others have emphasised the importance of "inclusive governance" as an instrument of such a growth path. These are energising slogans, but it is not clear that the prefix "inclusive" adds very much value.

The idea of inclusion is a derivative of the concept of "social exclusion" which, it is important to recall, has its origins in the domain of politics and policy, rather than social science.[8] John Pierson identifies the origin of this term in the French *les exclus*, as opposed to *les citoyens*, to describe "the condition of certain groups on the margins of society who were cut off from both regular sources of employment and the income safety nets of the welfare state."[9] The idea of social exclusion became part of the

[8] Cf. Byrne, *Social Exclusion*, chapter 3.

[9] Pierson, *Tackling Social Exclusion*, 4.

social policy of the European Union and was picked up by the British Labour Party when it came to power in 1997. Indeed, its most influential usage is in the policy discourse of "New Labour" in which it is strongly identified with the material inequalities of class – poverty and low income; lack of access to the jobs market; thin networks of social support; the effect of neighbourhood; and exclusion from services – and devoid of any reference to symbolic or cultural forms of exclusion such as discrimination.[10]

Levitas' *The Inclusive Society* (1998) interprets the social politics of the Labour Party in the UK as having moved from RED (its traditional redistributionist discourse in the 1960s and 1970s) to a combination of MUD (moral underclass/dependency) and SID (social integrationist) discourse. On this account, the shift was underwritten by the Labour Party's concern to distinguish itself from the uncaring quality of Thatcherism while remaining actively committed to neo-liberal agendas of globalisation, and the policies of privatising public services that these entailed. This diagnosis is taken further in the linguistic analysis of social exclusion discourse by Fairclough, who demonstrates clearly the use of the idea of social exclusion to help Labour step back from its programmatic commitment to the more radical project of equality:

> The long-standing Labour Party objective of greater equality has been displaced in "New Labour" by the objective of greater social inclusion. The objective of equality in left politics has been based on the claim that capitalist societies by their nature create inequalities and conflicting interests. The objective of social inclusion by contrast makes no such claim – by focusing on those who are excluded from society and ways of including them, it shifts away from inequalities and conflicts of interest amongst those who are included and presupposes that there is nothing inherently wrong with

[10] Ibid., 8–9.

contemporary society as long as it is made more inclusive through government policies.[11]

The rhetorical elisions entailed in the vocabulary of exclusion and inclusion have been persuasively interpreted by Amartya Sen, who points to "the plasticity of the language of exclusion". For instance, Sen argues, the Marxian idea of exploitation is actually about the "unfair inclusion" of the labourer in the relations of production rather than about exclusion. As such, there is a need to register both unfair exclusions and unfair inclusions, and to not confound the two.[12] Elsewhere, Sen writes: "the language of exclusion is so versatile and adaptable that there may be a temptation to dress up every deprivation as a case of social exclusion. There is, I fear, some evidence in the vast – and rapidly growing – literature on social exclusion that the language has run well ahead of the creative ideas involved."[13] A similar caution is advised by Iris Marion Young, who emphatically places limits on widening its scope beyond the political: "The concepts of exclusion and inclusion lose meaning if they are used to label all problems of social conflict and injustice. Where the problems are racism, cultural intolerance, economic exploitation, or a refusal to help needy people, they should be so named."[14]

Given thus the association of the idea of inclusion with (a) policies that represent a neo-liberal compromise with past commitments to equality, and (b) a tendency to (mis)name every form of deprivation as exclusion, how might the idea of citizenship be a superior guarantor of human development than inclusion? There is obviously some overlap between these two concepts, for full citizenship should logically imply full inclusion. Full or substantive citizenship encompasses not only legal and political

[11] Fairclough, *New Labour*, 65.

[12] Sen, "Exclusion and Inclusion", 19.

[13] Sen, "Social Exclusion", 9.

[14] Young, *Inclusion and Democracy*, 13.

citizenship (which are the usual elements of formal citizenship) but also, among others, social, economic, gendered, cultural, and cosmopolitan citizenship, and could conceivably go beyond these forms of citizenship to encompass newer and emerging contestations such as those around ecological or biological citizenship. One way or another, substantive citizenship here denotes the fullest condition of belonging in a political community.

Leaving aside the "genetic taint" in the lineage of the concept of inclusion, the notion of substantive citizenship obviates many of the conceptual and philosophical discomforts surrounding the idea of inclusion, five of which are identified below.

First, the idea of social *inclusion* presumes boundedness and therefore *exclusion*. The exclusion of some is a necessary condition for defining and fixing the category of the included. Those who have been or can be included are thus somehow fenced off from those outside the circle of inclusion, viz. the excluded, or even the potentially excludable. Literally defined, citizenship suffers from the same problem, but a substantive conception of citizenship is, unlike the idea of inclusion, capacious enough to accommodate the moral rights of even, for instance, stateless people. By and large, citizenship theory accepts the nation-state as the relevant unit for theorising and tends to focus its attention on those who *are* already citizens, but there is today a critical mass of scholarship that reflects a concern for the rights of refugees and other stateless people. It is also a concern memorably articulated by Hannah Arendt: "*the right to have rights,* or the right of every individual to belong to humanity, *should be guaranteed by humanity itself.*" Of course, she added anxiously that it was "by no means certain whether this is possible".[15] More recently, theorists of global justice and cosmopolitan citizenship have affirmed that the *moral* claims of such people are valid and may be addressed to humanity at large, even if it is not very clear to whom their *legal* claims,

[15] Arendt, *The Origins of Totalitarianism*, 298. Emphasis added.

possibly requiring a modification in international law, should be addressed.[16] Clearly, the idea of citizenship, at its most expansive, is more inclusive than the idea of inclusion itself.

Secondly, citizenship is a more specifiable concept. It is typically specified in terms of different dimensions – the political, legal, economic, social, ecological, biological, gendered, and global, among others. Inclusion, on the other hand, tends to be used in somewhat vague and under-specified ways, generally referring to the political community and often serving only to register the gap between formal and substantive citizenship, as for example when pleas for inclusion are made for groups that are formally included but substantively excluded. This is well illustrated in Young's caution about the tendency to name every social problem – from racial discrimination to economic exploitation – as exclusion, and her own explicit focus on *political* inclusions and exclusions in the decision-making processes in a democracy.[17]

Thirdly, inclusion suggests an act of incorporation, and therefore presumes a hierarchy, as between a dominant group which is initiating or directing the inclusion of the hitherto excluded. Citizenship is – at least conceptually – non-hierarchical. Unequal citizenship is, linguistically and normatively, an oxymoron, even if it is a widely and easily recognised empirical phenomenon. Citizenship invokes the imperative to equality in a way that inclusion does not. Equality is perfectly in consonance with citizenship, but not required by the ideal of inclusion. Logically, inclusion can be accomplished without simultaneously providing equality. Empirically, it is precisely this that is signalled by the discomfort, noted earlier, with the use of the concepts of exclusion and inclusion in British politics.

Fourthly, in an interesting inversion of the meaning ascribed to these concepts in British politics, the way in which the language

[16] Benhabib, *The Rights of Others*.

[17] Young, *Inclusion and Democracy*, 13.

of exclusion and inclusion has been deployed in political discourse in recent times has effectively destroyed the association of these terms with class inequality, forging instead a closer association with identity-related difference. This underscores the tendency, noted earlier, to (mis)label every form of deprivation as exclusion and its obverse as inclusion. Apart from the reservations expressed by both Sen and Young, it could be argued that the idea of exclusion in fact helps to identify situations of "incomplete citizenship", so encouraging us to address the citizenship deficits that call for inclusion.[18] As such, inclusion may be viewed as a strategy, even an instrument, for the fuller realisation of citizenship.

Finally, insofar as inclusion presumes a singular entity into which incorporation or inclusion is accomplished, it also contains a presumption of homogeneity. The plurality of the social universe, on the other hand, makes multiple citizenships both necessary and inevitable. For instance, a Sri Lankan woman chartered accountant who does environmental advocacy in her free time practises citizenship at various levels other than the national-political – economic citizenship, ecological citizenship, and gendered citizenship. The idea of inclusion does not prima facie appear to permit the recognition of plural memberships, as it is generally presumed that the recognition and redressal of exclusion implies that pluralities must be recognised as a prelude, and chiefly a prelude, to their incorporation in the larger collective, but singular, entity. One caveat to this claim would be Young's proposal for a pluralisation of the sites of representation, which would enable citizens to authorise different representatives relating to different aspects of their own lives.

Not only are there multiple *forms* of citizenship, there are also, at any given point in time, multiple *notions* of citizenship contending for pre-eminence. It is possible to identify the chief characteristics of particular dominant conceptions of citizenship

[18] Gore, "Markets, Citizenship".

and to collate these, as some scholars have done, as "citizenship regimes".[19] A citizenship regime specifies, among other things, who is a citizen; the terms of inclusion and exclusion; whether and how citizenship is identified with cultural identity; the recognised unit of citizenship – individuals or groups; and the substance of citizenship rights, especially social citizenship. The shift from one citizenship regime to another may be contested and politically negotiated, and the interaction between state institutions, state policies, and societal initiatives shapes and influences the evolution of the citizenship regime. In India, a decisive shift has taken place between the citizenship regime *circa* 1950 and the citizenship regime *circa* 2000, of which new inclusions and new exclusions are an important, but arguably not the only, dimension. I will return to this shift towards the end of this chapter, after a brief discussion in the next section of cultural difference, inequality, and human development in India.

Difference, Inequality, and Human Development in India

The relationship between exclusion and human development in India is alarmingly symmetrical. The cultural diversity of the Indian nation is not a composite of multiple ethnically distinct units. It is rather a product of cross-cutting and overlapping identities based in region, language, religion, sect, caste, and tribe. The social universe of most Indian citizens is composed of multi-layered identities encompassing language, region, caste, and religion, as well as the more "modern" secular identities of being an Indian, a woman, or an urban professional.

This overlapping quality of social cleavages in India is rendered even more complex by the fact that cultural identity frequently overlaps with other, material forms of disadvantage. As elsewhere,

[19] The idea of "citizenship regimes" was first spelt out, in the Canadian context, by Jenson and Phillips, "Regime Shift". It has subsequently been developed upon for the Latin American context in Yashar, *Contesting Citizenship*.

cultural diversity does not remain confined to the realm of culture alone – identities often carry, encoded within them, other types of disadvantage and discrimination. In India, there is frequently an overlap between cultural and material inequalities; between, on the one hand, inherited symbolic or cultural disadvantages of caste or religious identity, and, on the other, of economic disadvantage.

The data regarding human development indicators and poverty amongst various social groups clearly establish that levels of deprivation – in terms of human development – are highest for the Scheduled Castes, followed by the Scheduled Tribes, followed by Muslims. Most human development indicators show that the Scheduled Castes are at the bottom, the Scheduled Tribes just above them, and Muslims just slightly better off than the other two. However, while the Scheduled Castes and Tribes have guaranteed representation – in legislatures, public employment, and public education – Muslims are under-represented in all these areas.[20] The close linkage between the poverty statistics and human development indicators of these three groups is evidence of overlapping and even mutually reinforcing patterns of inequality.[21]

The Scheduled Castes or Dalits constitute 16.2 per cent of India's population. Human development indicators show their literacy rate as 41.5 per cent, as against an all-India average of 53.5 per cent; their enrolment rate as 62.5 per cent, compared to 72 per cent for Hindus. The gender gap in literacy is also high: only about 25 per cent of women belonging to the Scheduled Castes and Scheduled Tribes are literate, as opposed to 50 per cent of men. Though the gender *gap* is the same among other social groups, there is an important difference here, because in those other groups 50 per cent of women are literate, as compared with about

[20] Cf. Government of India, "Social Economic and Educational Status", better known as the Sachar Committee Report, after the name of its Chairperson, former Justice Rajinder Sachar.

[21] This section draws on Jayal, "The Transformation of Citizenship".

75 per cent of men. In other words, the gap between Scheduled Caste women and other women is also disconcertingly the same. Women belonging to these groups have higher levels of fertility, as also of morbidity and mortality.

Turning to material inequalities, though the chief source of income for most Scheduled Castes is agriculture, ownership of land is lowest among these groups (47 per cent as against 70 per cent for Hindus). The same disparity is found in the ownership of durables such as television sets, radios, and bicycles. As if this were not enough, the Scheduled Castes suffer the degrading burdens of discrimination, humiliation, and even untouchability, which remains prevalent sixty years after it was declared illegal.[22]

The Scheduled Tribes or Adivasis constitute 8.2 per cent of India's population and fall far below the national average on human development indicators. The literacy rate in these groups is 39.3 per cent as against the Indian average of 53.5 per cent. It is lower even than that for the Scheduled Castes at 41.5 per cent, Muslims at 49.4 per cent, and Christians at 80.8 per cent. Not surprisingly, the Scheduled Tribes have the lowest enrolment rate of 60.3 per cent, compared to 72 per cent for the general Hindu population. Health data also show a higher Morbidity Prevalence Rate among Scheduled Tribes, including a high incidence of diarrhoea, fever, and tuberculosis, which tends to be correlated with levels of literacy, village development, and immunisation, all of which are low among these groups.

Thus, levels of educational deprivation are highest among rural female Scheduled Castes and Scheduled Tribes and lowest among urban males who do not belong to these social groups. The number of deaths of children under the age of one year (per 1000 live births) is 121.4 for Scheduled Castes and Scheduled Tribes in rural areas, as opposed to 110 for people outside these groups. If rural poverty for those not in the Scheduled Caste/Scheduled

[22] Shah, *et al.*, *Untouchability.*

Tribe category is close to 40 per cent, it is almost 60 per cent for rural Scheduled Castes and Scheduled Tribes. The incidence of poverty, as also its intensity, is higher among the Scheduled Castes and Scheduled Tribes as compared to the national average.

Finally, at 13.4 per cent of India's population, Muslims are the largest religious minority in India. Compared to Hindus, this group has lower literacy rates (including female literacy), a lower work participation rate, lower per capita incomes (the percentage difference being 18 per cent), and also a higher percentage of people below the poverty line, with 43 per cent Muslims as opposed to 39 per cent Hindus below the poverty line in 2000.

These three groups together account for close to 38 per cent of India's population. It is indisputably clear that their economic impoverishment mirrors their social marginalisation. Of course, it is obviously not the case that all those in these groups are poor, or that there is no poverty in the other groups, but only that there is a high degree of overlap between being poor and being in these groups. These are also the groups which generally work in the informal economy, which is inflected by inequalities of caste, religion, and gender – as, for instance, when certain caste groups alone engage in occupations that are considered polluting or dirty by higher castes. Traditional and historical forms of social inequality thus coexist with, and are reinforced by, inequalities arising out of the sphere of production and economic activity.

The founders of the Indian republic were well aware of the particular vulnerability of these groups, which is why the citizenship regime, *circa* 1950, embedded in the Constitution as well as in the dominant ideological consensus of the time, sought to balance the demands of universalist citizenship with the special needs of communities. The Indian nation-state was the primary, architectonic, and essentially secular locus of civic identity, transcending all ascriptive identities of religion, language, or caste affiliation. There were however two significant exceptions to the principle of equal rights for all individual citizens. These were, first, the recognition of cultural rights for minority religious communities – such as the right to practice and propagate religion, to have separate personal laws and so forth – in respect of which the communities, rather than individuals, would be the bearers of rights; and second, the provisions for compensatory discrimination for historically disadvantaged groups. The latter took the form of affirmative action for the Scheduled Castes and Tribes in public employment, representative institutions, and public education.

In the citizenship regime *circa* 1950, universalist citizenship, qualified in the way just described, was also complemented by the constitutional vision of social citizenship, expressed in the welfare orientation of the state, which assumed primary responsibility for development and was enjoined, by the Directive Principles of State Policy, to work towards a just and egalitarian society. Over the last six decades, there has been a plethora of additional legislative and policy interventions designed to make these protections more robust. Institutions dedicated to the task of monitoring these interventions – such as the National Commissions on Minorities, Scheduled Castes, and Scheduled Tribes – have been established, with quasi-judicial powers to punish violations. Above all, the framework of democratic politics has provided opportunities for Dalit and other backward castes to mobilise in the political arena to elect leaders representing their group interests in order to obtain more responsive and accountable governance.

The persistence of poor human development indicators for these disadvantaged groups calls for an explanation. Possessing (and mostly even demanding) only cultural rights, the Muslim minority was denied any real opportunities for its material improvement, though the publication of the Sachar Committee Report (2006), recording the abysmal conditions of economic and educational backwardness of this community, seemed to promise programmes of a redistributive nature. The increased insecurity of not only the Muslim, but also the Christian, minority – and the vulnerability of both these to violence – remains a serious concern.

As far as the Scheduled Castes and Scheduled Tribes are concerned, it is clear that institutional quotas have failed to substantively address the disadvantages that mark the condition of the vast majority in these groups. Despite modest success in expanding access to domains from which such groups were previously excluded, the extent to which such access has been universalised *within* such groups remains unclear.

Even in terms of culture alone, the entire plethora of interventions has proved to be ineffectual in two ways. First, the interventions have remained confined to the domain of culture. When political parties claiming to authentically represent disadvantaged groups such as Dalits have come to power in the states, they have frequently chosen to invest public expenditure in symbolic rather than substantive goods. The importance of symbolic recognition, especially for groups that have been stigmatised and discriminated against, can never be overestimated, but it could nevertheless be argued that it is inadequate until supplemented by material improvements in the quality of people's lives. The absence of demands on leaders of backward castes as well as Dalits to provide enduring welfare outcomes in addition to dignity gains is a reflection of the weak capacity of poor citizens to make effective claims through the political process.

Second, not only have these interventions remained confined to the domain of culture, they have been contentious even within that domain. The constitutional provision of cultural rights for minorities has been embattled, as many challenges to Indian secularism have shown. Similarly, upper-caste resistance to the mobilisation by disadvantaged caste groups is now seen also among the category of the backward castes, often the more proximate enemy of the Dalits. The resilience of ideologies of social inequality, and therefore the persistence of practices of discrimination, is a reality that cannot easily be wished away.

On the whole, greater opportunities for voice have not led to material improvement, so that those at the bottom of the ritual order, on the margins of society, continue to carry multiple burdens of denial and deprivation, both cultural as well as economic. Despite constitutional protection and legal intervention, thus, despite democracy and guaranteed representation, despite their often energetic participation in the political process, the human development indicators of these groups remain poor. There has been inadequate policy recognition of the fact that questions of rights and basic needs are not divorced from questions of dignity and exclusion; and questions of cultural rights are not divorced from those of social and economic rights. These multiple and mutually compounding forms of disadvantage should suggest that the groups that need our special attention are those that are doubly disadvantaged – i.e. culturally, as also in terms of their human development indicators. Some – e.g. poor Dalit or Muslim women – may even be simultaneously disadvantaged in three ways, by gender, class, and caste/religion.

The Case for Substantive Citizenship and Human Development

As a prelude to bringing together the multiple and even disparate strands of this argument, a signalling of the three big changes of the 1990s may be apposite. Each of these changes – the rise of majoritarian Hindutva politics, the political mobilisation of the Dalits and backward classes, and the liberalisation of the Indian economy – has played a central role in shaping the citizenship regime *circa* 2000.[23]

There is no doubt, firstly, that the exclusions advocated by the politics of Hindutva, especially against the Muslim community, have become more deeply entrenched through a wider dissemination of Hindu nationalist ideology in society. Secondly, the democratic mobilisation of the 1990s has rightly been credited

[23] This section draws upon Jayal, "The Transformation of Citizenship".

with effecting new inclusions, but the evidence on this is also not unambiguous. Conflicts between Dalits and OBCs and assertions by sub-groups within the backward classes, such as the Most Backward Classes, are only the most visible among a plethora of voluble political assertions that threaten to fragment the presumed unity of many of the categories of official sociology on the basis of which resources such as quotas have long been allocated. Competition for such scarce resources is increasingly spawning new, and sometimes even unconvincing, demands based on the most feeble claims of exclusion.

Finally, while it is the middle and upper classes that have visibly been the chief beneficiaries of economic reforms, and while large numbers of the poor have been "falling into poverty",[24] excluded not just from access to the market but often also from their already precarious livelihoods, there is, nevertheless, reason for ambivalence here. Sociological research suggests that *lower*-middle-class groups, especially women, experience a new feeling of economic freedom and even inclusion simply by being able to enter the employment market and bring home a salary. More substantively, however, social citizenship – in terms of social-security measures – has to some extent been, as expected, a casualty of economic reform, though the fact that *the* landmark legislation guaranteeing employment to the poor has also been enacted in the wake of economic reforms can scarcely be ignored.

The citizenship regime *circa* 2000 thus expresses new inclusions as well as new exclusions. However, concurrently with these shifts, other developments have occurred that have had a modest but promising expansionary impact on citizenship. Take the example of revived institutions of local governance, the *panchayats*, the new institutional public spaces for the practice of local democracy, for

[24] Krishna, *et al.*, "Falling into Poverty"; Krishna, *et al.*, "Falling into Poverty in a High Growth State"; Krishna, *et al.*, "Falling into Poverty in Villages of Andhra Pradesh".

the local determination of developmental priorities, and for the assertion of citizenship claims by women and Dalits in particular. Several studies have shown that, even in the most socially backward states, women representatives have repeatedly demanded schooling for the girl child, reflecting a clear recognition of their own inadequacy, now – after many confrontations with agenda papers and minutes of meetings – perceived as a serious handicap. They have also begun to actively monitor schools and primary health centres, which cannot but have a positive long-term impact on human development indicators.

A second example is the recognition, by the state, of claims of social citizenship articulated by popular campaigns. These campaigns have variously demanded rights to housing, education, food, information, and employment. The Right to Education, the Right to Information, and the provision of the Right to Work through the National Rural Employment Guarantee Act, are examples of how civil society mobilisation, along with political commitment to welfare, can translate into effective initiatives for social citizenship and therefore improvements in human development. Both of these are testimony to the vital importance of democracy in advancing the project of substantive citizenship.

Quite apart from its intrinsic value, India's democracy has incontestably, and in ways both intended and unintended by its Constitution makers, furthered the project of greater inclusion. There is, if not adequate, certainly much greater representation of disadvantaged groups in India's public institutions, partly effected through affirmative action policies, and partly through the political opportunities offered by a democratic political framework.

Nevertheless, these modest successes are clearly not adequately reflected in improvements in human development. The slow gains in this area may suggest that democracy is a necessary, but not perhaps a sufficient, condition for human development. Democracy can and has, in India, provided opportunities for demanding and obtaining more effective inclusion, making good some, but only some, of the promise contained in the constitutional framework. Mostly defined in cultural and political terms, inclusion is evidently inadequate for the realisation of human development objectives.

This cannot, however, lead us to advance the reckless claim that the concept of citizenship can, except under specific and perhaps even utopian conditions, be equality-producing. The rather limited claim here is that citizenship can certainly enable the accomplishment of a more modest but nonetheless desirable objective – namely, human development. As a relationship between citizen and state, as also among citizens, citizenship does not demand absolute equality, but it does demand at least the recognition of

- Political equality for members of culturally different groups and the appropriate recognition of difference – in sum, cultural (or multicultural) citizenship; and
- Social citizenship in terms of addressing at least basic needs and therefore superior human development outcomes.

If our objective is to redress both cultural and economic inequalities, and thereby to achieve human development outcomes that do not vary by social group or cultural identity, substantive citizenship is likely to be a more robust and effective way of addressing human development deficits than that provided by the idea of inclusion. This is obviously unlikely to spell the end of structural inequalities in Indian society, which may well endure till more fundamental changes occur in economy and society. In the meanwhile, the more visible and even inhuman impacts of these may be mitigated and eroded through an emphasis on substantive citizenship. Above all, as that which enables future claim-making by citizens, such citizenship also has the potential to renew itself continuously in response to new needs.

7

An Immense and (In)complete Democracy

A Tocquevillian Perspective on India's Experiment with Democratic Citizenship

If the ratification of the U.S. Constitution (1789) is taken as the date on which American democracy was inaugurated, and the adoption of the Indian Constitution (1950) as that of India's democracy, the gap in years between Tocqueville's account of the former and my account of the latter is not dissimilar.[1] This chapter interprets the Indian experience of democratic citizenship with reference to two interrelated aspects of Tocqueville's argument in *Democracy in America.* The first is his argument about the relationship between social equality and democracy; and the second is his account of (what is now described as) civil society or the associational sphere for the performance of citizenship. The two arguments are, of course, intimately linked, as social equality is the prime guarantor of the robustness of democracy and the premise of the performance of citizenship.

It is interesting, however, that neither of these arguments – the equality–democracy thesis or the theory of citizenship – was invoked by Tocqueville in his narrative of the "two unlucky races",

[1] The title of this chapter refers to India, playing on Tocqueville's description of America as "an immense and complete democracy". *Democracy in America*, 316. I am taking 1840, the year of the publication of vol. II of *Democracy in America*, as the relevant date for Tocqueville.

or indeed of women. This chapter remarks, in a comparative vein, on Indian constitutional discourse and state policies on comparably disadvantaged groups, including women. Further, taking a cue from Dana Villa's interpretation – that the central distinction for Tocqueville was not between *société politique* and *société civile,* but between centralised and local organisations of power with their implications for politics and participation in public life – the chapter situates the argument about differentiated citizenship in the local.[2]

The tension between political equality, on the one hand, and social and economic inequality, on the other, is an old and weary one, with the question being typically framed in two ways: first, can democracy take root in a society marked by deep inequalities? And second, under what conditions can democracy produce a more egalitarian social and economic order? The first question suggests an interest in assessing the impact of background inequalities on the very possibility of democracy, while the second signals the impact of democracy on the production or mitigation of inequality. Neither has yet been conclusively answered, not least because democracy has long borne, and continues to be invested with, the burden of so much hope.

On the first question – under what conditions can democracy take root in a society marked by deep inequalities – it is well known that Tocqueville credited the relatively egalitarian society of America with having provided the necessary social and historical background for a flourishing democratic polity: ". . . the social state of America is a very strange phenomenon. Men there are nearer equality in wealth and mental endowments, or, in other words, more nearly equally powerful, than in any other country of the world or in any other age of recorded history."[3] This was in spite of, and unrelated to, his

[2] Villa, "Tocqueville and Civil Society", 219.

[3] Tocqueville, *Democracy in America*, 56.

pessimistic view of the inequality and exclusion that marked the condition of native Indians and African slaves. Its obverse was the cautionary injunction of Dr B.R. Ambedkar who, at the adoption of India's Constitution, warned that India was

> going to enter into a life of contradictions. In politics we will have equality and in social and economic life we will have inequality. In politics we will be recognising the principle of one man one vote and one vote one value. In our social and economic life, we shall, by reason of our social and economic structure, continue to deny the principle of one man one value. How long shall we continue to live this life of contradictions? How long shall we continue to deny equality in our social and economic life? If we continue to deny it for long, we will do so only by putting our political democracy in peril. We must remove this contradiction at the earliest possible moment or else *those who suffer from inequality will blow up the structure of political democracy which the Assembly has so laboriously built up.*[4]

The second question – under what conditions can democracy be an effective mechanism to produce a more just and equal social and economic order – clearly privileges political organisation, and so places on democracy itself the onus of creating a more egalitarian society. This instrumentalist view of democracy was expressed by Ambedkar when he described democracy as a form of government in which "revolutionary changes in the economic and social life of people are brought about without bloodshed", a vehicle that could take citizens towards a more egalitarian society. Tocqueville made a similar argument from the opposite end when he showed

[4] B.R. Ambedkar, *Constituent Assembly Debates*, 29 November 1949, https://www.constitutionofindia.net/constitution_assembly_debates/volume/11/1949-11-25, 11.165.325. Emphasis added.

how and why all classes in a democracy – the rich, the poor, and those in between – were equally averse to revolution.[5]

Albeit separated by a hundred years or so, Tocqueville and Ambedkar both recognised the potential role of social inequalities in undermining the egalitarian promise of democracy. For Tocqueville, the explanation for America's democratic achievements lay in its relatively egalitarian society and the historical absence of a feudal social order. Looking forward, Ambedkar recognised that the deep social inequalities that marked Indian society would be a serious obstacle in the way of creating a robust democracy in which every citizen could enjoy substantive political equality. However, as the chief architect of the constitution of a new republic, Ambedkar hoped that social inequalities would be diminished over time, in and through the practice of democracy. Writing about a manifestly different context, Tocqueville was evidently less sanguine about the prospects of the poor using the resources of democracy to divest the rich of their power.

This tension between (in)equality and democracy is an important if clichéd part of the explanation for the limitations of Indian democracy today. Despite a half-century of affirmative action policies for, and political mobilisation by, disadvantaged groups, Ambedkar's fears continue to resonate, and a later section of this chapter suggests why.

The second Tocquevillian argument addressed here is about citizenship. Distinguishing between two dimensions of the citizenship question – (a) who is or can be a citizen and (b) how is citizenship performed – it would appear that Tocqueville is chiefly concerned about the second, while the attention of many scholars, including Rogers Smith, is on the prior question of the bearers of citizenship, on which Tocqueville evidently had little to say.[6] Part

[5] Tocqueville, *Democracy in America*, 635–8.
[6] Smith, *Stories of Peoplehood*.

of Tocqueville's fascination was with the – for him unusual – civic fluency of Americans. Citizens, he gushed, knew their rights and how to exercise them; they knew also the customs of the political world. This knowledge was, however, only partly derived from books, which did not furnish it but merely prepared the citizen to receive it. "It is by taking a share in legislation that the American learns to know the law; it is by governing that he becomes educated about the formalities of government. The great work of society is daily performed before his eyes, and so to say, under his hands."[7]

These habits of public life were further carried over into the private lives of citizens, such that you would find "the idea of a jury in children's games, and parliamentary formalities even in the organization of a banquet!"[8] In Volume II, Tocqueville applauded political associations as being "great free schools to which all citizens come to be taught the general theory of association" and described "the technique of association" as "the mother of every other technique: everyone studies and applies it."[9]

How did it come about that a people so obsessed with the individualistic pursuit of physical pleasures did not abdicate public affairs or leave them hostage to despots? How could the same individual be so divided that one moment he appeared to be motivated purely by selfish greed and the next moment only by selfless patriotism? Enlightened self-interest, more or less, was Tocqueville's answer:

> Americans in fact do regard their freedom as the best tool of and the firmest guarantee for their prosperity. *They love them both for the sake of each other.* They are therefore by no means inclined to suppose that it is no business of theirs to meddle in public affairs. On the contrary, they think it their most important concern to secure a government which will

[7] Tocqueville, *Democracy in America*, 304.

[8] Ibid., 305.

[9] Ibid., 522.

> allow them to get the good things they want and which will not stop their enjoying those they have in peace.[10]

Tocqueville's question thus is *what citizens do – how, why, and to what effect,* but not *who is, should be, or can be a citizen.* He is interested in how citizens in America are prepared for the tasks of citizenship and what makes them so public-minded, but he appears on the whole to take the boundaries and exclusions of citizenship as given and does not seriously interrogate them.

In his account of "the two unlucky races" – groups that he rather embarrassingly identifies as Negroes and Indians – Tocqueville characterises their misfortunes as being alike insofar as both groups are located at two extremes of freedom (Indians) and slavery (blacks).[11] The enslaved cannot handle freedom, while the free cannot be civilised.[12] On the Indians, Tocqueville is critical of the failure to follow the "noble and virtuous policy" of "kindness and generosity" towards them, as promised by George Washington.[13] As for the slaves, he deems it a delusion that they could ever mingle with the whites. Even if, he argues, slavery were to retreat, the prejudices from which it arose are immutable.[14] Conversely, even if the inequalities of law were to be corrected, the inequalities of nature and mores would remain.[15] If, he said, referring specifically to the American South, they were refused freedom, they would

[10] Ibid., 541. Emphasis added.

[11] Ibid., 317–18. I have retained Tocqueville's usage for Native Americans and Blacks.

[12] Ibid., 318, 326.

[13] Ibid., 334.

[14] Tocqueville acknowledges that slavery has also deepened prejudice, and made slavery more enduring. "Increasing enlightenment in the South makes the people there see that slavery is harmful to the master, and the same enlightenment makes them see, more clearly than they had seen before, that it is almost impossible to abolish it." Ibid., 361. Similar arguments have been made in relation to reservation policies for disadvantaged castes in India, pointing to the entrenchment of caste divisions as a negative outcome of these.

[15] Ibid., 342.

seize it; but if granted it, they would surely abuse it.[16] "The Negroes might remain slaves for a long time without complaining, but as soon as they join the ranks of free men, they will soon be indignant at being deprived of almost all the rights of citizens; and *being unable to become the equals of the whites, they will not be slow to show themselves their enemies.*"[17]

Tocqueville's narrative of his simultaneous encounter with the three races – Indian, black, and white – in a forest in Alabama metaphorically brings them together, as he represents it, in a bond of affection that "united oppressors and oppressed". He recounts how, while he rested beside a spring in the forest, an Indian woman came holding a little white girl by the hand, followed by a black woman. The Indian and the black woman both lavished on the child "fond caresses as mothers give". The little white girl's very movements showed superiority and even condescension. "Crouched down in front of her mistress, anticipating her every desire, the Negro woman seemed equally divided between almost maternal affection and servile fear, whereas even in the effusions of her tenderness, the savage woman looked free, proud, and almost fierce."[18] Here, Tocqueville contrasts the role of nature in bringing the three races together with the gap introduced by prejudice and laws.[19] It is interesting that the protagonists in his narrative – each representing one of the three races – are, firstly, encountered in the wilderness, and, secondly, all female. The gendered stereotype of motherhood is presented as transcending the stereotypical servility of the black woman and the equally clichéd proud barbarism of the Indian. Most notably, the girl child – all of six years old and described as charming – manages to reinforce white racial supremacy by her very presence. This is a curiously deterministic view of the natural world, including not just the forest and the spring, but also race.

[16] Ibid., 363.

[17] Ibid., 360. Emphasis added.

[18] Ibid., 320.

[19] Ibid.

This intriguing vignette apart, women were for the most part excluded from Tocqueville's account of the equality that reigned around the domestic hearth as relations between fathers and sons were reinvented within a democratic framework.[20] However, democracy played a curiously double role in relation to women: on the one hand, democratic institutions and mores were a danger to women; on the other, a democratic education such as American women received, was the best protective shield against these dangers.[21] Protestantism influenced the provision of education and freedom to American girls, and consequently the confidence with which they spoke and acted. It was these reasoning powers that American women could draw upon "to defend feminine chastity".[22] Why American women should be particularly imperilled by the individual freedom afforded by a democracy and by the unsettled quality of public opinion – a certain untamed quality of democracy? – is not entirely clear, but Tocqueville did attribute to their "cold and austere powers of reasoning" a stoic submission, after marriage, to their husbands.[23] He salutes the quiet fortitude and indomitable spirit with which women in America bear the privations forced upon them by marriage – such as their husbands' propensity to go into the wilderness in search of fortunes! But equally he applauds American men for having "wonderfully understood the true conception of democratic progress" by maintaining the social inferiority of women and keeping them confined to the domestic sphere, while at the same time "making" women their moral and intellectual equals.[24] Tocqueville observes (and approves of) American women receiving a demo-

[20] Ibid., 587.

[21] Ibid., 590–2.

[22] Ibid., 591.

[23] Ibid., 593.

[24] Ibid., 603. This resonates strongly with Partha Chatterjee's account of the educational and literary accomplishments of the bourgeois woman, the *bhadramahila*, in colonial India. Chatterjee, "The Nationalist Resolution", 247.

cratic education; democratic participation could not be further from his mind. This is surprising because he could not but have been acquainted with the contemporary debate around political rights for women in France. In this debate, women's claims to political rights had frequently been countered with the argument that their exclusion was temporary, till such time as the flaws in their education had been remedied.[25] The political organisation of French women – whether in the French Revolution or the Jacobin period, whether for the right to bear arms or for bread – appears not to have struck Tocqueville as an important contrast with the American case.

It is clear then that none of these three groups is even remotely perceived by Tocqueville as being a future claimant to citizenship. Nor is the condition of any of the three viewed as in any way undermining the quality of American democracy, much less inviting a revision of their status in American society. They are firmly on the margins of that society, and any challenge posed by their existence is purely social, not political.

In the American context, Rogers Smith has posited the idea of differentiated citizenship – particularly with respect to gender and race – as a way of administering a corrective to what he describes as "the crude Tocquevillian story" about citizenship in America. This chapter revisits Tocqueville's argument about citizenship through the experience of a considerably younger democratic polity that gave implicit recognition to the idea of differentiated citizenship in 1950.

Differentiated Citizenship: Some Indian Questions

The idea of group-differentiated citizenship (GDC) has become a widely accepted strategy of reconciling the project of the universal rights of citizenship with that of providing recognition to diverse

[25] Wallerstein, "Citizens All?", 654.

ethnic groups in multicultural societies.[26] It has helped to assuage the discomfort with liberal, difference-blind accounts of citizenship, and their inability to accommodate the very real challenge of citizenship in culturally diverse societies. In her early critique of "universality as sameness", Iris Marion Young made a distinction between groups defined by their interests or political position, and social groups defined in terms of their "comprehensive identities and ways of life".[27] She identified the chief instruments of GDC as affirmative action; comparable worth policies; and bilingual, bicultural education and service.[28] The Indian constitutional accommodation clearly avowed some of these principles, and many of the justifications offered in the Constituent Assembly in the late 1940s, as in present-day political discourse, have harked back to the same reasoning. As in Young's account, these are mostly arguments about just compensation for past histories of discrimination and exclusion.

Even before India attained independence and enacted a republican Constitution, the imperial British government in India had already quite successfully flirted with forms of GDC that could scarcely – given the colonial context and the rather skeletal and empty forms of legislative opportunities this afforded – be described as citizenship. The colonial state had carefully separated out and delinked from each other the principles of differentiation and of citizenship, giving recognition to the first and obviously ignoring the second. The structures of governance in the colonial period provided for the articulation of the communitarian interests of the Muslim minority through the institutionalisation of separate electorates.[29] Such political safeguards were all along resented by

[26] Young, "Polity and Group Difference"; Kymlicka, *Multicultural Citizenship*; Carens, *Culture, Citizenship and Community*.

[27] Young, "Polity and Group Difference", 195.

[28] Ibid., 200–1.

[29] In a separate electorate, a particular group is represented by a legislator chosen by an electorate composed solely of members of that group. Thus, both the electorate

Hindu nationalists, who viewed these as a manifestation of the British policy of "divide and rule"; and the separate electorates did not survive into independent India.

Another quite unique form of "recognition" was initiated in the colonial treatment of caste as "the institutional keystone of Indian society".[30] The census became the main instrument of gathering information about the "caste system", fixing caste identities in previously unknown ways, and feeding these into the organisation of, for instance, the British Army in India, whose regiments (e.g. the Jat regiment, the Sikh regiment) were caste/community based, depending on the colonial state's stereotyping of certain communities as "martial races". With their identities so fixed, caste groups began to form caste associations, some of which would periodically petition the colonial government to reconsider their rank in the caste hierarchy. The arbiters of the caste system were thus no longer part of the ritual order, but rather external to it.

In 1909, when the Morley–Minto Reforms granted the Muslims separate or communal electorates, the politics of numbers brought forth similar claims from the Depressed Classes.[31] Caste Hindus were keen that these classes be counted as Hindus, while the Muslims argued that they should not. In the Government of India Act of 1919, the Depressed Classes were given representation – albeit as non-official nominated members – in the Central Legislative Assembly as well as the Provincial Legislatures. This legislation was the first official recognition of the status of the Depressed Classes as a distinct and disadvantaged group. The

---

and the candidate belong to the same community. In a reserved or quota seat, by contrast, the candidates must belong to the particular social group, but the electorate is a mix of all the social groups that happen to live within the constituency.

[30] Fuller, "Caste", 481.

[31] This was the name by which the "untouchable" castes were then known. Gandhi subsequently gave them the name "Harijan"" (People of God), but both of these have now been overridden by the two currently dominant usages: the official category 'Scheduled Castes" and the political category "Dalit" (the oppressed).

devolution of powers to elected governments in the provinces, and the three-fold increase in the size of the Indian electorate – both mandated by the Government of India Act of 1935 – gave a new salience to the question of community identity. Ambedkar's demand for separate electorates for the untouchables had already generated new fears among the (mostly upper-caste Hindu) nationalists, since these groups represented between 15 and 20 per cent of the population, not a proportion to be scoffed at in the electoral arithmetic.[32] Gandhi's opposition to this was fierce, and the compromise formula arrived at in the Poona Pact of 1932 was to keep Hindus and the Depressed Classes in the same electorates but reserve a proportion of seats in the assemblies for candidates belonging to the latter group. The arrangement was formalised in the Communal Award of 1932, whereby a fixed number of seats in every provincial legislature were to be reserved for members of the Depressed Classes, as well as of the religious minorities. It was clearly an important precursor to the provisions of the Constitution of independent India, as was the procedure of creating "schedules" for tribes and castes deserving of such reservation. Initiated in the Government of India Act of 1935, "scheduling" attempted to identify and list every "depressed" (i.e. disadvantaged) community in every province, and the initial list contained 400 untouchable groups, apart from many tribes. This is the origin of the terms Scheduled Castes and Scheduled Tribes.[33]

The Constitution of independent India sought to sanctify the founding idea of India as an intrinsically diverse and plural nation-state. Though defined in "national-civic" rather than "national-ethnic" terms,[34] national identity remained a rather fragile construct, a complex "national-civic-plural-ethnic" combination that did not apparently strike its authors as being chaotic or unruly,

[32] This was particularly the case in Bengal and the Punjab, in both of which the Hindu and Muslim populations were fairly evenly balanced in terms of numbers.

[33] Bayly, *Caste, Society and Politics*, 260–3.

[34] Beiner, *Theorizing Citizenship*.

much less inconsistent.[35] The Indian Constitution privileged the conception of universal citizenship as a critical component of the project of "nation-building". At the same time, and for important historical reasons, it consciously sought to accommodate the claims of minorities and disadvantaged groups on the grounds, variously, of protection or compensation for disadvantage, rather than on the grounds that these were distinctive interests that needed special representation in the political system. The normative weight, as between the universalist and particularist dimensions of citizenship, clearly belonged to the former, with the latter merely facilitating the realisation of the background conditions of equality, and so advancing the eventual accomplishment of the universalist ideal. Conflicts between these two dimensions were perhaps inevitable; as Lloyd and Susanne Rudolph have summarised it, "The contradiction in India's concept of secularism was its *simultaneous* commitment to communities and to equal citizenship."[36] There was also a conviction – perhaps nowhere better expressed than in the *locus classicus* of the unity-in-diversity approach, Jawaharlal Nehru's *Discovery of India* – that identities were retrograde phenomena which would surely be transcended by the alliance of science, reason, and economic development.

The institutions of governance were on the whole designed to conform to the liberal-individualist conception of equal citizenship, encompassing equal rights for all citizens and upholding the principle of equality before the law. There were two significant exceptions to this universality: (a) the recognition of certain categories of rights for which (cultural) communities rather than individuals would be the bearers of rights; and (b) the provisions for compensatory discrimination for historically disadvantaged

[35] Of course, the idea of a purely civic nationhood is a contested one. Rogers Smith, for instance, disagrees with the proposition that "political communities can be sustained by agreement on shared political principles alone". Smith, *Stories of Peoplehood*, 190.

[36] Rudolph and Rudolph, *In Pursuit of Lakshmi*, 178. Emphasis added.

groups. Thus, instead of adopting an identical strategy of accommodation towards different cultural communities, the state in independent India devised different institutional mechanisms for giving recognition to their interests. This is why there are different policy provisions for different types of "differences", each justified in terms of some criterion of appropriateness.

The constitutional attempt to balance the demands of universal citizenship with the special needs of communities took the form, first, of the recognition that, along with equal civil and political rights for all citizens, it is important to secure and guarantee the rights of religious minorities. This was done through guarantees for the freedom of religion, including the freedom to practice and propagate it, as well as through providing for separate personal laws for members of minority communities, alongside a universally applicable criminal law. The promise of equality, secondly, was also given greater content through constitutional provisions for affirmative action for the Scheduled Castes and Tribes, both in public employment as well as in representative bodies.[37] Finally, at the macro-institutional level, consociational practices were adopted, along with a federal framework designed in a way that was broadly congruent with linguistic divisions. Unlike the federal structure, which was intended to be enduring, the separate personal laws as also policies of compensatory discrimination were seen as interim measures on the path to a society in which greater social equality and processes of secularisation would eventually lead to the universalist norms of citizenship becoming firmly entrenched, rendering special provisions redundant.

[37] The view that the Constitution was, in this respect, a charter of social transformation has been contested by Jaffrelot, who argues that the Scheduled Castes, under the colonial resolution of this question, actually had greater voice in the choice of their representatives than within the framework of reserved seats in the legislatures provided in the constitutional settlement after independence. Jaffrelot, "Containing the Lower Castes", 255.

Despite the apparent similarities, there is reason to insert a caution in the use of the term "group-differentiated citizenship" to describe the policies of positive or compensatory discrimination legislated by the Indian Constitution. A multi-layered theoretical interpretation is available of the conflicting conceptions of representation at work in the debates in the Constituent Assembly.[38] Three mechanisms were proposed, any or all of which could qualify as (imperfect) forms of GDC. The first proposal, to continue with separate electorates, was opposed on the grounds of universal citizenship and political equality of individual citizens, but most strongly on grounds of "national unity" and a common political community. Proportional representation (PR), secondly, was advocated because it would enable the representation of minorities and minority opinions, and so make legislatures more representative of diversity. It is interesting that the opposition to proportional representation – including from Ambedkar himself – was essentially institutional. PR was considered unworkable chiefly because of its association with governmental instability, but also because it was unsuited to an unlettered electorate and even viewed by some as a reinvention of separate electorates. The consensus of the Assembly was on the third alternative, viz., reservation of seats (quotas), and these were couched in the language of transition.[39] In other words, universal citizenship based on the political equality of individual citizens was the default position; GDC was a temporary deviation, justified not by the purpose of giving these groups a voice in legislation but for improving their condition of social and economic "backwardness" through a form of emphatically political affirmative action.[40]

The time-bound quality of these constitutional provisions is evident in the domain of both the cultural rights of religious minorities as well as the quotas for Scheduled Castes and Scheduled

[38] Bajpai, "Minority Representation".

[39] Ibid., 377.

[40] Ibid., 379.

Tribes. With respect to the former, the long-term objective of a uniform civil code was quietly tucked away along with other good intentions in the chapter on Directive Principles of State Policy, to be realised when secularisation processes would make its retrieval less contentious. The provisions for reservations for the Scheduled Castes and Tribes were given an unwarrantedly optimistic ten-year term that has consequently had to be formally extended once in every decade. Both these proved to be highly contentious issues in Indian politics in the 1990s. The first created unexpected paradoxes, as when the endorsement of religious personal law by the State in the celebrated Shah Bano case entailed acquiescing in the violation of individual rights and principles of gender justice. Similarly, though policies of affirmative action have been extended to castes previously outside their fold, they have often led to bitter contestation, imitative mobilisation, and even the formation of new elites within the formerly excluded groups.

The Indian experience of what could be described as an early form of GDC provokes at least three important questions which may have implications for theories of such forms of citizenship. Briefly stated, these are: (a) Can differentiated citizenship accommodate multiple and overlapping inequalities; (b) Can differentiated citizenship be an effective instrument for addressing inequalities other than cultural and symbolic; and (c) Can the idea of GDC accommodate the project of a civic community?

Firstly, regardless of the criteria and principles for determining which groups are entitled to differentiated citizenship, and for defining the boundaries of such entitlements, it is generally accepted that GDC is constructed along singular axes of social difference such as gender or race. Iris Marion Young proposed the criterion of oppression, which included exploitation, marginalisation, powerlessness, cultural imperialism, and the experience of being victims of violence motivated by hatred and fear. In the American context, these criteria yielded the following plausible candidates for differentiated citizenship: "women, blacks, Native Americans,

Chicanos, Puerto Ricans and other Spanish-speaking Americans, Asian Americans, gay men, lesbians, working-class people, poor people, old people, and mentally and physically disabled people."[41] However, in a telling example of the inconsistencies and temporalities entailed in such characterisations, Young apparently dropped Asian-Americans from a later republication of this paper.[42]

In India, the justification for differentiated citizenship has customarily rested upon two, often intertwined, criteria: historical injustice, discrimination, and the backwardness flowing from it on the one hand, and ascriptive identity on the other. It could be argued, as Young has done for working-class people, poor people, and the elderly, that injustice in the present – even if it is not historical – is, so long as it is an attribute of a group, equally deserving of differentiated citizenship. Equally, it could be argued that disadvantages that are not associated with ascriptive identity are also deserving of such consideration. Legal and policy provisions in India did not adequately account for the complex and overlapping nature of social inequalities, and in particular the overlap between cultural and material inequalities; between, on the one hand, inherited symbolic or cultural disadvantages of caste or religious identity, and, on the other, economic disadvantage.

The data on human development indicators and poverty amongst various social groups in India clearly show that levels of deprivation are highest for the Scheduled Castes, followed by the Scheduled Tribes, followed by the Muslims. These three groups together account for close to 38 per cent of India's population, and traditional and historical forms of social inequality thus coexist with, and are reinforced by, inequalities arising out of the sphere of production and economic activity. These forms of multiple and mutually compounding disadvantage present challenges of both recognition and redistribution, suggesting that the groups that

[41] Young, "Polity and Group Difference", 195.

[42] Joppke, "Multicultural Citizenship", 247.

need our special attention are those that are doubly disadvantaged – both culturally, as also in terms of their human development indicators. Some – for example, poor Dalit or Muslim women – may be simultaneously disadvantaged in three ways, by gender, class, and caste/religion. In this sort of context, the theoretical and normative strategies for determining appropriate criteria and delimiting boundaries for the application of differentiated citizenship are necessarily complicated.

The task becomes even more complex when we consider the difficulty of building in multiple types of disadvantage into the categories of differentiated citizenship. For instance, should a poor Dalit woman be entitled to differentiated citizenship on the basis of her poverty or her caste or her gender or indeed all of these? Is her entitlement conditional upon her being a member of a similarly disadvantaged *group* of citizens, such that she becomes entitled to redress not as an individual but only as a member of a similarly defined collective? Can differentiated citizenship be constructed so as to take account of multiple disadvantages? Building cross-cutting inequalities into a conception of differentiated citizenship is clearly a more challenging task than a uni-dimensional notion of differentiated citizenship, grounded in a single indicator of disadvantage, may suggest.

Secondly, the Indian experience suggests the need to devise criteria not only for determining which groups should or should not be entitled to GDC, but also for the empirical assessment of actual outcomes of such policies. Where the inequalities encountered are purely symbolic, the politics of recognition may suffice. However, in contexts where symbolic and material inequalities overlap, redistributive policies may also be called for. Drawing upon the distinction made in feminist scholarship between the descriptive representation of women (DRW) and their substantive representation (SRW), it may be useful to consider the outcomes of exclusively or substantially quota-based approaches for all disadvantaged groups. In feminist debates on representation, there is some consensus that "judgements needed to be made about the 'quality' of SRW, in order to assess the outcomes of SRW."[43] An empirical study of women's representation in thirty-six countries came to the rather disturbing conclusion that "descriptive representation is severely limited as an avenue for providing substantive representation."[44]

In India, the persistence of poor human development indicators for disadvantaged groups is depressing testimony to the fact that institutional quotas – the dominant strategy of differentiated citizenship thus far – have failed to substantively address the disadvantages that mark the condition of the vast majority of such groups. It is not clear that this strategy has either adequately expanded access to domains from which such groups were previously excluded or universalised access within such groups. One study showing the widespread persistence of the practice of untouchability in several states of India – despite the constitutional and legal provisions making it a punishable offence – suggests that those at the bottom of the ritual order and on the margins of society continue to carry multiple burdens of denial and deprivation, both cultural as well as economic.[45] As for the Muslim minority, possessing only cultural rights, it has been denied any real opportunities for its material improvement,[46] though the publication of the Sachar Committee Report (2006), recording the abysmal conditions of economic and educational backwardness of this community, led to expectations of programmes of a redistributive nature.

[43] Mackay, "Thick Conceptions", 126.

[44] Weldon, "Beyond Bodies", 1171.

[45] Shah, *et al.*, *Untouchability*. Pointing to the limitations of the constitutional strategy, Gopal Guru has also argued that "constitutional provisions are necessary for positional good but not sufficient for achieving cultural goods like recognition and dignity . . . In fact, the Constitution consciously or unconsciously creates tensions between the positional and cultural notion of justice." Guru, "Constitutional Justice", 244.

[46] Khalidi, *Muslims in Indian Economy*.

Some symbolic inequalities have begun to be more effectively addressed through political mobilisation, leading for instance to a higher numerical presence of backward-caste representatives in the legislatures. However, inequalities engendered by poverty or unequal access to resources such as land and education have not received the policy attention they deserve. While the importance of symbolic recognition cannot be overstated – especially for groups that have been the victims of the most reprehensible forms of stigmatisation and discrimination – this may be inadequate until supplemented by material improvements in the quality of people's lives.

New claims to GDC tend to become issues of political management rather than of the theoretical arbitration and application of criteria. This is not only because they are politically constructed but also because they need to be weighed against other competing claims. The Gujjars in Rajasthan – seeking "ritual" downgrading in order to become eligible for quotas in categories where the pressure on these is relatively lower – have chosen strategies of protest that are disruptive and not squeamish about the use of violence. They have therefore received much greater political attention than the arguably more legitimate claims of Dalit Christians and Muslims, which are yet to be seriously debated, let alone accommodated. These challenges indicate the need for much greater clarity on the questions of determining not merely the most just criteria for GDC, but also the most effective institutional mechanisms for implementing it, and the most appropriate criteria for evaluating its effectiveness. In all these, it is useful to bear in mind Nancy Fraser's caution (articulated in the context of feminism, but with connotations beyond it) that, in neo-liberal times, governments often find symbolic political solutions less challenging than policies that call for the redistribution of power and material resources:

> The shift to a culturalised politics of recognition occurred at precisely the moment when neoliberalism was staging its

> spectacular comeback. Throughout this period, academic feminist theory was largely preoccupied with debates about "difference" [and] . . . tended to remain on the terrain of recognition, where subordination was construed as a problem of culture and dissociated from political economy. The effect was to leave us defenceless against free-market fundamentalism, which had meanwhile become hegemonic.[47]

Finally, there is the question of the bases of political community, and the social unity and cohesion this bespeaks. Can the idea of GDC accommodate the idea of a civic community? In spite of recognising and even expanding the scope of GDC, India has found it manifestly hard to reconcile claims of cultural communities with the project of creating and nurturing a civic community. Today, the fragmentation and entrenchment of a variety of identities – based on religion, caste, and region – and in particular the increased insecurity of minorities and their vulnerability to violence, call into question the future of the civic project, of an overarching conception of the common good putatively shared by all citizens, or even of a shared space in which such a common good may be determined through public reasoning and debate.

It is possible to hazard a historical explanation for this, such that in nations where the national-civic was already formed and consolidated, differentiated citizenship may have provided a much-needed, but not socially destabilising, corrective to the homogenising and uniformising definition of universal citizenship. By contrast, in a relatively young nation like India, where the project of constructing a national identity went hand in hand with the anti-colonial struggle, the idea of the national-civic was somewhat more fragile. Notwithstanding the attempt to build in mechanisms for GDC for at least certain groups, the tension between the national-civic

[47] Fraser, *Scales of Justice*, 106.

and multiple national-ethnics has remained raw and palpable. As Tocqueville might have remarked, despite laws and policies to address disadvantage, the prejudices and mores of society have remained resilient.

As an aside, some of the caste-related contentions actually encourage a comparison with Tocqueville's "permanent associations": in the context of the *ancien regime,* these were the estates that signified a permanent and unchangeable social hierarchy, though in the context of America Tocqueville used the term for legally established political entities such as towns, cities, and counties.[48] Castes in India have attributes of both: the hierarchical and involuntary quality of the first French usage, as well as the episodic and voluntary quality of the second American usage. They represent both hierarchically arranged ascriptive groups into which one is born, as well as voluntary political groups in which one participates by choice. Tocqueville did view these permanent and political associations, rather than civil associations, as the seedbed of civic virtue and the sites where citizens learnt lessons in citizenship. The reinvention of caste in the context of democratic politics in India, enhancing its political salience while reducing its more traditional social salience, suggests an interesting comparison. Scholars of Indian politics have, since the late 1960s, noted that democracy provided new opportunities for political mobilisation based upon identities, such as caste, that were relatively fixed.[49] Horizontal linkages created translocal caste identities, and eventually the creation of federative caste associations for representation and reservations. A study suggests that while caste continues to be consequential in Indian society, its role in political mobilisation and as the basis for political representation has far outstripped its role as the signifier of ritual hicrarchy.[50]

[48] Villa, "Tocqueville and Civil Society", 224.

[49] Rudolph and Rudolph, *The Modernity of Tradition*; Kothari, *Caste in Indian Politics*.

[50] Sheth, "Caste and Class".

Notwithstanding the quasi-empirical questions raised about differentiated citizenship in this section, there can be little disagreement about the necessity, in principle, for differentiated forms of citizenship. In a diverse and complex world, it is scarcely possible to argue for a relentlessly uniform and universal conception of citizenship. The challenge is to identify the criteria by which different types of claims to differentiated citizenship can be mediated in a way that is normatively just and satisfactory.

The next section outlines the important exclusion of women as a group that has had a fraught and contested relationship with the idea of differentiated citizenship since before independence and to the present day.

Women as Inappropriate Subjects of Differentiated Citizenship

Apart from institutions of local governance, in which quotas were introduced in 1992, women have not been considered a plausible category for GDC in India. Indeed, the striking irony is that when, in the early years of the twentieth century, women's organisations were agitating for universal franchise and equal political status, they were awarded reserved constituencies. However, since they began, in the last decade of the same century, asking for reservations in legislatures to enhance women's participation, they have been repeatedly thwarted in their efforts to obtain these.

In the first few decades of the twentieth century, women's claims to political recognition primarily took the form of demanding the franchise, with a simultaneous rejection of special provisions such as separate electorates or quotas. The first women's delegation to wait upon the Secretary of State and the Viceroy (Montagu and Chelmsford) in 1917 asked the colonial government to give women the vote, and thereby grant them the status

[51] Forbes, *Women in Modern India*, 92.

of "people".[51] The following year, Sarojini Naidu, who had led that delegation, argued eloquently at the Congress session for the rational, scientific, and political soundness of enfranchising women. She simultaneously reassured her audience – which passed the resolution by a resounding three-fourths majority – that this was no transgression of tradition and that women would not, by participating in politics, become less feminine! Her views were echoed by other women leaders, such as Saraladevi Chaudhurani, who defined the sphere of women as including politics and "comradeship with men in the rough and tumble of life".[52] These claims were accompanied by a strong rejection of any preferential treatment as violative of their demand for absolute political equality. In fact, women's organisations even rejected the prevailing property qualification for the vote and demanded universal adult franchise in joint electorates and on equal terms with men. The language of strident universal citizenship, and resentment at being treated as a "reservable" category rather than as equal, pervades the documents that emanated from women's organisations through the 1930s, the ultimate touchstone of these arguments being the declaration of the Fundamental Rights of Citizenship in India passed in the famous Karachi session of the Indian National Congress in 1931.

Women's demands for enfranchisement were strongly influenced by the ideas of the British suffragists, many of whom, such as Eleanor Rathbone and Millicent Fawcett, were in touch with the women's movement in India. Rathbone disagreed with Indian women's insistence on universal adult franchise, which she believed would materialise in due course anyhow. She prioritised representation as being more important for social reform, and suggested to Indian women colleagues that they accept reservations. Eventually, this turned out to be the only concession that women could in fact extract.

[52] Ibid., 94.

The denial of the franchise on the grounds that it was "premature" triggered angry activity and depositions before many official committees in England as well as in India. Even as they claimed to speak on behalf of all Indian women, British officials dismissed them as elite exceptions to the vast majority of women in India – stereotypically characterised as veiled, uneducated, and ignorant – and therefore representing only their own limited class. Though small numbers of women were admitted into the provincial legislative assemblies over the next decade or so, the women's campaign for the franchise was effectively thwarted by both colonial officialdom and the nationalist leadership. Where women leaders demanded a proportion of 1:5 female to male voters, the White Paper of 1933 recommended an increase from the existing 1:20 to 1:10. The repudiation, in 1933, by the All India Women's Conference, of both separate electorates and reserved seats was justified thus:

> We look upon nominations, reservation of seats, and co-option in any sphere of activity as a pernicious and humiliating system which must run counter to all real progress. However impartially carried out it must, by its very nature, engender an inferiority complex amongst those for whom it caters, a contingency to be avoided at all costs . . . We realise to the full and with immeasurable sorrow to what an extent this canker amongst men has retarded and is retarding the progress of our beloved land.[53]

The official nationalist position supported the women's demand for enfranchisement no more than did the colonial state.[54] Gandhi

[53] Dhanda, *Reservations for Women*, 5.

[54] The apparently widely shared understanding that women themselves dropped their political demands out of deference to Gandhi (Singer, *"A Constituency Suitable for Ladies"*, 36) has been variously represented. In Radha Kumar's characterisation, "Gandhian feminism which developed in the 1920s became majority feminism in the 1930s." Kumar, *History of Doing*, 67. Chatterjee's argument (in "The Nationalist

himself enjoined women to first join forces with men in the fight against the greatest common enemy, British rule, the removal of which would bring with it the right to vote among all other rights. In the 1930s, even as Gandhi's opposition to Ambedkar's proposal for separate electorates for the Scheduled Castes was sustained, women came to be treated – like Muslims – as a discrete constituency. Both Muslims and women received the right to vote in separate Muslim-only and women-only constituencies respectively, with Muslim women finding themselves under considerable pressure by the Muslim League to support community candidates and disavow gender affiliations. The Indian National Congress too supported only those women who contested for reserved seats, with Nehru also using nationalism to trump women's demands. In the 1937 elections to the provincial assemblies, four million women voters were enfranchised, though only a quarter of them actually voted – and about sixty women contested elections from reserved constituencies.[55] Sacrificing their political demands, thousands of women participated in large numbers in the anti-colonial movement, many of them going to jail with their infants. The women's movement was effectively swallowed up by the independence movement.

In the years before independence, thus, women's claims to universal citizenship were clearly premised on the idea of separate spheres – "separate goals, separate destinies" – for men and

---

Resolution", for a somewhat earlier period) that nationalism domesticated the issue of women by confining it to the home, and refusing to make it a matter of political negotiation with the state, is implicitly echoed in Forbes' view that prominent nationalists preferred that women busy themselves with issues of civil rights and franchise instead of engaging in culturally disloyal discussions on patriarchy and subordination. Indeed, Lord Montagu actually expressed his reluctance to offend (male) nationalists on religious grounds by conceding the demands of women. Forbes, *Women in Modern India*, 99. One way or the other, women were encouraged towards, and largely accepted, political quiescence.

[55] Singer, "*A Constituency Suitable for Ladies*", 39–45.

women.[56] While the influence of the public realm on the private sphere of family and household went largely unremarked, citizenship was viewed as belonging to the public sphere to which women would, through their enfranchisement, bring the values and virtues of the private sphere, without in any way threatening men's exercise of their functions and civic duties. The public sphere was presented as a domain where rights were exercised, while the private sphere was represented as a domain of responsibilities towards families, children, etc. As in many other colonial and post-colonial societies, women's responsibilities in the private sphere also entailed their role as mothers of the nation, imparting civic education to their children.

In the Constituent Assembly, as in the years before it, women members opposed reservations for themselves as "an impediment to our growth and an insult to our very intelligence and capacity."[57] It is well known that while the Fundamental Rights were enacted in a way intended to be gender-neutral, social rights were placed in the non-justiciable Directive Principles of State Policy. The visibility of women is greater in this chapter of the Constitution, with many rights explicitly mentioning women being located here – for example, the right to equal pay for equal work, the right to an adequate livelihood, just and humane conditions of work and maternity relief, and, of course, the contentious uniform civil code.

The provision of universal adult franchise in the Indian Constitution gave women the right to political equality with men, but other aspects of gender inequality were for the first time confronted in *Towards Equality* (1974), the Report of the Committee on the Status of Women in India. This landmark report favoured reservations for women only in institutions of local governance. However, a dissenting opinion by the pioneering feminist scholars Lotika Sarkar and Vina Mazumdar began with the statement that

[56] Naidu, quoted in Forbes, *Women in Modern India,* 94.

[57] Quoted in John, "Reservations and the Women's Movement", 50.

"as members of the pre-Independence generation, we have always been firm believers in equal rights for women."[58] They went on to argue that they had never before supported reservations or "class representation" in any form. However, in their travels and meetings with women across India, they found that the actual life conditions of Indian women had not changed very much, and now felt that the presence of only a small number of women, mostly from the upper strata of society, lay at the root of this failure. Sarkar and Mazumdar therefore recommended special protections – in the form of reservation of seats in legislative bodies – to redress the under-representation of women and the denial of substantive equality of opportunity to them.[59]

It was the Beijing effect, and the recognition that women had rarely exceeded 8 per cent of the membership of Parliament, that led to some rethinking and the formulation of the Women's Reservation Bill in 1996, providing for one-third of the seats in the federal and state legislatures to be reserved for women.[60] At the higher levels of the political system, independent India has had no dearth of women leaders. It had a woman Prime Minister for approximately a fourth of its sixty-year history, and today the President of the republic, the President of the ruling Congress Party, and two state chief ministers are women. However, successful women political leaders have often been linked by blood or marriage to powerful male politicians. While it is possible that the enactment of the Women's Reservation Bill may not provide absolute safeguards against this phenomenon, the resistance to the Bill suggests that autonomous women's politics is perceived as a threat. Despite the support of women politicians cutting across political parties, thus, the passage

[58] Dhanda, *Reservations for Women*, 11.

[59] Ibid., 13–16.

[60] The Beijing Declaration, emanating from the United Nations World Conference on Women in 1995, urged governments to enhance the representation of women in leadership positions in all spheres of power and decision-making, including legislative bodies.

of this Bill has been repeatedly obstructed by openly sexist comments in parliamentary debate and even minor violence (as when a copy of the bill was torn by an enraged male parliamentarian).

In contemporary India, it is only in the institutions of local governance that constitutional recognition for differentiated citizenship – based on gender, caste, *and* tribal identity – obtains. For Tocqueville, of course, the attraction of the local was a consequence of his abhorrence for a centralised state like that of France. But it was also partly an argument about the practice and pedagogy of citizenship: the idea that it was by taking a share in legislation and governing that Americans became educated in the formalities of government and the law. So while education in Europe was intended to prepare individuals for their private lives, education in America was designed to prepare citizens for their participation in public affairs.

A constitutional amendment of 1992 mandated the creation of, and regular elections to, the *panchayats* – institutions of rural local governance (three tiers at the sub-state level) – providing for guaranteed representation of 33 per cent for women at every level of these institutions, including in the post of chairperson at each level. Similar quotas – in proportion to their percentage in the population – were provided for members of the Scheduled Castes and Scheduled Tribes. In terms of sheer numbers, the women's quota yielded breathtaking results, as approximately 1.2 million women entered the *panchayats*. Early studies of their performance reported tokenism and surrogate or proxy representation (by fathers, husbands, brothers, etc.) on a massive scale. Practices of men contesting elections in the name of their wives, attending meetings on their behalf, even signing official papers, have been widespread. Over time, however, many exceptions have been observed, as also many women who have gradually grown into their role as elected representatives, recognising that this entails their doing not what their husbands or fathers-in-law want them to do, but what their electors expect them to do.

The use of institutional mechanisms to undermine women's leadership has also been widespread. Women representatives have been unseated by manipulated motions of no-confidence, or been threatened, intimidated, or simply marginalised. Meetings have been called without even informing the woman chair of the *panchayat* and decisions taken have been sent home for her official endorsement. These problems have been particularly acute in the case of Dalit and tribal women, reinforcing the point made earlier about multiple and overlapping forms of disadvantage. In a famous case, a Dalit woman head of a village *panchayat* in Madhya Pradesh went to court because she was restrained from hoisting the national flag on Independence Day, a task that was rightfully hers and an honour that she valued. She won the case in court and returned the following year to perform her role.

Notwithstanding these difficulties, the developmental achievements of women-headed *panchayats,* or those in which women members are more active, have been impressive. Indeed, a gender distinction has often been observed between the types of development works prioritised by women and men. While male leaders tend to give importance to the building of roads, electricity, and other infrastructure, women are found to be more attentive to primary education and health, drinking water, playgrounds and schools, as also to the conservation and sustainable use of common property resources like forests and ponds.[61] A 23-state survey on the participation of women in *panchayats* revealed that there is a mere 2 per cent gap in community perceptions of the effectiveness of male and female leaders.[62]

What may be called the "empowerment" impacts of women's participation in local governance are obviously less easy to establish or document. Many women entering *panchayats* have given up

[61] Jayal, "Engendering Local Democracy", 29.

[62] Government of India, "Study on Elected Women".

the veil or purdah. There is also some evidence that relationships within the family, including the division of labour within the household, are being renegotiated. Women find that their opinions receive greater respect not only within, but also outside, the household. For instance, their influence on decisions regarding when the children should marry has now increased. Most importantly, the inability to read agenda papers or minutes of meetings has brought with it a recognition that illiteracy is a major handicap, and this in turn has led to a greater awareness of the importance of girls' education and higher levels of aspirations for girl children.[63]

The very women who needed to be virtually coerced to contest elections are now eager to attend *panchayat* meetings themselves, and to participate in processes of decision-making. Many women representatives, especially Dalit and tribal women, say that they would like to contest elections again, some saying that they would like to contest for positions of a higher level than the ones they currently hold. There are already some instances of women having served a term on a reserved seat and then having returned to office through open competition in the election. In the community, women's involvement in *panchayat* work is perceived as having reduced corruption and favouritism, encouraged a greater awareness of education, and even created a greater recognition of women's rights. Many women representatives perceive a change in the attitude of people (men and women) belonging to their own as well as other castes. Backward-caste women, for example, see as an indicator of their new status the number of invitations they now get to weddings, especially from upper-caste families. Of course, none of these should encourage us to romanticise such gestures, for Dalit women hardly ever report a change in the behaviour of higher-caste people towards them. They are often satisfied with small gains, as when upper-caste people no longer expect them

[63] Jayal, "Engendering Local Democracy".

to sit on the floor but offer a seat at the same level as themselves. Nevertheless, a new sense of self-confidence is perceptible.

The impact of women's participation in institutions of local governance varies significantly across states and regions, with regional, historical, and cultural factors accounting for some of these variations. In regions where the structures of caste and patriarchy are more deeply entrenched, for instance, women encounter more formidable obstacles to participation. By contrast, in regions where the customary status of women is somewhat higher – whether because of a social-reform movement in the nineteenth century or male migration in search of employment – women's quotas have been relatively more successful.

More centrally, and in ways that recall Tocqueville's discontent with the centralised state, there are important structural factors that shape the possibilities of local citizenship. Different states have interpreted the constitutional mandate differently – some have devolved more powers, functions, and finances to the *panchayats* than others. As such, the same formal institutional structures operate more effectively in some areas than in others, and accordingly render more or less difficult the effective participation of women. In the absence of adequate powers, the impact of *panchayats* – whether headed by women or by men – is naturally minimal, but this is clearly not a gender-specific phenomenon.

Despite the many negative trends (such as surrogate representation and tokenism) observed in the practice of women's participation as elected representatives in *panchayats*, it is clear that these institutions are performing – slowly, but unmistakably – a transformatory role. To speak of their powerlessness, as some women have done, is already to squarely, and for the first time, recognise it. This recognition may presently be confined to an awareness of powerlessness in the public sphere, but it cannot be long before the powerlessness within the home also comes to be recognised.

Conclusion

The discussion so far has recorded the contrasting state strategies for incorporating disadvantaged groups such as the Scheduled Castes, Scheduled Tribes, Muslims, and women into fuller membership of the Indian polity. As noted, prior to independence Muslims and women were treated alike, though women, unlike Muslims, did not themselves favour special treatment in this particular form of separate electorates. In this period, also, the Scheduled Castes were accorded reservations in the general electorate, though it is worth underlining that this franchise was also restricted by property and gender qualifications.

After independence, two types of exception were made to the principle of universal citizenship. The first of these pertained to Scheduled Caste/Scheduled Tribe groups who were given quotas in recognition of, and compensation for, historical injustice and the social backwardness induced by it. Muslims received constitutional protections for the rights of cultural community, including the right to be governed by Muslim Personal Law in civil matters. We have already observed the lack of substantive outcomes of both sets of laws and policies, in terms of the poor human development indicators of the former group, and the abysmal conditions of educational and economic backwardness of the latter. Women – those belonging to these groups as well as others – have remained under-represented in all public institutions, except the institutions of local governance where they are beneficiaries of guaranteed representation. As members of the Scheduled Caste and Tribe communities, their human development indicators – from maternal mortality to health and literacy – are the worst of any section of the Indian population. As members of the Muslim minority community, they have frequently been targets of the most retrogressive policies of community leaders, with all considerations of gender justice being cheerfully sacrificed at the altar of community rights. As members of the majority Hindu community, they have been participants in terrible practices like female foeticide that bespeak the power of patriarchy. They have also, in alliance with religion, been complicit in extremely conservative Hindu revivalist politics.

Differentiated citizenship for women at the local level is clearly inadequate to the task of combating these diverse but equally formidable forces of patriarchy, often conjoined with religion. It does however represent a beginning in terms of, for instance, enabling a recognition of the need for literacy and education. The problem of the local is emblematic of the larger challenge of carefully evaluating the multiple burdens of disadvantage borne by women more than perhaps any other section of the Indian citizenry. The questions that arise are particularly relevant for women, though they can be generalised to apply to other disadvantaged groups as well. Are quotas the only, or even the best, way forward? Do they need to be buttressed by other policy strategies or institutional mechanisms? Should citizenship differentiated by religion be allowed to trump citizenship differentiated by gender? Are policies of differentiated citizenship based exclusively on recognition on the basis of caste adequate for addressing material disadvantages that arise out of, but are not limited to, that particular caste condition – such as access to land, water, forests, and livelihoods – as also the disabilities that attach to women belonging to these groups?

As an internal minority within minority religious communities, women lack recognition and autonomy. As the most disadvantaged sections of the most socially and economically disadvantaged groups, their need for redistributive policies is the most acute. Finally, despite being politically equal citizens, they are poorly represented in the polity. Deprived of recognition, redistribution, and representation, women remain only nominally citizens.

Notwithstanding a limited recognition of the principle of GDC, the incompleteness of the project of citizenship also renders grievously incomplete the Indian democratic experiment.

This could be read as a vindication of the Tocquevillian thesis on the relationship between equality and democracy, but also of the Ambedkar thesis on the vulnerability of the democratic project in the presence of deep social inequalities.

In India, practices of both undifferentiated citizenship (as in the case of women) and differentiated citizenship (tribes, castes, religious minorities) have encountered difficulties. The critique, in this chapter, of the empirical failures of policies and practices of differentiated citizenship should not be read as implying a celebration of its obverse, viz. universal, undifferentiated citizenship. In India, some forms of differentiated citizenship – e.g. reservations for the Scheduled Castes and Scheduled Tribes – were intended to be temporary and in the nature of rectification of past wrongs. Others, such as the constitutional provisions for minority rights, were intended to be more enduring. If neither has resulted in adequate material and cultural security for disadvantaged groups, that is not an argument against differentiated citizenship, but only for making provisions for it more effective. Because, conversely, the principle of gender-neutral citizenship – as evinced in the absence of special provisions for women, mostly advocated by women themselves – has also not resulted in improvements in either representation or material status for women.

Clearly, the undifferentiated ideal of universal citizenship is inadequate to the task of recognising and addressing the possibilities of disadvantage and discrimination that inhere in any plural society. On the other hand, not every form of difference necessarily implies a valid claim to differentiated citizenship. Over time, democracies encounter new claims and must adjust their policies and practices accordingly. The normative negotiation of such claims to differentiated citizenship may be viewed as a central and continuing task of the democratic project.

Conclusion

The chapters in this volume have offered a commentary on the increasingly exclusionary character of India's citizenship regime as it has unfolded over the past decade. In this note of conclusion, I endeavour to take stock of the question of Indian citizenship in the contemporary moment.

Recent years have been exceptionally consequential for the re-visioning of Indian citizenship, marking the considerable distance it has travelled from the constitutional conception. The preceding chapters have presented and analysed the major milestones on this journey, which constitute not just a departure but a foundational shift from the original idea of citizenship. It is too early to tell if the present moment, defined substantially by the Citizenship Amendment Act 2019, is just another alarming milestone or the end point of this dispiriting journey.

The rules of the Citizenship Amendment Act 2019 have not, at the time of writing, been notified, despite the government having already sought and obtained two extensions from Parliament for this purpose. The official reason for the delay – contrasting with the alacrity of the amendment's enactment – has been blandly attributed to administrative preoccupations over the 2020–1 pandemic, leaving abundant room for speculation that the stiff resistance to it in Delhi and elsewhere, as well as a possible electoral backlash in the impending state elections of mid 2021, have played a part in the political calculus. In its response to the Parliamentary Standing Committee, the Ministry of Home Affairs stated that "till now no decision has been taken to create (*sic*) National Register of Indian citizen (*sic*)."[1] In the meanwhile, the absence of the rules

[1] https://indianexpress.com/article/india/no-nrc-census-home-ministry-india-parliamentary-committee-7171420/. 2 February 2021.

has reportedly led to 243 Pakistani nationals – Hindus and Sikhs who would have been eligible for fast-track citizenship under the Act – being given permission to return to their country.[2]

While the widespread protests against the Act apparently failed to penetrate the tympanum of the state, the compulsions of electoral politics have laid bare some contradictions of citizenship bigotry. The BJP has discovered that its thunderous offer of the CAA against the "illegal immigrant" has limited purchase in Assam. This is because the dog-whistle illegality is being blown only to target Muslim immigrants, whereas Assamese nativism demands the expulsion of *all* who are culturally alien and will not suffer many of these being redesignated legitimate citizens by yet another variant mutation of the NRC. Once seen as a popular carrot, the substantial suffering caused by the NRC to every citizen in Assam has made the whole idea of a citizens' register look like a thoroughly disagreeable stick with which the state can strike citizens indiscriminately. The BJP's careful electoral calculations, too, seem for now to have advised discretion above valour in the effort to disenfranchise Muslim citizens, given how many more Hindu citizens have been imperilled by the drive.

The difficulty of managing this political contradiction is compounded by another in the simultaneously poll-bound state of West Bengal. Here, even as fear of the NRC has already driven many poorly documented citizens to suicide, the Matuas, a Dalit community of substantial numbers that migrated from East Pakistan during and after the Partition, have been eagerly awaiting notification of the rules of the CAA 2019 in order to become legal citizens. In an election speech, the Home Minister assured them that the CAA would be implemented once the vaccination programme for Covid-19 has been completed.[3] In the age of social

[2] https://thewire.in/external-affairs/hindu-sikh-pakistani-refugees-indian-citizenship.

[3] https://www.ndtv.com/india-news/caa-will-be-implemented-after-covid-vaccination-ends-amit-shah-in-bengal-2368516?pfrom=home-ndtv_topstories. 11 February 2021.

media, with the amplification of the speeches of political leaders across states, the art of mixed messaging – promising the CAA to some while maintaining a strategic silence amongst others – is no longer easy or credible.

One way or another, with or without the notification of the rules, the CAA stays on the statute book. Until the rules are formulated, the amendment will remain a grim reminder to the Muslim minority of the tenuousness and precariousness of their membership of the constitutional political community. When they are formulated – possibly followed by the implementation of the NPR and NRC – an arguably unconstitutional hierarchy of citizenship will have been established, unless the courts step in to undo it. At the time of writing, the country's constitutional court, the Supreme Court, has shown such a clear disinclination to pronounce on immediate constitutional questions that its decision-making trajectory looks, to put it euphemistically, timid. There is no disguising the fact that recent majoritarian politics has resulted in a sharp increase in social violence, and if even the apex court sees its immunity within such an ethos as largely theoretical, if not materially threatened, it cannot be faulted. In the meantime, rhetorical or otherwise, the threat of a nationwide NRC shows that the fig leaf of illegal immigration is being used to bring the citizenship of all Muslim citizens into question; while Muslim migrants, beginning with those in Assam, are fast becoming a pretext to fabricate and advance a much more ambitious and nationwide project of 'othering'.

These shifts encourage us to revisit the argument about group-differentiated citizenship that frames Chapter 5. Earlier claims to differentiated citizenship, such as quotas on the basis of caste-based backwardness, were made by historically disadvantaged groups asking for group-differentiated citizenship as a mode of redress – effectively, demanding the conditions of equal citizenship. Today, it is the state that is using group identity (albeit religious community rather than caste) as the basis for differentiating between citizens, and as a pretext for the denial of equal and universal citizenship. As such, this new form of differentiated citizenship works to the manifest detriment of the excluded rather than to their advantage. The idea of differentiated citizenship consequently bears a different type of normative burden in these two examples. In the first, group-differentiated citizenship was a normatively justifiable and appealing strategy to overcome the difference-blindness of conventional liberal practice, and thereby open the doors to greater equality. In the second, differentiated citizenship promises to undermine equal citizenship and make some citizens less equal than others. Instead of making possible greater equality, it actively promotes the production of inequality.

The CAA 2019 also amended a provision relating to Overseas Citizens of India. Since India does not recognise dual citizenship, the OCI is not quite a citizen. Nevertheless, recent prime ministers have been solicitous of the OCI, none more so than Narendra Modi, who has performed in big-ticket events in the US and the UK, and whose election campaigns in India have witnessed the enthusiastic participation of members of the diaspora travelling thousands of miles to volunteer for his campaigns. The CAA 2019 amended Section 7D to say that if the OCI cardholder violates any provision of the Citizenship Act, or indeed any other laws, she could be deprived of OCI status, although she would be given "a reasonable opportunity of being heard".[4]

On 4 March 2021, the Ministry of Home Affairs issued a notification abridging the rights of OCIs, superseding the notifications of 2005, 2007, and 2009. The new notification requires

[4] The amendment provoked fear amongst Goans who had taken Portuguese citizenship for economic mobility, banking on their OCI status to enable their return home after retirement. Given that many Goans participate actively in opposing development projects that compromise the coastal ecosystem and ways of life of fishing communities, there is a fear that they could now be vulnerable to punishment as political dissenters: https://thewire.in/rights/citizenship-amendment-act-oci-cardholder, 25 April 2020.

OCIs to get special permits if they wish to visit India to undertake research, missionary activity, Tabligh activities, and even journalism or mountaineering.[5] The protections already available to doctors, dentists, lawyers, architects, and chartered accountants remain. The suspicion that the change is intended to rein in just a couple of well-known OCI journalists (based in India and abroad) who have taken positions strongly critical of the government is not altogether unfounded, and evident from a headline: "'No journalism or conversion without permission' – Modi Govt breaks the spine of OCI card holding anti-nationals".[6] The story even describes such journalists: "Now the Union government has come up with a permanent solution against Tablighis and journalists who carry out propaganda that harms the interest of the nation, and the conversion mafia. The newly notified rules will keep such OCI cardholders in check and would safeguard the nation's interests."[7]

Even amongst the wealthy, frequently supportive of the BJP and especially appreciative of Narendra Modi's leadership, there is a noticeable trend towards what could plausibly be described as secessionary citizenship. Data from a global citizenship and residence advisory firm, Henley and Partners, show that, the pandemic notwithstanding, high-net-worth individuals from India top the 2020 list of those seeking "residence by investment" or "citizenship by investment" overseas. In the first six months of 2020 alone, there was an 111 per cent increase in the number of enquiries this firm received from Indians, as compared to the same period the previous year.[8] Another news report, based on data from the Regional Passport Office in Ahmedabad, shows that the number of Gujaratis surrendering their Indian passport – a legal requirement when an

[5] Ministry of Home Affairs: Notification dated 4 March 2021: http://egazette.nic.in/WriteReadData/2021/225647.pdf

[6] TFI Post, 6 March 2021: https://tfipost.com/2021/03/no-journalism-or-conversion-without-permission-modi-govt-breaks-the-spine-of-oci-card-holding-anti-nationals/

[7] Ibid.

Indian acquires citizenship of another country – had jumped 400 per cent, from 60 in 2018 to 312 in 2020.[9]

On the whole, it appears that tinkering with the citizenship law has become the preferred weapon of transforming India's already fragile democracy, by enfeebling minority rights and punishing dissenters. The CAA 2019, with the accompanying threat of the NPR and the NRC, created paths to statelessness for Indian Muslims, disfavoured only on the basis of their faith, even as it opened up paths to citizenship for favoured groups of migrants only on grounds of their faith and their countries of origin. The latest notification for OCI cardholders weaponises the status of the OCI to clamp down on dissent. Meanwhile, the wealthy may exercise their freedom of choice and legal right to exit without fear of their nationalist credentials being questioned.

[9] https://ahmedabadmirror.indiatimes.com/ahmedabad/cover-story/five-fold-rise-in-no-of-gujaratis-who-gave-up-their-indian-passports/articleshow/80778257.cms, 10 February 2021.

Bibliography

Aggarwal, Ankita, "Direct Benefit Transfer: More Chaos than Benefit in Jharkhand Pilot", *Catch News*, 10 April 2018, http://www.catchnews.com/india-news/direct-benefit-transfer-more-chaos-than-benefit-in-jharkhand-pilot-107086.html, accessed 10 October 2018.

Ambedkar, Dr Babasaheb, *The Annihilation of Caste* (1936), rpntd in Vasant Moon, comp., *Dr Babasaheb Ambedkar: Writings and Speeches*, vol. 1, Government of Maharashtra, Education Department, 1979.

Arendt, Hannah, *Men in Dark Times*, New York: Harcourt, Brace & World, Inc., 1970.

Arendt, Hannah, "The Decline of the Nation-State and the End of the Rights of Man", in idem, *The Origins of Totalitarianism*, Cleveland: A Meridian Book, The World Publishing Company, 1962.

Arendt, Hannah, *The Origins of Totalitarianism*, New York: Harcourt, Brace and Jovanovich, 1962.

Austin, Granville, *Working a Democratic Constitution: The Indian Experience*, New Delhi: Oxford University Press, 1999.

Bajpai, Rochana, "Minority Representation and the Making of the Indian Constitution", in Rajeev Bhargava, ed., *Politics and Ethics of the Indian Constitution*, New Delhi: Oxford University Press, 2008.

Balagopal, K., "A Tangled Web: Subdivision of SC Reservations in AP", *Economic and Political Weekly*, vol. 35, no. 13, 25–31 March 2000.

Banerjee, Anil Chandra, ed., *Indian Constitutional Documents, Volume II (1858–1917)*, 1946; rpntd, 3rd edn, Calcutta: A. Mukherjee and Co., 1961.

Bardhan, Pranab, "Symposium on Democracy and Development", *Journal of Economic Perspectives*, vol. 7, no. 3, Summer 1993.

Barrier, N. Gerald, "The Punjab Government and Communal Politics, 1870–1908", *The Journal of Asian Studies*, vol. 27, no. 3, May 1968.

Basu, Amrita, *Violent Conjunctures in Democratic India*, New York: Cambridge University Press, 2015.

Basu, Tapan, Pradip Datta, Sumit Sarkar, Tanika Sarkar, and Sambudha Sen, *Khaki Shorts and Saffron Flags: A Critique of the Hindu Right*, Tracts for the Times 1, New Delhi: Orient Longman, 1993.

Bayly, Susan, *Caste, Society and Politics in India from the Eighteenth Century to the Modern Age* (The New Cambridge History of India IV.3), Cambridge: Cambridge University Press, 1999.

Beiner, Ronald, ed., *Theorizing Citizenship*, Albany: State University of New York Press, 1995.

Benhabib, Seyla, *The Rights of Others: Aliens, Residents and Citizens*, Cambridge: Cambridge University Press, 2004.

Béteille, André, *The Backward Classes and the New Social Order.* Delhi: Oxford University Press, 1981.

Bhadrakumar, M.K., "India has Wounded Afghan and Bangladeshi Self-respect", https: //www.rediff.com/news/ column/india-has-wounded-afghan-and-bangladeshi-self-respect/20191212.htm, accessed 29 June 2020.

Bhat, Mohsin Alam, "Stateless and Hyperlegalized: The Indian State Weaponizes Paperwork", *The Baffler*, 3 January 2020, https:// thebaffler.com/logical-revolts/stateless-and-hyperlegalized-alam, accessed 30 June 2020.

Bhatt, Chetan, *Hindu Nationalism: Origins, Ideologies and Modern Myths*, Oxford: Berg, 2001.

Bosniak, Linda, *The Citizen and the Alien: Dilemmas of Contemporary Membership*, Princeton, NJ: Princeton University Press, 2006.

Byrne, David, *Social Exclusion*, Maidenhead: Open University Press, 2005.

Carens, Joseph, *Culture, Citizenship and Community: A Contextual Exploration of Justice as Evenhandedness*, Oxford: Oxford University Press, 2000.

Centre for Equity Studies and Delhi Research Group, "Labouring Lives: Hunger, Precarity and Despair Amid Lockdown", A Report, June 2020.

Centre for the Study of Developing Societies and Azim Premji University, *Society and Politics Between Elections: A Report*, Delhi: Centre for the Study of Developing Societies, 2017.

Chatterjee, Partha, "The Nationalist Resolution of the Women's Question", in Kumkum Sangari and Sudesh Vaid, eds. *Recasting Women: Essays in Colonial History*, New Delhi: Kali for Women, 2006.

Constituent Assembly Debates, Lok Sabha Secretariat, 1986.

Constitution of India 1950, https:// www.india.gov.in /sites/upload_files/npi/files/coi_part_full.pdf.

Corbridge, Stuart, "Competing Inequalities: The Scheduled Tribes and the Reservations System in Jharkhand, India", in Stuart Corbridge, Sarah Jewitt, and Sanjay Kumar, *Jharkhand: Environment, Development, Ethnicity*, New Delhi: Oxford University Press, 2004.

Daga, Mohitkumar, and Parag Mohanty, "Modi May Have Repackaged 23 UPA Schemes, But Most Are Working Better Now", *The Wire*, 13 September 2017, https:// thewire.in/politics/ modi-may-repackaged-23-upa-schemes-working-better-now, accessed 12 October, 2018.

Dahrendorf, Ralf, "Citizenship and Social Class", in Martin Bulmer and Anthony M. Rees, eds, *Citizenship Today: The Contemporary Relevance of T.H. Marshall*, London: UCL Press, 1996.

Deshpande, Ashwini, "The Covid-19 Pandemic and Lockdown: First Effects on Gender Gaps in Employment and Domestic Work in India", Discussion Paper Series in Economics, DP No. 30, Department of Economics, Ashoka University, June 2020, ftp://52.172.205.73/ash/ wpaper/paper30.pdf.

Dhanda, Meena, ed., *Reservations for Women*, New Delhi: Women Unlimited, 2008.

Dhavan, Rajeev, *Reserved! How Parliament Debated Reservations 1995–2007*, New Delhi: Rupa & Co., 2008.

Drèze, Jean and Amartya Sen, *India: Development and Participation*, New Delhi: Oxford University Press, 2002.

Drèze, Jean, "Ill fares Aadhaar", *The Indian Express*, 2 October 2018.

Drèze, Jean, and Amartya Sen, *India: Economic Development and Social Opportunity*, New Delhi: Oxford University Press, 1996.

Drèze, Jean, Nazar Khalid, Reetika Khera, and Anmol Somanchi, "Aadhaar and Food Security in Jharkhand: Pain without Gain?", *Economic and Political Weekly*, vol. LII, no. 50, 16 December 2017, pp. 50–9, https:// www.epw.in/ system/files/pdf/2017_52/50/SA_LII_50_161217_Jean_Drèze.pdf.

Fairclough, Norman, *New Labour, New Language?* London: Routledge, 2000.

Forbes, Geraldine, *Women in Modern India*, The New Cambridge History of India, vol. IV.2, New Delhi: Foundation Books for Cambridge University Press, 2004.

Fraser, Nancy, *Scales of Justice: Reimagining Political Space in a Globalizing World*, Cambridge: Polity Press, 2008.

Fuller, Christopher J., "Caste", in Veena Das, ed., *The Oxford India Companion to Sociology and Social Anthropology*, Delhi: Oxford University Press, 2003.

Gandhi, M.K., "Answers to Questions" (1942), in *Collected Works of Mahatma Gandhi*, vol. 83: 7 June 1942–26 January 1944, http://www.gandhiserve.org/cwmg/VOL083.PDF

Gore, Charles, "Introduction: Markets, Citizenship and Social Exclusion", in Gerry Rodgers, Charles Gore, and Jose B. Figueiredo, eds, *Social Exclusion: Rhetoric, Reality, Responses*, Geneva: International Institute for Labour Studies and UNDP, 1995.

Government of India, "Report of the High Level Committee on the Indian Diaspora", chairperson: L.M. Singhvi <http://indiandiaspora.nic.in/contents.htm> accessed 26 October 2014.

Government of India, "Social, Economic and Educational Status of the Muslim Community in India: A Report", Prime Minister's High Level Committee, chairperson: Justice Rajinder Sachar Cabinet Secretariat, 2006.

Government of India, "Study on Elected Women Representatives in Panchayati Raj Institutions", Ministry of Panchayati Raj, 2008.

Government of India, *Report of the Backward Classes Commission*, vol. I, New Delhi, 1956.

Government of India, *Report of the Backward Classes Commission*, New Delhi, 1980.

Government of NCT of Delhi, "Report of the DMC Fact-Finding Committee on North-East Delhi Riots of February 2020", July 2020.

Guru, Gopal, "Constitutional Justice: Positional and Cultural", in Rajeev Bhargava, ed., *Politics and Ethics of the Indian Constitution*, New Delhi: Oxford University Press, 2008.

Haider, Suhasini, "Mr. Modi's Diaspower", *The Hindu*, 14 November 2015, https://www.thehindu.com/opinion/mr-modis-diaspower/article7874522.ece, accessed 12 October 2018.

Hasan, Mushirul, "The Myth of Unity: Colonial and National Narratives", in David Ludden, ed., *Contesting the Nation: Religion, Community, and the Politics of Democracy in India*, Philadelphia: University of Pennsylvania Press, 1996.

Hirschman, Albert O., *Exit, Voice, and Loyalty: Responses to Decline in Firms, Organizations, and States*, Cambridge, MA: Harvard University Press, 1970.

Holmes, Stephen, and Cass R. Sunstein, *The Cost of Rights: Why Liberty Depends on Taxes*, New York: W.W. Norton & Co., 2000.

Jaffrelot, Christophe, "Containing the Lower Castes: The Constituent Assembly and the Reservation Policy", in Rajeev Bhargava, ed., *Politics and Ethics of the Indian Constitution*, New Delhi: Oxford University Press, 2008.

Jaffrelot, Christophe, *Dr. Ambedkar and Untouchability: Analysing and Fighting Caste*, Ranikhet: Permanent Black, 2005.

Jaffrelot, Christophe, ed., *Hindu Nationalism: A Reader*, Ranikhet: Permanent Black, 2007.

Jayal, Niraja Gopal, *Citizenship and Its Discontents*, Ranikhet and Cambridge, Mass.: Permanent Black and Harvard University Press, 2013.

Jayal, Niraja Gopal, "Engendering Local Democracy: The Impact of Quotas for Women in India's Panchayats", in *Democratization*, vol. 13, no. 1, February 2006.

Jayal, Niraja Gopal, "Faith-Based Citizenship", *The India Forum*, 1 November 2019, https://www.theindiaforum.in/article/faith-criterion-citizenship.

Jayal, Niraja Gopal, *Representing India: Ethnic Diversity and the Governance of Public Institutions*, London: Palgrave Macmillan and UNRISD, 2006.

Jayal, Niraja Gopal, "The 2016 Citizenship Amendment Bill Consolidates a Trend Towards a Majoritarian and Exclusionary Concept of Indian Citizenship", *Caravan*, 20 February, 2017, http://www.caravanmagazine.in/vantage/2016-citizenship-amendment-bill-majoritarian-exclusionary, accessed 10 October 2018.

Jayal, Niraja Gopal, "The Transformation of Citizenship in India in the 1990s and Beyond", in Stuart Corbridge, John Harriss, Sanjay

Reddy, and Sanjay Ruparelia, eds, *India: The Great Transformation?*, London: Routledge, 2011.

Jenson, Jane, and Susan D. Phillips, "Regime Shift: New Citizenship Practices in Canada", *International Journal of Canadian Studies*, vol. 14, Fall/Autumn 1996.

John, Mary, "Reservations and the Women's Movement in Twentieth Century India", in Meena Dhanda, ed., *Reservations for Women*, New Delhi: Women Unlimited, 2008.

Joppke, Christian, "Multicultural Citizenship", in Engin F. Isin and Bryan S. Turner, eds, *Handbook of Citizenship Studies*, London: Sage Publications, 2002.

Karmakar, Rahul, "30 'Foreigners' Dead in Assam's Detention Centres", *The Hindu*, 12 April 2020, https://www.thehindu.com/news/national/30-foreigners-dead-in-assams-detention-centres/article31325045.ece, accessed 29 June 2020.

Kazmin, Amy "Dodgy Data Makes it Hard to Judge Modi's Job Promises", *Financial Times*, 8 October 2018.

Khalidi, Omar, *Muslims in Indian Economy*. Gurgaon: Three Essays Collective, 2005.

Kothari, Rajni, ed., *Caste in Indian Politics*, Delhi: Orient Longman, 1970.

Krishna, Anirudh, *et al.*, "Falling into Poverty", in *Economic and Political Weekly*, vol. 38, no. 6, 2003.

Krishna, Anirudh, *et al.*, "Falling into Poverty in a High Growth State", in *Economic and Political Weekly*, vol. 38, no. 49, 2003.

Krishna, Anirudh, *et al.*, "Falling into Poverty in Villages of Andhra Pradesh", in *Economic and Political Weekly*, vol. 39, no. 29, 2004.

Kumar, Radha, *The History of Doing: An Illustrated Account of Movements for Women's Rights and Feminism in India*, New Delhi: Zubaan, 1993.

Kymlicka, Will, "Introduction: An Emerging Consensus", *Ethical Theory and Moral Practice*, vol. 1, no. 2, Special Issue on Nationalism, Multiculturalism, and Liberal Democracy, June 1998.

Kymlicka, Will, *Multicultural Citizenship*, Oxford: Oxford University Press, 1996.

Kymlicka, Will, and Wayne Norman, "Citizenship in Culturally Diverse Societies: Issues, Contexts, Concepts", in idem, eds., *Citizenship in Diverse Societies*, Oxford: Oxford University Press, 2000.

Kymlicka, Will, and Wayne Norman, "Return of the Citizen: A Survey of Recent Work on Citizenship Theory", in Ronald Beiner, ed., *Theorizing Citizenship*, Albany: State University of New York Press, 1995.

Levitas, R., *The Inclusive Society: Social Exclusion and New Labour*, Basingstoke: Palgrave Macmillan, 1998.

Macedo, Stephen, "The Moral Dilemma of U.S. Immigration Policy: Open Borders Versus Social Justice?", in Carol M. Swain, ed., *Debating Immigration*, Cambridge: Cambridge University Press, 2007.

Mackay, Fiona, "'Thick' Conceptions of Substantive Representation: Women, Gender and Political Institutions", *Representation*, vol. 44, no. 2, 2008.

Marshall, T.H., *Citizenship and Social Class*, 1950; rpntd London: Pluto Press, 1992.

Meyer, William J., "The Politics of Differentiated Citizenship", in Karen Slawner and Mark E. Denham, eds, *Citizenship after Liberalism*, New York: Peter Lang Publishing, 1998.

Ministry of Overseas Indian Affairs, "Overseas Citizenship of India Scheme", <http://moia.gov.in /services.aspx?id1=35&id=m3&idp=35&mainid=23> accessed 26 October 2014.

Muralidharan, K., Paul Niehaus, and Sandip Sukhtankar, "Direct Benefits Transfer in Food: Results from One Year of Process Monitoring in Union Territories", San Diego: University of California, 2017, 5.

Pai, Sudha, and Sajjan Kumar, *Everyday Communalism: Riots in Contemporary Uttar Pradesh*, New Delhi: Oxford University Press, 2018.

Parthasarathy, D., "Citizenship (Amendment) Act: The Pitfalls of Homogenising Identities in Resistance Narratives", *Economic and Political Weekly*, vol. 55, issue 25, 20 June 2020, https://www.epw.in/engage/article/citizenship-amendment-act-pitfalls-homogenising-identities-resistance-narratives, accessed 29 June 2020.

Pierson, John, *Tackling Social Exclusion*, London: Routledge, 2002.

Przeworski, Adam, and Fernando Limongi, "Political Regimes and Economic Growth", *Journal of Economic Perspectives*, vol. 7, no. 3, Summer 1993.

Pieterse, Marius, "Eating Socioeconomic Rights: The Usefulness of Rights Talk in Alleviating Social Hardship Revisited", *Human Rights Quarterly* 29, 3, August 2007.

Prakash, Amit, *Jharkhand: Politics of Development and Identity*, New Delhi: Orient Longman, 2001.

Przeworski, Adam, Michael E. Alvarez, Jose Antonio Cheibub, and Fernando Limongi, *Democracy and Development: Political Institutions and Well-Being in the World, 1950–1990*, Cambridge: Cambridge University Press, 2000.

Rathore, Aakash Singh, *Ambedkar's Preamble: A Secret History of the Constitution of India*, Gurugram: Penguin Random House, 2020.

Rodrigues, Valerian, ed., *The Essential Writings of B.R. Ambedkar*, New Delhi: Oxford University Press, 2002.

Rousseau, Jean-Jacques, *The Social Contract and Discourses* (1750), trans. and with an Introduction by G.D.H. Cole, rpntd London: J.M. Dent & Sons, 1979.

Rudolph, Lloyd I., and Susanne Hoeber Rudolph, *In Pursuit of Lakshmi: The Political Economy of the Indian State*, New Delhi: Orient Longman, 1987.

Rudolph, Lloyd I., and Susanne Hoeber Rudolph, *The Modernity of Tradition,* Chicago: The University of Chicago Press, 1967.

Sadiq, Kamal, *Paper Citizens: How Illegal Immigrants Acquire Citizenship in Developing Countries*, New York: Oxford University Press, 2009.

Savarkar, V.D., *Essentials of Hindutva*, n.p., 1923, http://www.savarkar.org/content/pdfs/en/essentials_of_hindutva.v001.pdf.

Shachar, Ayelet, "Citizenship and Membership in the Israeli Polity", in T. Alexander Aleinikoff and Douglas Klusmeyer, eds, *From Migrants to Citizens: Membership in a Changing World*, Washington, D.C.: Carnegie Endowment for International Peace, 2000.

Seervai, H.M., *Constitutional Law of India*, vol. 1, 4th edn, Delhi: Universal Book Traders, 2002.

Sen, Amartya, "Exclusion and Inclusion", *Mainstream*, vol. XXXIX, no. 49, 24 November 2001.

Sen, Amartya, "Social Exclusion: Concept, Application, and Scrutiny", Social Development Papers No. 1, Office of Environment and Social Development, Asian Development Bank, 2000.

Shah, Ghanshyam, Harsh Mander, Sukhdeo Thorat, Satish Deshpande, and Amita Baviskar, *Untouchability in Rural India*, New Delhi: Sage Publications, 2006.

Sheth, D.L., "Caste and Class: Social Reality and Political Representations", in Ghanshyam Shah, ed., *Caste and Democratic Politics in India*, Delhi: Permanent Black, 2002.

Singer, Wendy, *"A Constituency Suitable for Ladies" and Other Social Histories of Indian Elections*, New Delhi: Oxford University Press, 2007.

Sixteenth Lok Sabha, "Report of the Joint Committee on the Citizenship (Amendment) Bill 2016", presented to the Lok Sabha on 7 January 2019, https://www.prsindia. org/sites/default/files/bill_files/Joint%20 committee%20report%20on%20citizenship%20%28A%29%20 bill_0.pdf.

Smith, Rogers M., *Civic Ideals: Conflicting Visions of Citizenship in US History*, New Haven: Yale University Press, 1997.

Smith, Rogers M., *Stories of Peoplehood: The Politics and Morals of Political Membership*, Cambridge: Cambridge University Press, 2003.

Stranded Workers Action Network, "32 Days and Counting: Covid-19 Lockdown, Migrant Workers, and the Inadequacy of Welfare Measures in India", https://covid19socialsecurity.files.wordpress. com/2020/05/32-days-and-counting_swan.pdf?fbclid=IwAR0-ku Fz9pV9drrshn7NLnOUOuVbkv7NbrGzcqMLBMwyel0isEsao LO-dw0.

Supreme Court of India, *Sarbananda Sonowal vs. Union of India and Anr*, Writ Petition (Civil) 131 of 2000, AIR 2005 SC 2920.

Tocqueville, Alexis de, *Democracy in America*, vol. 1, 1835; vol. 2, 1840, trans. George Lawrence, ed. J.P. Mayer, rpntd New York: Anchor Books, 1969.

United Nations Development Programme (UNDP), *Human Development Report 2007/08: Fighting Climate Change: Human Solidarity in a Divided World*, New York: United Nations, 2007.

Varieties of Democracy Institute, "Autocratization Surges – Resistance Grows: Democracy Report 2020", March 2020.

Varictics of Democracy Institute, "Democracy for All? V-Dem Annual Democracy Report 2018", May 2018.

Villa, Dana, "Tocqueville and Civil Society", in Cheryl B. Welch, ed., *The Cambridge Companion to Tocqueville*, Cambridge: Cambridge University Press, 2006.

Wallerstein, Immanuel, "Citizens All? Citizens Some! The Making of the Citizen", *Comparative Studies in Society and History*, vol. 45, 2003.

Weldon, Laurie S., "Beyond Bodies: Institutional Sources of Representation for Women in Democratic Policymaking", in *The Journal of Politics*, vol. 64(4), 2002.

Wolpert, Stanley A., *Morley and India, 1906–1910*, Berkeley: University of California Press, 1967.

Yashar, Deborah, *Contesting Citizenship in Latin America: The Rise of Indigenous Movements and the Postliberal Challenge*, Cambridge, Mass.: Cambridge University Press, 2005.

Young, Iris Marion, *Inclusion and Democracy*, 2000; rpntd Oxford: Oxford University Press, 2002.

Young, Iris Marion, "Polity and Group Difference: A Critique of the Ideal of Universal Citizenship" (1989), in Ronald Beiner, ed., *Theorizing Citizenship*, Albany: State University of New York Press, 1995.

Zamindar, Vazira Fazila-Yacoobali, *The Long Partition and the Making of Modern South Asia: Refugees, Boundaries, Histories*, New York: Viking Books, 2007.

Zelliot, Eleanor, "Gandhi and Ambedkar – A Study in Leaderhip", in J. Michael Mahar, ed., *The Untouchables in Contemporary India*, Tucson, Arizona: The University of Arizona Press, 1972.

Index